George Rawlinson

Egypt and Babylon

From scripture and profane sources

George Rawlinson

Egypt and Babylon

From scripture and profane sources

ISBN/EAN: 9783337231743

Printed in Europe, USA, Canada, Australia, Japan

Cover: Foto ©ninafisch / pixelio.de

More available books at **www.hansebooks.com**

EGYPT AND BABYLON,

From Scripture and Profane Sources.

BY THE REV.
GEORGE RAWLINSON, M.A.

CANON OF CANTERBURY; CAMDEN PROFESSOR OF ANCIENT HISTORY, OXFORD;
CORRESPONDING MEMBER OF THE ROYAL ACADEMY OF TURIN.

London:
HODDER AND STOUGHTON,
27, PATERNOSTER ROW.

MDCCCLXXXV.

[*All rights reserved.*]

CONTENTS.

PART I.

Biblical Notices of Babylon.

CHAPTER I.
NOTICES OF BABYLON IN GENESIS . . 3

CHAPTER II.
NOTICES OF BABYLON IN THE BOOKS OF KINGS AND CHRONICLES 19

CHAPTER III.
NOTICES OF BABYLON IN THE BOOKS OF KINGS AND CHRONICLES (*continued*) 37

CHAPTER IV.
NOTICES OF BABYLON IN DANIEL 53

CHAPTER V.

NOTICES OF BABYLON IN DANIEL (*continued*) . . 71

CHAPTER VI.

NOTICES OF BABYLON IN DANIEL (*continued*) . . 89

CHAPTER VII.

NOTICES OF BABYLON IN JEREMIAH AND EZEKIEL . 109

CHAPTER VIII.

FURTHER NOTICES OF BABYLON IN EZEKIEL . 127

CHAPTER IX.

NOTICES OF BABYLON IN DANIEL (*resumed*) . . 147

CHAPTER X.

NOTICES OF BABYLON IN DANIEL (*continued*) . 165

CHAPTER XI.

FURTHER NOTICES OF BABYLON IN DANIEL, ISAIAH, JEREMIAH, AND EZEKIEL 181

CHAPTER XII.

FURTHER NOTICES OF BABYLON IN ISAIAH AND JEREMIAH 199

PART II.

Biblical Notices of Egypt.

CHAPTER I.
NOTICES OF EGYPT IN GENESIS . . . 217

CHAPTER II.
NOTICES OF EGYPT IN GENESIS (*continued*) . . . 237

CHAPTER III.
NOTICES OF EGYPT IN EXODUS . . 255

CHAPTER IV.
NOTICES OF EGYPT IN EXODUS (*continued*) . . . 273

CHAPTER V.
NOTICES OF EGYPT IN EXODUS AND NUMBERS . 291

CHAPTER VI.
NOTICES OF EGYPT IN EXODUS (*continued*) . . 309

CHAPTER VII.
NOTICES OF EGYPT IN THE FIRST BOOK OF KINGS 327

CONTENTS.

CHAPTER VIII.
NOTICES OF EGYPT IN THE SECOND BOOK OF KINGS . 345

CHAPTER IX.
NOTICES OF EGYPT IN THE BOOK OF THE PROPHET
ISAIAH 363

CHAPTER X.
NOTICES OF EGYPT IN THE BOOKS OF JEREMIAH AND
EZEKIEL 381

CHAPTER XI.
NOTICES OF EGYPT IN DANIEL . 399

CHAPTER XII.
NOTICES OF EGYPT IN DANIEL (*continued*) . 417

PART I.
BIBLICAL NOTICES OF BABYLON.

CHAPTER I.

THE NOTICES OF BABYLON IN GENESIS.

CHAPTER I.

THE NOTICES OF BABYLON IN GENESIS.

"CUSH begat Nimrod; he began to be a mighty one in the earth. He was a mighty hunter before the Lord: wherefore it is said, Even as Nimrod, the mighty hunter before the Lord. And the beginning of his kingdom was Babel, and Erech, and Accad, and Calneh, in the land of Shinar" (Gen. x. 8-10).

That this passage refers to Babylon will scarcely be disputed. The words "Babel" and "Shinar" are sufficient proof. "Babel," elsewhere generally translated "Babylon" (2 Kings xx. 12, xxiv. 1; 2 Chron. xxxii. 31, xxxiii. 11; Ps. cxxxvii. 1, etc.), is the exact Hebrew equivalent of the native *Babil*, which appears as the capital of Babylonia in the cuneiform records from the time of Agu-kak-rimi (about B.C. 2000) to the conquest of the country by Cyrus (B.C. 538). "Shinar" is probably an equivalent of "Mesopotamia," "the country of the two rivers," and in Scripture always designates the lower part of the Tigris and Euphrates valley, the alluvial plain through which the great rivers flow before reaching the Persian Gulf.

Four facts are recorded of Babylonia in the passage :—1, That it became at a very early date a settled government under a king ; 2, that it contained, besides Babylon, at least three other great cities—Erech, Accad, Calneh ; 3, that among its earliest rulers was a great conquering monarch named Nimrod ; and 4, that this monarch, and therefore probably his people, descended from Cush —*i.e.*, was a Cushite, or Ethiopian.

The first of these facts is confirmed by Berosus, by Diodorus Siculus, and by the monuments. Berosus declared that a monarchy had been set up in Babylon soon after the flood, which he regarded as a real occurrence, and counted 208 kings from Evechous, the first monarch, to Pul, the predecessor of Tiglath-Pileser. Diodorus believed that Babylon had been built by Semiramis, the wife of Ninus, at a date which, according to his chronology, would be about B.C. 2200. The monuments furnish between eighty and ninety names of kings anterior to Tiglath-Pileser, and carry back the monarchy by actual numerical statements to B.C. 2286, while the superposition of the remains is considered by the explorers to indicate an even greater antiquity. An early Babylonian kingdom, once denied on the authority of Ctesias, is now generally allowed by historians; the researches of Sir Henry Rawlinson, Mr. George Smith, Professor Sayce, Mr. Pinches, and others, having sufficiently established the fact previously questioned.

The second fact—the early existence of several large cities in Babylonia, cities ranking almost upon a par—is also strongly supported by the native records. In the most ancient times to which the monuments go back, the chief cities, according to Mr. George Smith,[1] were Ur, Nipur, Karrak, and Larsa, all of them metropolitan, and all of them places giving their titles to kings. Somewhat later, Babylon and Erech rose to greatness, together with a city called Agadé, or Accad, according to the same authority.[2] If this last identification be allowed, then three out of the four cities mentioned in Genesis as metropolitan at this early date will have the same rank in the native records, and one only of the four names will lack such direct confirmation. Certainly, no name at all resembling Calneh occurs in the primitive geography of Babylonia. There are, however, grounds for regarding Calneh as another name of Nipur,[3] and one which superseded it for a time in the nomenclature of the inhabitants. In this case we

---

[1] "History of Babylonia" (edited by Rev. A. H. Sayce), ch. iii., pp. 63—74.
[2] Ibid., p. 61.
[3] Smith's "Dictionary of the Bible," *ad voc.* Calneh.

may say that all the four cities of Genesis x. 10 are identified, and shown to have had (about B.C. 2000) the eminence ascribed to them in that passage. Mr. George Smith's reading of " Agadé " is, however, questioned by some, who read the name " Agané." If this latter reading be correct, the city Accad must be regarded as at present not identified.

The third fact—the reign of a powerful king, called Nimrod, over Babylonia—has not as yet received any confirmation from the monuments. It is suspected that the monarch so called had two names, and that, while Scripture uses one of them, the Babylonian documents employ the other. Mr. George Smith proposed to identify the scriptural Nimrod with a certain Izdubar, a semi-mythical, semi-historical personage, very prominent in the primitive legends. But the identification is a pure conjecture. The monuments must be regarded as silent with respect to Nimrod, and we must look elsewhere for traces of his existence and authority. Such traces are numerous in the traditions of the East, and among the early Jewish and Arabic writers. Josephus tells us that Nimrod lived at the time when the attempt was made to build the Tower of Babel, and represents him as the prime mover in that impious enterprise. The Mohammedans have a tradition that he lived somewhat later, and was brought into contact with Abraham, whom he attempted to burn to death in a furnace of fire. In Arabian astronomy he appears as a giant who at his decease was translated to heaven, and transformed into the constellation which the Arabs called *El Jabbar*, " the Giant," and the Greeks Orion. These tales have, of course, but little value in themselves ; they are merely important as showing how large a space this monarch occupied in the imaginations of the Eastern races, a fact only to be accounted for by his having once filled a prominent position. That position is declared in the "Nabathæan Agriculture," an Arabic work of great antiquity, to have been the position of a king, the founder of a dynasty which long bore sway over the land. Another sign of the reality of Nimrod's rule is to be found in the attachment of his name to various sites in the Mesopotamian region. The remarkable ruin generally called Akkerkuf, which lies a little to the south-west of Baghdad, is known to many as the " Tel-Nimrúd ; " the great dam across the Tigris below Mosul is the " Sahr-el-Nimrúd ; " one of the chief of the buried cities in the same neighbourhood is called " Nimrúd" simply ; and the name of " Birs-Nimrúd " attaches to the grandest mass of ruins in the lower country.[1]

The fourth fact—that Nimrod, and therefore probably his people, was of Cushite origin, has been

---

[1] See Rich's " Journey to Babylon," p. 2, note.

strenuously denied by some, even among modern critics.[1] But ancient classical tradition and recent linguistic research agree in establishing a close connection between the early inhabitants of the lower Mesopotamian plain and the people, which, under the various names of Cushites, Ethiopians, and Abyssinians, has long been settled upon the middle Nile. Memnon, king of Ethiopia, according to Hesiod and Pindar, led an army of combined Ethiopians and Susianians to the assistance of Priam, king of Troy. Belus, according to the genealogists, was the son of Libya (or Africa); he married Anchinoe, daughter of Nilus, and had issue Ægyptus. Names which are modifications of Cush have always hung about the lower Mesopotamian region, indicating its primitive connection with the Cush upon the Nile. The Greeks called the Susianians "Kissii," and a neighbouring race "Kossæi." The early Babylonians had a city, "Kissi," and a leading tribe in their country was called that of the "Kassu." Even now the ancient Susiania is known as 'Khuzistan," the land of Khuz, or of the Cushites. Standing alone, these would be weak arguments; but weight is lent them by the support which they obtain from the facts of language. Sir Henry Rawlinson, the first translator of primitive Babylonian documents, declares the vocabulary employed to be

---

[1] See Bunsen's "Philosophy of History," vol. iii., pp. 190,

"decidedly Cushite or Ethiopian," and states that he was able to interpret the inscriptions chiefly by the aid which was furnished to him from published works on the Galla (Abyssinian) and the Mahra (South Arabian) dialects.[1]

"The whole earth was of one language and of one speech. And it came to pass, as they journeyed from the east (eastward, *marg.*), that they found a plain in the land of Shinar; and they dwelt there. And they said one to another, Go to, let us make brick, and burn them throughly. And they had brick for stone, and slime had they for mortar. And they said, Go to, let us build us a city and a tower, whose top may reach unto heaven; and let us make us a name, lest we be scattered abroad upon the face of the whole earth. And the Lord came down to see the city and the tower, which the children of men builded. And the Lord said, Behold, the people is one, and they have all one language; and this they begin to do; and now nothing will be restrained from them, which they have imagined to do. Go to, let us go down, and there confound their language, that they may not understand one another's speech. So the Lord scattered them abroad from thence upon the face of all the earth; and they left off to build the city. Therefore is the name of it called Babel, because the Lord did there confound

---

[1] See the author's "Herodotus," vol. i., p. 441.

the language of all the earth ; and from thence did the Lord scatter them abroad upon the face of all the earth " (Gen. xi. 1-9).

We have here the scriptural account of the meaning of the name " Babel," the primitive term which the Greeks converted into " Babylon," but which remains even now attached to a portion of the ruins that mark the site of the great city, almost in its original form.[1] The etymology was not accepted by the Babylonians themselves, who wrote the word in a way which shows that they considered it to mean "the Gate of God." This has been regarded by some as a contradiction of the scriptural account; but we may reconcile the two by supposing either that the name was first given in scorn, and that afterwards a better meaning was found for it, or (more probably that the word, having been intended by the Babylonians themselves in the sense of " the Gate of God," was from the first understood in a different sense by others, who connected it with the " confusion " of tongues. The word is capable of both etymologies, and may from the first have been taken in both senses by different persons.

The account of the origin of the name is connected with an historical narrative, of which the following are the chief incidents :—1. A body of men, who had occupied the plain of Shinar, disliking

---

[1] The northernmost of the three great mounds which mark the ruins of Babylon is called by the Arabs *Babil*.

the idea of that dispersion which was continually taking place, and scattering men more and more widely over the earth, determined to build a city, and to adorn it with a lofty tower, in order that they might get themselves a name, and become a centre of attraction in the world. 2. The materials which they found to their hand, and which they employed in building, were burnt brick and "slime," or bitumen. 3. They had built their city, and raised their tower to a certain height, when God interfered with their work. By confounding the language of the workmen, He made it impossible for them to understand each other's speech, and the result was that the design, for the time at least, fell through. The people "left off to build the city," and the mass of them dispersed, and "were scattered abroad upon the face of the earth."

It would not have been surprising if profane history had contained no notice of this matter. It belongs clearly to a very remote antiquity, a time anterior—as it might have been supposed—to records, and lost in the dark night of ages. But the fact seems to be, that the Babylonians either recorded at the time, or at any rate bore in memory, the transaction. Two Greek writers, who drew their Babylonian histories from native sources, noticed the occurrence, and gave an account of it, which is in most respects very close to the biblical narrative. Alexander Polyhistor said, that "Once upon a time,

when the whole race of mankind were of one
language, a certain number of them set to work to
build a great tower, thinking to climb up to heaven;
but God caused a wind to blow, and cast the tower
down, at the same time giving to every man his own
peculiar speech. On which account the city was
called Babylon."[1] Abydenus, a somewhat later
historian, treated the subject at greater length. "At
this time," he said, " the ancient race of men were so
puffed up with their strength and tallness of stature,
that they began to despise and contemn the gods,
and laboured to erect that very lofty tower, which
is now called Babylon, intending thereby to scale
heaven. But when the building approached the sky,
behold, the gods called in the aid of the winds, and
by their help overthrew the tower, and cast it to the
ground. The name of the ruins is still called Babel;
because until this time all men had used the same
speech, but now there was sent upon them a confusion of many and diverse tongues."[2]

These passages have long been known, and have
been adduced as probable evidence that the native
Babylonian records contained a notice respecting the
tower of Babel and the confusion of human speech,
But it is only recently that such a record has been
unearthed. Among the clay tablets brought from
Babylonia by Mr. George Smith, and deposited in

[1] Ap Euseb. "Chron. Can.," part i, c. 4, § 1.
[2] Ap. eod., part i., c. 3.

the British Museum, is one, unfortunately much mutilated, which seems clearly to have contained the Babylonian account of the matter. The main portions of this document are as follows :—

"Babylon corruptly to sin went, and
　　Small and great were mingled on the mound;
Babylon corruptly to sin went, and
　　Small and great were mingled on the mound.
　　　　*　　*　　*　　*
Their work all day they builded;
But to their stronghold in the night
　　Entirely an end God made.
In His anger also His secret counsel He poured forth;
　　He set His face to scatter;
He gave command to make strange their speech;
　　Their progress He impeded.
　　　　*　　*　　*　　*
In that day He blew, and for [all] future time
　　The mountain (was demolished ?);
Lawlessness stalked forth abroad;
　　And, though God spake to them,
Man went *his* ways, and strenuously
　　Opposed themselves to God.
He saw, and to the earth came down;
　　No stop He made, while they
Against the gods revolted. . . . .
　　　　*　　*　　*　　*
Greatly they wept for Babylon;
　　Greatly they wept."[1]

"It came to pass in the days of Amraphel, king of Shinar, Arioch, king of Ellasar, Chedorlaomer, king of Elam, and Tidal, king of nations, that these

---

[1] See "Records of the Past," vol. vii., pp. 131, 132.

made war with Bera, king of Sodom, and with Birsha, king of Gomorrha, Shinab, king of Admah, and Shemeber, king of Zeboiim, and the king of Bela, which is Zoar. All these were joined together in the vale of Siddim, which is the salt sea. Twelve years they served Chedorlaomer" (Gen. xiv. 1-4).

The chief fact relating to Babylon, which this passage contains, is its subjection in the time of Abraham to a neighbouring country, called here Elam. Amraphel, the king of Shinar, the country whereof Babylon was the capital (Gen. x. 10, xi. 2—9), is plainly, in the entire narrative (Gen. xiv. 1—17), secondary and subordinate to Chedorlaomer, king of Elam. The conquered monarchs "serve" Chedorlaomer (ver. 4, not Amraphel; Chedorlaomer leads both expeditions, the other kings are "with him" (ver. 5, 17), as subordinate allies, or, more probably, as tributaries. This is an inversion of the usual position occupied by Babylonia towards its eastern neighbour, of which, until recently, there was no profane confirmation.

Recently, however, traces have been found of an Elamitic conquest of Babylon, and also of an Elamitic dynasty there at an early date, which show that there were times when the more eastern of the two countries which lay side by side upon the Lower Tigris had the greater power, and exercised dominion over the more western. Asshur-bani-pal, the son of Esarhaddon, relates that in his eighteenth year (B.C. 651) he restored to the Babylonian city of Erech, certain images of gods, which had been carried off from them as trophies of victory 1635 years previously by Kudur-Nakhunta, king of Elam, to adorn his capital city of Susa.[1] The primitive Babylonian monuments also show a second conquest of Babylon from the same quarter, and the establishment of a dynasty there, which is known as "Elamite,"[2] about B.C. 1600, or a little later. This dynasty consisted of two kings, Kudur-Mabuk and Rim-agu (a name which has been compared with "Arioch").

It is thus evident that Elam was, in the early period of Babylonian history, a country of about equal power with Babylon, and one which was able from time to time to exercise dominion over her neighbour. It appears also that its kings affected, as one of the elements in their names, the word "Chedor" or "Kudur," which is believed to have meant "servant,"—Chedorlaomer (or Chedor-Lagamer, as the word might be transliterated) being "the servant of Lagamer," a Susianian god; Kudur-Nakhunta, "the servant of Nakhunta," another god; and Kudur-Mabuk, "the servant of Mabuk," a goddess. We may add, that "Amar" (=Amra in "Amra-phel") appears also as a root in the early

---

[1] "Ancient Monarchies," vol. i., p. 446; "Origin of Nations," p. 37.
[2] George Smith's "History of Babylonia," pp. 11, 74.

Babylonian titles,[1] while Arioch is perhaps identical with the name of Rim-agu (or Eri-aku), Kudur-Mabuk's son and successor. Thus the notice in Gen. xiv. 1—4, without being directly confirmed by the monuments, is in close harmony with them, both linguistic and historical.

---

[1] George Smith's " History of Babylonia," p. 10.

CHAPTER II.

THE NOTICES OF BABYLON IN THE BOOKS OF KINGS AND CHRONICLES.

CHAPTER II.

THE NOTICES OF BABYLON IN THE BOOKS OF KINGS AND CHRONICLES.

SCRIPTURE is silent on the subject of Babylon through the whole period from Genesis to Kings.[1] Israel, during the sojourn in Egypt, the wanderings in the wilderness, the time of the Judges, and the greater part of the time of the Kings, was never brought in contact with Babylonia or Babylonians; and Scripture, which traces the religious history of the people of God, has therefore no occasion to mention the southern Mesopotamian power. Another power has interposed itself between Israel and Babylon—the great empire of Assyria—and has barred the path by which alone they could readily communicate. It is not till Assyria, under the Sargonidæ, is seriously threatening the independence of both countries, that a common danger brings them together, and Babylon once more claims the attention of the sacred historians. The first

---

[1] The "Babylonish garment" coveted by Achan (Josh. vii. 21) scarcely constitutes an exception.

notice of Babylon in the Books of Kings is the following :—

".At that time" (the time of Hezekiah's illness) "Berodach-Baladan, the son of Baladan, king of Babylon, sent letters and a present unto Hezekiah : for he had heard that Hezekiah had been sick. And Hezekiah hearkened unto them, and showed them all the house of his precious things, the silver, and the gold, and the spices, and the precious ointment, and all the house of his armour, and all that was found in his treasures : there was nothing in his house, nor in all his dominion, that Hezekiah showed them not" (2 Kings xx. 12, 13.

The same circumstance is related, almost in the same words, by the prophet Isaiah, in one of his historical chapters. Isaiah says—

"At that time Merodach-Baladan, the son of Baladan, king of Babylon, sent letters and a present to Hezekiah; for he had heard that he had been sick, *and was recovered*. And Hezekiah *was glad of them*, and showed them the house of his precious things, the silver, and the gold," etc. (Isa. xxxix. 1, 2.

The author of Chronicles, without relating the circumstance, makes a short comment upon it. After describing the riches, honour, and prosperity of Hezekiah, he adds—

"Howbeit in the business of the ambassadors of the princes of Babylon, who sent unto him to inquire of the wonder that was done in the land, God left him to try him, that He might know all that was in his heart" (2 Chron. xxxii. 31).

The reign of a Babylonian monarch, called Merodach-Baladan, at about the period indicated —the latter part of the eighth century B.C.—is recorded in the famous "Canon of Ptolemy," which assigns him the years between B.C. 722 and B.C. 710. That the same monarch, after being deprived of his throne, was restored to it, and had a second reign of six months' duration, is related by Alexander Polyhistor, the friend of Sulla.[1] This latter reign appears to have belonged to the year B.C. 703. So much is known to us from the classical writers. From the Assyrian monuments we learn that the relations between Babylonia and Assyria, during the reign of Merodach-Baladan, were hostile. Sargon relates that he attacked this king, whom he viewed as a rebel, in his first year,[2] defeated his ally, the king of Elam, and ravaged his territory, but without coming into contact with the Babylonian monarch himself. After this, troubles elsewhere forced him to leave Merodach-Baladan in peace for eleven years; but in his twelfth year he

---

[1] Ap. Euseb. "Chron. Can.," part. i., c. 5. Both reigns are noticed in a recently deciphered Babylonian tablet ("Proceedings of the Society of Bibl. Archæology" for 1884, pp. 197—8).

[2] George Smith, "History of Babylonia," p. 116.

again invaded Babylonia, took Babylon, and made Merodach-Baladan a prisoner.[1] Five years after this, as we learn from Sennacherib's annals,[2] on the death of Sargon, Babylonia revolted. Merodach-Baladan, escaping from the custody in which he was held, hastened to Babylon, and re-established his authority over the whole southern kingdom. But Sennacherib at once marched against him, defeated his forces, recovered Babylon, and drove him to take refuge in the marshes of southern Chaldæa; whence, after a short time, he fled across the Persian Gulf to southern Elam, where he died in exile.

The embassy of Merodach-Baladan to Hezekiah falls, by Archbishop Usher's chronology, which is here founded upon Ptolemy's Canon, into the year B.C. 713. It would thus have taken place between Sargon's first and second attack, very shortly before the latter. The monuments do not mention it; but they show that at this time Merodach-Baladan was expecting the Assyrians to invade his country, was looking out for allies, and doing his best to strengthen his position. Under these circumstances it would be natural that he should seek the alliance of Hezekiah, who, at the opposite end of the Assyrian dominions had ' rebelled against the king of Assyria, and served him not " (2 Kings xviii. 7). That he should cloak

---

[1] "History of Babylonia," p. 123.   [2] Ibid., p. 125.

his design under the double pretext that his object was to congratulate the Jewish king on his recovery from a dangerous illness (Isa. xxxix. 1), and to inquire concerning the astronomical "wonder done in the land" (2 Chron. xxxii. 31), is intrinsically probable, being consonant with diplomatic practice both in the East and in the West. An astronomical marvel, such as that of the going back of the shadow on the dial of Ahaz (2 Kings xx. 11; Isa. xxxviii, 8), would naturally attract attention in Babylonia, where the phenomena of the heavens were observed with the utmost diligence from a very remote period.

It must not be concealed that there is one important discrepancy between the Scriptural narrative and the history of Merodach-Baladan, as recorded upon the Assyrian monuments. Merodach-Baladan is stated, both by Isaiah and by the compiler of the Book of Kings, to have been "the son of Baladan"—on the monuments he is always called "the son of Yakina," or "Yakin." Mr. George Smith has suggested that Yakin was the name of the tribe whereto Merodach-Baladan belonged;[1] but it can scarcely be argued that he was called "son of Yakin" on this account. Yakin must have been a person; and if not the actual father of Merodach-Baladan, at any rate one of his progenitors. Perhaps the true explanation is, that Yakin was a more or less remote progenitor, the

---

[1] "History of Babylonia," p. 113.

founder of the house, and Baladan (Bel iddina?) the actual father of Merodach-Baladan. By the former designation he was popularly known, by the latter in his official communications.

"The Lord spake to Manasseh and to his people, but they would not hearken. Wherefore the Lord brought upon them the captains of the host of the king of Assyria, which took Manasseh among the thorns, and bound him with fetters, and carried him to Babylon. And when he was in affliction, he besought the Lord his God, and humbled himself greatly before the God of his fathers; and prayed unto Him, and He was intreated of him, and heard his supplication, and brought him again to Jerusalem into his kingdom" (2 Chron. xxxiii. 10-13).

It appears by this passage, 1, that Manasseh, after having provoked God by a long course of wicked conduct, was attacked and made prisoner by the generals of a king of Assyria, who "took him among the thorns," or rather "took him with hooks," and bound him with fetters, and so carried him with them to Babylon; 2, that after having suffered captivity for a time, and repented of his wickedness, he was allowed by the king of Assyria to quit Babylon, and return to Jerusalem, where he was once more established in his kingdom. Three things are especially remarkable in this narrative: (*a*) the generals of the Assyrian monarch conduct Manasseh to their master, not at Nineveh, but *at Babylon*; (*b*) they bring him into the royal presence "*with hooks*," and *fettered;* (*c*) by an act of clemency, very unusual in the East, the Assyrian king pardons him after a time, and goes so far as to reinstate him in his government. We have to consider what light profane history throws upon these facts.

And, first, how comes a king of *Assyria* to hold his court at *Babylon?* Nineveh is the Assyrian capital, and ordinarily the court is held there. If not there, it is held at Dur-Sargina, where Sargon built himself a palace, or at Calah (Nimrud), where were the palaces of Asshur-izir-pal, Shalmaneser II., and Tiglath-Pileser II. What has caused the anomaly of a transfer of the court to the capital of another country? The Assyrian records fully explain this circumstance. Sennacherib, Hezekiah's contemporary, was succeeded by his son, Esar-haddon, who would thus be Manasseh's contemporary. The Assyrian monuments tell us that this monarch inaugurated a new policy with respect to Babylonia. Most Assyrian kings who found themselves strong enough to reduce that country to subjection, governed it by means of a native or Assyrian viceroy ; and this was the plan adopted by Sennacherib, Esar-haddon's father. But Esar-haddon, when he came to the throne, acted differently. He assumed the double title of "King of Assyria and Babylonia," appointed no viceroy, but, having built himself a palace in Babylon, reigned there in person, holding his court sometimes at the northern, sometimes at the southern capital. Towards the end of his life, he relinquished Nineveh altogether to his eldest son, Asshur-bani-pal, and contented himself with ruling the southern kingdom from his palace in Babylon.[1] The anomaly is thus fully explained, and what once appeared a difficulty turns out a confirmation.

What our translators intended to be understood by the expression, "which took Manasseh among the thorns," is perhaps doubtful. But they convey to most minds the idea of a caitiff monarch endeavouring to hide himself from his pursuers in a thorny brake, but detected, and dragged from his concealment. The words in the original have no such meaning. החוחים (khôkhim), the term translated "thorns," is indeed capable of that rendering; but it has also another sense, much more suitable to the present context. Gesenius[2] explains it as "instrumentum ferreum, circulus vel hamus, in modum spinæ aculeat.e, quo olim captivi figebantur, et quo Turcæ suos captivos detinent vinctos." In the singular number the word is translated "hook" in Job xli. 2; and a term nearly identical, khâkh has the same rendering in 2 Kings xix. 28, Isa. xxxvii. 29, Ezek. xxix. 4, xxxviii. 4, etc. These passages sufficiently fix the meaning of the phrase used in Chronicles. The captains of the king of Assyria "took Manasseh

---

[1] G. Smith's "History of Babylonia," pp. 141, 142.
[2] "Hebrew Lexicon," *ad voc.* חוח

away with hooks" (comp. Amos iv. 2), and having also "bound him with fetters," brought him into the presence of Esar-haddon.

The practice of bringing prisoners of importance into the presence of a conquering monarch by means of a thong attached to a hook or ring passed through their upper or their under lip, or both, is illustrated by the sculptures both of Babylonia and Assyria. Sargon is seen in his palace at Khorsabad receiving prisoners whose lips are thus perforated ;[1] and one of the few Babylonian sculptures still extant shows us a vizier conducting into the presence of a monarch two captives held in durance in the same way.[2] Cruel and barbarous as such treatment of a captured king seems to us, there is no doubt that it was an Assyrian usage. To put a hook in a man's mouth, and a bridle in his jaws (2 Kings xix. 28), was no metaphor expressive of mere defeat and capture, but a literal description of a practice that was common in the age and country—a practice from which their royal rank did not exempt even captured monarchs.

The pardon extended by Esar-haddon to Manasseh, little consonant as it is with general Oriental practice, agrees well with the character of this particular monarch, whose rule was remarkably mild, and who is proved by his inscriptions to have been equally merciful on other occasions. When a son of Mero-

---

[1] See "Ancient Monarchies," vol. i., pp. 243, 292 (2nd ed.).
[2] Ibid., vol. iii., p. 7.

dach-Baladan, who had been in revolt against his
authority, quitted his refuge in Susiania, and presented
himself before Esar-haddon's footstool at Nineveh,
that monarch received him favourably, accepted his
homage, and appointed him to the government of a
large tract upon the Persian Gulf, previously ruled
by his father, and afterwards by his elder brother.[1]
Again, when the chief of the Gambalu, an Aramæan
tribe upon the Euphrates, after revolt, submitted himself, and brought the arrears of his tribute, together
with a present of buffaloes, Esar-haddon states that
he forgave him, strengthened his city with fresh works
and continued him in the government of it.[2]

"Jehoiakim was twenty and five years old when he
began to reign, and he reigned eleven years in Jerusalem; and he did that which was evil in the sight
of the Lord his God. Against him came up Nebuchadnezzar, king of Babylon, and bound him in
fetters, to carry him to Babylon. Nebuchadnezzar
also carried off the vessels of the house of the Lord
to Babylon, and put them in his temple at Babylon"
(2 Chron. xxxvi. 5-7).

With this notice may be compared the following,
which relates to the same series of occurrences:—

"In the third year of the reign of Jehoiakim
king of Judah came Nebuchadnezzar king of Babylon
unto Jerusalem and besieged it. And the Lord gave

---

[1] "Ancient Monarchies," vol. ii., p. 188.
[2] Ib. I., p. 191.

Jehoiakim king of Judah into his hand, with part of the vessels of the house of God ; which he carried into the land of Shinar to the house of his god : and he brought the vessels into the treasure house of his god " (Dan. i. 1, 2).

In these passages we have brought before us, 1, the independence of Babylon, which, when last mentioned (2 Chron. xxxiii. 11), was subject to the king of Assyria ; 2, its government by a prince named " Nebuchadnezzar," or, as Ezekiel transliterates the word from the Babylonian, " Nebuchadrezzar " (Ezek. xxvi. 7) ; 3, the fact that this prince made a great expedition into Palestine in the third year of Jehoiakim, king of Judah, besieged Jerusalem, and took it, and made Jehoiakim a prisoner ; 4, the further fact, that he carried off from the Jewish temple a certain portion of the holy vessels, conveyed them to Babylon, and placed them there " in the house of his god."

With respect to the first point, profane history tells us by the mouth of a large number of writers,[1] that towards the close of the seventh century B.C. the Assyrian empire came to an end, Nineveh was destroyed, and Babylon stepped into a position of greatly augmented power and authority. The exact date of the change is undetermined ; but it was certainly not earlier than B.C. 625, and not later than

---

[1] As Herodotus (i. 106, 178), Polyhistor, Abydenus, the writer of the Book of Tobit (xiv. 13), and others.

B.C. 610. The third year of Jehoiakim seems to have been B.C. 605. Thus the independence of Babylonia, distinctly implied in the above passages, was beyond all doubt a *fait accompli* at the time mentioned.

The second point—the government of Babylonia at this exact time by a prince named Nebuchadnezzar or Nebuchadrezzar—is to some extent a difficulty. The name indeed is abundantly confirmed. Nine-tenths of the baked bricks found in Babylonia bear the stamp of "*Nabu-kudurri-uzur*, the son of *Nabu-pal-uzur*, king of Babylon." And Berosus, Abydenus, and Alexander Polyhistor, all give the name with little variation. But Babylonian chronology made Nebuchadnezzar ascend the throne, not in B.C. 605, but in B.C. 604; and Berosus expressly stated that the first expedition conducted by Nebuchadnezzar into Syria, Palestine, and the north-eastern parts of Egypt, fell into the lifetime of his father, Nabopolassar, and preceded his own establishment on the Babylonian throne.[1] The difficulty is sometimes met by the supposition that Nebuchadnezzar was associated in the kingdom by his father before setting out upon his expedition (and association was certainly a practice not unknown to the Babylonians); but the more probable explanation is, that the sacred writers call Nebuchadnezzar "king of Babylon," on first making mention of him, because he became such; just as

---

[1] Berosus, Fr. 14.

we ourselves might say, " King George the Fourth received the allied sovereigns on their visit to England after Waterloo;" or "The Emperor Louis Napoleon was long a prisoner in the fortress of Ham ;" although George the Fourth received the sovereigns as prince regent, and Louis Napoleon was not emperor till many years after his imprisonment was over.[1] Or, it may have been assumed by the Jews, that the leader of the great expedition was the king of the people whom he led against them, and the sacred writers may have received no directions to correct the popular misapprehension.

The expedition itself, and its synchronism with Jehoiakim's third year is generally allowed. Berosus related that in the last year of Nabopolassar's reign, which by the Canon of Ptolemy was B.C. 605, he sent his son Nebuchadnezzar to crush a revolt of the western provinces. Nebuchadnezzar was successful, conquered Syria and Phœnicia, and had invaded Egypt, when news of his father's death reached him, and forced him to return to his own capital.

The fourth point—one of comparative detail— receives very curious illustration from the Babylonian monuments. Nebuchadnezzar is said to have placed the holy vessels which he carried off from Jerusalem "in *his temple* at Babylon," " *the* house of *his god*," and to have " brought them into *the* treasure-house of *his*

See Dr. Pusey's "Daniel," p. 400.

god." These expressions are at first sight surprising, considering that the Babylonian religion was polytheistic, that Babylon had many temples, and that the kings, as a general rule, distributed their favours impartially among the various personages of the pantheon. It is, however, an undoubted fact that Nebuchadnezzar formed an exception to the general rule. He was a devotee of Merodach. He calls Merodach "his lord," "his gracious lord," "his maker," "the god who deposited his germs in his mother's womb," "the god who created him, and assigned him the empire over multitudes of men." One of the foremost of his own titles is "Worshipper of Merodach." He regards Merodach as "the great lord," "the lord of lords," "the chief of the gods," "the king of heaven and earth," "the god of gods." Even on the cylinders which record his dedication of temples to other deities it is Merodach whom he principally glorifies.[1] Sir H. Rawlinson says: "The inscriptions of Nebuchadnezzar are for the most part occupied with the praises of Merodach, and with prayers for the continuance of his favour. The king ascribes to him his elevation to the throne: 'Merodach, the great lord, has appointed me to the empire of the world, and has confided to my care the far-spread people of the earth;' 'Merodach, the great lord, the senior of the gods, the most ancient, has

---

[1] See "Records of the Past," vol. vii., pp. 71—78.

given all nations and people to my care,' etc. The prayer also to Merodach, with which the inscriptions of Nebuchadnezzar always terminate, invokes the favour of the god for the protection of the king's throne and empire, and for its continuance through all ages to the end of time."[1]

The temple of Merodach at Babylon is properly called "Nebuchadnezzar's temple," because he completely rebuilt and restored it. It was the *great* temple of Babylon, and known to the Greeks as the "temple (or tower) of Belus." To its ruins the name of "Babil" still attaches. Nebuchadnezzar describes his restoration of it at great length in his "Standard Inscription;"[2] and his statement is confirmed by the fact that all the inscribed bricks which have ever been found in it bear his name. Special mention of the "treasure-house" attached to the temple has not been found in the Babylonian remains; but it was probably the building at the base of the great tower, which is described by Herodotus as a "second temple," and said to have contained furniture and figures in solid gold, together with many other offerings.[3]

---

[1] Rawlinson, "Herodotus," vol. i., p. 652 (3rd edition).
[2] See "Records of the Past," vol. v., pp. 116—120.
[3] "Herod." i. 183.

CHAPTER III.

NOTICES OF BABYLON IN THE BOOKS OF KINGS AND CHRONICLES. (Continued.)

CHAPTER III.

NOTICES OF BABYLON IN THE BOOKS OF KINGS AND CHRONICLES. (Continued.)

THE numerous expeditions of the Babylonians against Jerusalem, subsequently to the first attack in B.C. 605, receive no direct confirmation from the cuneiform monuments, probably owing to the fact that no general historical inscription descriptive of the events of Nebuchadnezzar's reign has been as yet discovered. The records of his time which modern research has unearthed, consist almost entirely either of invocations addressed to the gods, or of descriptions and measurements connected with his great works.[1] Alexander Polyhistor, however, noticed an expedition of Nebuchadnezzar's into these parts, which appears to have been that conducted in the year B.C. 597, against Jehoiakim, whereof we

---

[1] Until the year 1878, no historical inscription of Nebuchadnezzar's had come to light. In that year a small and mutilated cylinder, giving an account of some events belonging to his thirty-seventh year, was purchased by the British Museum. Further reference will be made to this cylinder in a future chapter.

have the following notice in the Second Book of Kings:—

"The Lord sent against him" (*i.e.*, Jehoiakim) "bands of the Chaldees, and bands of the Syrians, and bands of the Moabites, and bands of the children of Ammon, and sent them against Judah to destroy it, according to the word of the Lord, which He spake by His servants the prophets" (2 Kings xxiv. 2).

Polyhistor tell us [1] that the expedition was one in which Nebuchadnezzar called in the aid of his allies, among others, of the Median king called by him Astibaras, who seems to represent Cyaxares. The number of troops employed was unusually great, amounting, according to the same authority, to ten thousand chariots, one hundred and twenty thousand horsemen, and one hundred and eighty thousand infantry. These numbers imply an army gathered from many nations, and account for the expressions, "bands of the Chaldees, and bands of the Syrians, and bands of the Moabites, and bands of the children of Ammon," in the passage of Kings, as well as for the following in Ezekiel:—

"Then *the nations* set against him on every side from the provinces, and spread their net over him: he was taken in their pit" (Ezek. xix. 8).

The context of this passage shows that the monarch intended is Jehoiakim.

---

[1] "Fragm. Hist. Gr.," vol. iii., p. 229, Fr. 24.

On passing from the reign of Jehoiakim to that of Jehoiachin, the author of Kings makes the following remark :—

"And the king of Egypt came not again any more out of his land ; for the king of Babylon had taken from the river of Egypt unto the river Euphrates all that pertained to the king of Egypt" (2 Kings xxiv. 7).

This remark, though interposed at this point, belongs, so far as it bears on Babylon, to an anterior time. The king of Egypt, the writer intends to say, did not at this time lend any help to Jehoiakim against Nebuchadnezzar, did not even set foot beyond his borders, because some years previously the Egyptians had been worsted in an encounter with the Babylonians, and had lost to them the whole of their Asiatic dominions—the entire tract between the torrent (*nakhal*) of Egypt, or the Wady el Arish, and the Euphrates. The event glanced at is among the most important in the history of the East. When Necho, king of Egypt, in B.C. 608, carried the Egyptian arms triumphantly from the Nile valley to the Upper Euphrates, it seemed as if the old glories of the Thothmeses and Amenhoteps were about to be renewed, as if Egypt was about to become once more the dominant power in western Asia, and to throw the hordes of Asiatic invaders back upon their own continent. A permanent advance of Egypt, and retrocession of Babylon, at this time would greatly have complicated the political problem, and might seriously have checked that aggressive spirit which was already moving Asia to attempt the conquest of Europe. When Nabopolassar, therefore, in the last year of his reign, sent his son Nebuchadnezzar to challenge Necho to a trial of strength, and the hosts of Africa and Asia met in battle array at the great frontier fortress of Carchemish (Jer. xlvi. 2), the issue raised was of no small importance, being nothing less than the question whether African power and influence should or should not maintain itself in Syria and the adjoining regions, should or should not establish its superiority over the power of Asia, should or should not step into a position which would have brought it shortly into direct contact with the civilization of the Greeks. The battle of Carchemish, as it is called, decided these questions. The armies of Nebuchadnezzar and Pharaoh-Necho met in the vicinity of Carchemish (now Jerablus), in B.C. 605, which was the last year of Nabopolassar and the accession year of Nebuchadnezzar, and contended in a great battle, wherein ultimately the Babylonians were victorious. The battle is prophetically, but very graphically, described by the prophet Jeremiah ;

"Order ye the buckler and shield, and draw near to battle," he says ; " harness the horses, and get up, ye horsemen" (or rather, " mount, ye chariotmen") "and stand forth with your helmets; furbish the spears; put on the brigandines. Wherefore have I seen them dismayed and turned away back? Their mighty men are beaten down, and are fled apace, and look not back; for fear was round about, saith the Lord. Let not the swift flee away, nor the mighty man escape; they shall stumble, and fall toward the north by the river Euphrates. Who is this that cometh up as a flood, whose waters toss to and fro as the rivers? Egypt riseth up like a flood, and his waters are tossed to and fro like the rivers; and he saith, I will go up, and will cover the earth; I will destroy the city and the inhabitants thereof. Come up, ye horses; and rage, ye chariots; and let the mighty men come forth, Cush and Phut that handle the shield, and Lud that handle and bend the bow. For this is the day of the Lord God of hosts, a day of vengeance, that He may avenge Him of His adversaries: and the sword shall devour, and it shall be satiate and made drunk with their blood; for the Lord God of hosts hath a sacrifice in the north country by the river Euphrates. Go up into Gilead, and take balm, O virgin, the daughter of Egypt: in vain shalt thou use many medicines; for thou shalt not be cured. The nations have heard of thy shame, and thy cry hath filled the land: for the mighty man hath stumbled against the mighty, and they are fallen both together" (Jer. xlvi. 3—12).

A fierce struggle is here indicated, a hardly contested battle terminating in a complete defeat. Egypt is not surprised—not taken at disadvantage. She has ample time to call together her armed force of natives and auxiliaries, Cush and Phut and Lud. Her chariots are marshalled in their gallant array, together with her horsemen and her footmen: she "rises up like a flood," bent on conquest rather than on mere resistance. But all is in vain. "It is the day of the Lord God of hosts, a day of vengeance." By the river Euphrates the mighty men stumble and fall—they are dismayed and beaten down; in a short time they are compelled to fly—they "flee apace, and look not back." The mighty man hath met a mightier; the forces of Asia have proved too strong for those of Africa; the Nile flood is swept back on its own land.

Profane history, while touching the struggle itself only in a single sentence,[1] amply signalizes the result. With the battle of Carchemish, Babylon, for long ages oppressed and held in subjection, springs up to notice as an empire. Syria, Phœnicia, Palestine, hitherto threatened alternately by Egypt and Syria, now find a new foe in the great city on the Lower Euphrates, and become fiefs of the Babylonian crown. Egypt's attempt to recover, under the Psamatiks, the Asiatic dominion which had been hers under the Thothmeses and Amenho-

---

[1] Beros. ap Joseph., "Contr. Ap." i. 19, § 2.

teps, is rudely checked. Her own territory is invaded, and she becomes for a time a "base kingdom," the subject-ally and tributary of another. Babylon is recognized as one of the "great powers" of Asia, sends her armies within the Cicilian gates, wastes Tyre, destroys Jerusalem, makes alliances with Media and Lydia. The general position of affairs in Western Asia for the next sixty years was determined by the events of that campaign, wherein "the king of Babylon took from the river of Egypt unto the river Euphrates all that pertained unto the king of Egypt."

"They burnt the house of God, and brake down the wall of Jerusalem, and burnt all the palaces thereof with fire, and destroyed all the goodly vessels thereof: and them that had escaped from the sword carried he away to Babylon, where they were servants to him and his sons, until the reign of the kingdom of Persia" (2 Chron. xxxvi. 19, 20).

The complete destruction of Jerusalem, and transfer of its inhabitants from Palestine to Babylonia, momentous events as they were in the history of the Jewish nation, and in that discipline of severity which was to purge out its dross from the people of God, and fit them to hold up the torch of truth to the nations for another half millennium, did not greatly attract the attention of the world at large, or even obtain record generally at the hands of the historiographers who were engaged in chronicling the events of the time. In Babylon, indeed, it must have been otherwise. There, if nowhere else, the final capture and ruin of so great, so renowned, so ancient a city, after a siege which lasted eighteen months, must, beyond a doubt, have been entered upon the records, with the view of its being handed down to posterity. But, unfortunately, it happens that at present, as already observed, Nebuchadnezzar's historical inscriptions remain undiscovered; and consequently we are still deprived of such light as a Babylonian account of the capture of Jerusalem would naturally have thrown on the whole subject. The fragments of Berosus might have been expected to supply the deficiency; but, at the best, they are scanty, and for the time of Nebuchadnezzar they furnish nothing but a bare outline. They do just state that Nebuchadnezzar made an expedition into Palestine and Egypt, carried all before him, and, after burning the temple at Jerusalem, bore away into captivity the whole Jewish people, and settled them in different places in Babylonia;[1] but they give no further particulars. Not even is the name of the Jewish king mentioned, nor that of the general to whom Nebuchadnezzar entrusted the execution of his orders for the destruction of the city.

Direct illustration of the destruction of Jerusalem, and captivity of the Jewish people, is therefore at

---

" Fragm. Hist. Gr ," vol. ii. Fr. 14.

present impossible. Still history may be said to illustrate *indirectly* this portion of the sacred records by the examples which it sets forth of parallel instances. The complete destruction of a great city by the power which conquers it is a rare event, requiring as it does a dogged determination on the part of the conqueror, and a postponement of immediate gain to prospective advantage. But the complete destruction of Nineveh, which is abundantly attested, had taken place not very long before, and must have been fresh in the minds of men at the time, furnishing a precedent for such extreme severity, while a sufficient motive may be discerned in the important position of Jerusalem, and the persistency of the rebellious spirit in its inhabitants.

Transplantations of conquered nations are unknown in modern warfare, and scarcely belong to the history of the West. But in the East they were common anciently, and are still not wholly unknown. The Kurds, who protect the north-eastern frontier of Persia against the raids of the Turkomans, were transported thither by Nadir Shah, after a revolt in Kurdistan, being thus transferred from the extreme west almost to the extreme east of his empire. Sargon transported the Samaritans to Gozan and Media; Sennacherib carried off 200,000 Jews from Judæa; Esar-haddon placed Elamites, Susianians, and Babylonians in Samaria. Darius Hystaspis brought the nation of the Pæonians from Europe into Asia Minor,[1] removed the Barcæans to Bactria,[2] and the Eretrians to Ardericca, near Susa.[3] The forcible removal of large populations from their native countries to a remote region was a portion of the system under which great empires were administered in the Oriental world from the time of Sargon downwards, and was regarded as especially suited for the case where a race distinguished itself by persistence in revolt.

"It came to pass *in the seven and thirtieth year of the captivity of Jehoiachin*, king of Judah, in the twelfth month, on the seven and twentieth day of the month, that Evil-Merodach, king of Babylon, *in the year that he began to reign*, did lift up the head of Jehoiachin, king of Judah, out of prison; and he spake kindly to him, and set his throne above the thrones of the kings that were with him in Babylon; and changed his prison garments: and he did eat bread continually before him all the days of his life" (2 Kings xxv. 27—29).

Evil-Merodach was mentioned as the son and successor of Nebuchadnezzar by Berosus and Abydenus. His name has also been found on no fewer than eleven Babylonian contract tablets, and is transliterated by the best authorities, "Avil-Marduk." There can be no doubt of the position of this king

---

[1] Herod. v. 17.   [2] Ibid. iv. 204.
[3] Ibid. vi. 119.

in the Babylonian list between Nebuchadnezzar and Neriglissar, or Nergal-sar-uzur. As Jehoiachin was carried captive to Babylon by Nebuchadnezzar in the eighth year of his reign (2 Kings xxiv. 12), and Nebuchadnezzar reigned forty-three years, according to Berosus, Ptolemy, and the tablets—commencing his reign in B.C. 605, and ending it in B.C. 562—the "seven and thirtieth year of the captivity of Jehoiachin" would exactly coincide with the first regnal year of Evil-Merodach, which was B.C. 561.

The mild treatment of a rebel, whom Nebuchadnezzar had kept in durance for so many years, was perhaps regarded by the Babylonians as a wrongful departure from their customs. At any rate, we learn from Berosus that within two years of his accession Evil-Merodach was put to death by his subjects, on the charge of ruling in a *lawless* and intemperate fashion. As Jehoiachin "did eat bread continually before Evil-Merodach all the days of his (*i.e.* Jehoiachin's) life," we must suppose that he died within less than two years from his release. He would have been at the time between fifty and sixty years of age.

"Them that had escaped from the sword carried he" (*i.e.*, Nebuchadnezzar) "away to Babylon, where they were servants to him *and his sons* until the reign of the kingdom of Persia ; to fulfil the word of the Lord by the mouth of Jeremiah, until the land had enjoyed her sabbaths ; for as long as she lay desolate she kept sabbath, to fulfil *threescore and ten years* " (2 Chron. xxxvi. 20, 21).

The statement that the Israelites "were servants to Nebuchadnezzar *and his sons*" is at first sight contradictory to the Babylonian history, as delivered to us by profane authors. According to them, Nebuchadnezzar was succeeded by one son only, viz., Evil-Merodach, after whom the crown fell to a certain Neriglissar, or Nergal-sar-uzur, who was not a blood relation. Neriglissar, however, had married a daughter of Nebuchadnezzar, and having thus become a son-in-law, may conceivably be termed a "son." He was succeeded by his own son, Laborosoarchod, probably a grandson of Nebuchadnezzar, who would come under the term "son" by the ordinary Hebrew usage. The successor of Laborosoarchod was, we are told, "in no way related" to the family of Nebuchadnezzar. There are some reasons, however, for believing that he, too, married a daughter of the great monarch ; so that he, too, may have been regarded as "a son" in the same sense with Neriglissar.

The seventy years of the captivity, during which the land lay waste, and "enjoyed its sabbaths," may be counted from different dates. In this place the year of the final destruction of Jerusalem seems to be taken as the *terminus a quo*. This was B.C. 586, the nineteenth year of Nebuchadnezzar (2 Kings xxv. 3—8 ; Jer. lii. 6—12) ; and the passage would therefore seem to point to B.C. 516 as the termination of the captivity period. Now B.C. 516, the sixth of Darius Hystaspis, was, in fact, the close of the period of depression and desolation, so far as the temple was concerned (Ezra vi. 15). But the personal captivity, the desolation of the *land* through loss of inhabitants, both began and ended earlier. Jeremiah evidently intended his "seventy years" to count from the first capture of Jerusalem by Nebuchadnezzar (Jer. xxv. 1—12), which was in B.C. 605 ; and Daniel must have counted from the same date when he felt, in B.C. 538, that the time of release was approaching (Dan. ix. 2). It is questionable, however, whether the full term of the prophetic announcement, thus understood, was actually reached. If Nebuchadnezzar carried away his first captives from Jerusalem in B.C. 605, and Cyrus issued his edict for the return in his first year (2 Chron. xxxvi. 22 ; Ezra i. 1), which was B.C. 538, the seventieth year had certainly not then commenced. Even if the captives did not take immediate advantage of the edict, but made the journey from Babylonia to Palestine in the year following the proclamation, B.C. 537, which is not improbable, still the captivity had not endured seventy years, but only sixty-eight. It is usual to meet the difficulty by the supposition that the first year of Cyrus *in Scripture* is really the third year from his conquest of Babylon, Darius the Mede having been made viceroy of Babylon under Cyrus during the first two years after the conquest. This is, no doubt, a possible explanation. But it is perhaps as probable that the *round* number "seventy," in the prophecy of Jeremiah, was not intended to be exact, but approximate, and that the actual duration of the captivity fell short by a year or two of the threatened period.

That "the reign of the kingdom of Persia" immediately succeeded to that of Babylon, which was swallowed up by the Great Aryan power within seventy years of the accession of Nebuchadnezzar, is declared with one voice by the classical historians, and has been recently confirmed by more than one native document. Two inscriptions, brought from Babylonia within the last decade, describe the circumstances under which the great empire of Babylon collapsed before the arms of Cyrus the Great, and was absorbed into his dominions. The details of the subjection will have to be considered hereafter, when we comment on those passages of Scripture which treat directly of the fall of the city. At present we desire simply to note the confirmation by the monuments of the Persian conquest, effected by Cyrus the Great, in the seventeenth year of Nabonidus, which was the sixty-eighth year after the accession of Nebuchadnezzar and his first capture of Jerusalem.[1]

---

[1] See the "Transactions of the Society of Biblical Archæology," vol. vi., pp. 47—61.

CHAPTER IV.

NOTICES OF BABYLON IN DANIEL.

CHAPTER IV.

NOTICES OF BABYLON IN DANIEL.

THE history of the chosen people during the period of the Babylonian captivity is carried on in a book which we are accustomed to regard as prophetical, but in which the historical element decidedly preponderates. The first six chapters of Daniel contain a continuous and most important narrative. The scene of the history has been transferred from Jerusalem to Babylon. We are introduced into the court of the great King Nebuchadnezzar, and shown his grandeur, his pride, his cruelty, his relentings, his self-glorification, his punishment. We find the Jews his captives, scattered in various parts of his territories (ch. ix. 7), without organization or national life, a mere herd of slaves, down-trodden and oppressed for the most part. At the court, however, it is different. There four Jews, of royal, or at any rate noble blood, occupy a position of some importance, take rank among the courtiers, hold communication with the monarch, and are called upon to advise him in circumstances of difficulty (ch. i. 17—20). After a time they rise still higher in the king's favour, and are promoted to some of the chief governmental offices in the kingdom (ch. ii. 48, 49). One, the writer of great part of the book, if not even of the whole, becomes the very first person in the kingdom next to the king, and lives and prospers under four monarchs, called respectively, Nebuchadnezzar, Belshazzar, Cyrus, and Darius. We have thus a considerable body of Babylonian history in this (so-called) prophetical book; and numerous points present themselves on which some illustration of the history from profane sources is possible.

Let us take, first, the character of Nebuchadnezzar's court. It is vast and complicated, elaborate in its organization, careful in its etiquette, magnificent in its ceremonial. Among the most important personages in it are a class who profess to have the power of expounding dreams, and generally foretelling future events by means of magic, sorcery, and astrology (ch. ii. 2, 10, 27, etc.). Next to these are the civil administrators, " princes, governors, captains, judges, treasurers, councillors, sheriffs, and rulers of provinces " (ch. iii. 2), who are specially summoned to attend in full numbers on certain grand occasions. The king is waited on by eunuchs, sometimes of royal descent, who are subjected to a three years' careful training, and are under the superintendence of a " master of the eunuchs," who is an officer of high position (ch. i. 3—5). The monarch has, of course, a "body-guard," which is under the command of a "captain" (ch. ii. 14), another high official. Music is used at the court in ceremonials, and is apparently of an advanced kind, the bands comprising performers on at least six different musical instruments (ch. iii. 5, 7, 10, etc.).

The Babylonian and Assyrian remains amply illustrate most of these particulars. Magic holds a most important place in both nations, and the monarchs set a special value on it. Their libraries contained hundreds of tablets, copied with the utmost care, on which were recorded the exorcisms, the charms, the talismans and the astronomical prognostics, which had come down from a remote antiquity, and which were implicitly believed in. The celestial phenomena were constantly observed, and reports sent to the court from the observatories, which formed the groundwork of confident predictions.[1] Eclipses were especially noted, and, according to the month and day of their occurrence, were regarded as portending events, political, social, or meteorological.[2] We give a specimen from an astronomical calendar:—

"In the month of Elul (August), the 14th day, an eclipse happens; in the north it begins, and in the south and east it ends; in the evening watch it begins, and in the night watch it ends. To the king

---

[1] "Records of the Past," vol. i., pp. 153—157.
[2] Ibid., pp. 158—161.

of Mullias a crown is given. . . . There are rains in heaven, and in the channels of the rivers floods. A famine is in the country, and men sell their sons for silver.

"An eclipse happens on the 15th day. The king's son murders his father, and seizes on the throne. The enemy plunders and devours the land.. ..

"An eclipse happens on the 16th day. The king of the Hittites plunders the land, and on the throne seizes. There is rain in heaven, and a flood descends in the channels of the rivers.

"An eclipse happens on the 20th day. There are rains in heaven, and floods in the rivers. Country makes peace with country, and keeps festival.

"An eclipse happens on the 21st day. The enemy's throne does not endure. A self-appointed king rules in the land. After a year the Air god causes an inundation. After a year the king does not remain. His country is made small."[1]

The application of the ethnic term "Chaldæan" (Kasdim) to the learned caste, or class, which occupied itself with the subjects of magic and astrology, so frequent in Daniel (ch. ii. 2, 4, 5, 10 ; v. 11), is found also in profane writers, as Strabo, Diodorus, Cicero, and others,[2] who distinguish between Chaldæans and Babylonians, making the latter term the

---

[1] "Records of the Past," vol. i., p. 160.

[2] Diod. Sic. ii. 29 ; Strab. xvi. 1, § 6 ; Cic. *De Div.* i. 1, § 2 ; 42, § 93 : Plin. *H.N.* vi. 30, § 123, etc.

ethnic appellative of the nation at large, while they reserve the former for a small section of the nation, distinguished by the possession of abstruse and recondite learning. The distinction seems to have originated in the later period of the empire, and to have been grounded on an identification of the Chaldæans with the Akkad, and on the fact that the old Akkadian language and learning was in the later times the special possession of a literary class, who furnished to the nation its priests, astrologers, magicians, and men of science. What the real connection was between the Chaldæans and the Akkad is still uncertain ; but some ethnic affinity may be regarded as probable.

The division of the learned class into three distinct bodies, devoted to different branches of the mystic lore in which all participated, receives illustration from the native remains, where the literature of magic comes under three principal heads: (1) written charms or talismans, which were to be placed on the bodies of sick persons, or on the doorposts of afflicted houses ;[1] (2) formulæ of incantation, which had to be recited by the learned man in order to produce their proper effect ;[2] and (3) records of observations, intended to serve as grounds for the prediction of particular events, together with collections of prog-

---

[1] See " Records of the Past," vol. iii., p. 142.
[2] Ibid., vol. iii., pp. 147-152, and xi., 128-138.

nostics from eclipses or other celestial phenomena, regarded as having a general applicability.[1] The preparation of the written charms or talismans was probably the special task of the " magicians " or *khertummim*, whose name is formed from the root *kheret*, which signifies "an engraving tool," or "stylus." The composition and recitation of the formulæ of incantation belonged to the *ashshaphim* or *mecashaphim*, the " astrologers " and " sorcerers " of our version, whose names are derived from the root *ashaph* or *cashaph*, which means " to mutter."[2] The taking of observations and framing of tables of prognostics is probably to be assigned to the *gâzerim* or " dividers," in our version " soothsayers," who *divided* the heavens into constellations or " houses " for astronomical and astrological purposes.[3]

The attention paid to dreams (ch. ii. 1—46, iv. 5—27) by the Babylonian monarch is quite in accordance with what we know of the state of opinion, both in Babylonia and Assyria, about the time of Nebuchadnezzar. The Assyrians had a " dream deity," whom they called Makhir, and regarded as " the daughter of the Sun," and to whom they were in the habit of praying, either beforehand, to send them favourable dreams, or after they had dreamed to " confirm " their dream, or make it turn out

---

[1] " Records of the Past," vol. ix., pp. 153—163.
[2] Furst, " Concordant." p. 133.
[3] "Ancient Monarchies," vol. ii., p. 575.

favourably to them.[1] A late Assyrian monarch records that, in the course of a war which he carried on with Elam or Susiania, one of his "wise men" dreamed a remarkable dream, and forthwith communicated to him the particulars. "Ishtar," he said, "the goddess of war, had appeared to him in the dead of night, begirt with flames on the right hand and on the left; she held a bow in her hand, and was riding in a chariot, as if going forth to war. Before her stood the king, whom she addressed as a mother would her child . . . 'Take this bow,' she said, 'and go with it to the battle. Wherever thou shalt pitch thy camp, I will come to thee.' Then the king replied, 'O queen of all the goddesses, wherever thou goest, let me accompany thee.' She made answer, 'I will protect thee, and march with thee at the time of the feast of Nebo. Meanwhile, eat meat, drink wine, make music, and glorify my divinity, until I come to thee and this vision shall be fulfilled.'" Rendered confident by his dream, the Assyrian monarch marched forth to war, attacked the Elamites in their own country, defeated them, and received their submission.[2]

Not very long after the time of Nebuchadnezzar, Nabonidus, one of his successors, places on record the following incident:—"In the beginning of my long reign," he says, "Merodach, the great Lord, and

---

[1] "Records of the Past," vol. ix., p. 152.
[2] Ibid., vol. vii., p. 68.

Sin, the illuminator of heaven and earth, the strengthener of all, showed me a dream. Merodach spake thus with me: 'Nabonidus, king of Babylon, come up with the horses of thy chariot; build the walls of Ehulhul; and have the seat of Sin, the great lord, set within it.' Reverently I made answer to the lord of the gods, Merodach, 'I will build this house of which thou speakest. The Sabmanda destroyed it, and strong was their might.' Merodach replied to me, 'The Sabmanda of whom thou speakest, they and their country, and the king who rules over them, shall cease to exist.' In the third year he (*i.e.*, Merodach) caused Cyrus, king of Ansan, his young servant, to go with his little army: he overthrew the wide-spreading Sabmanda; he captured Istumegu (*i.e.*, Astyages), king of Sabmanda, and took his treasures to his own land."[1]

The civil organization of the Babylonian kingdom is very imperfectly known to us. Neither sacred nor profane authorities furnish more than scattered and incomplete notices of it. We gather from Daniel merely that it was elaborate and complicated, involving the employment by the crown of numerous officers, discharging distinct functions, and possessing different degrees of dignity. The names given to the various officers by Daniel can scarcely be those which were in actual use under the Babylonian monarch, since

---

[1] "Proceedings of the Society of Biblical Archæology," November, 1882, p. 7.

they are in many cases of Aryan etymology. Most likely they are the equivalents under the Medo-Persic system, which was established before David wrote his book, of the Babylonian terms previously in vogue. Still, in some instances, the names sufficiently indicate the offices intended. The "princes" (literally "satraps") of Dan. iii. 2, 3, 27, can only be governors of provinces (compare ch. vi. 1), chief rulers under the monarch of the main territorial divisions of his empire. Such persons had been generally employed by the Assyrian kings in the government of the more settled parts of their dominions, and were no doubt continued by the Babylonians when the territories of Assyria were divided between them and the Medes. Gedaliah held the office in Judæa immediately after its conquest by Nebuchadnezzar (2 Kings xxv. 22—25; Jer. xl. 5). Another such Babylonian governor is actually called a "satrap" by Berosus.[1] Babylonian witnesses to contracts still in existence often sign themselves "governor," sometimes "governor" of a province which they mention.[2] The *sagans* ("governors" in our version) may be "governors" of towns, who are often mentioned in the inscriptions as distinct from governors of provinces. The "judges" (literally "noble judges") are no doubt the heads of the judicature, which was separate from the executive in

[1] Ap. Joseph, "Contr. Apion.," i. 19.
[2] "Records of the Past," vol. ix., pp. 34, 92, 98, 107.

Babylonia, as in Persia.[1] They, too, appear in the inscriptions,[2] as do "treasurers" and "captains."[3] It is not intended to assert that the correspondence between Daniel's account of the civil administration and that indicated by the Babylonian remains is very close or striking, but the general features certainly possess considerable resemblance, and there is as much agreement in the details as could fairly be expected.

The employment of eunuchs at the Babylonian court, under the presidency of a "master of the eunuchs," is analogous to the well-known practice of the Assyrians, where the president, or "master," bore the title of rab-saris, or "chief eunuch" (2 Kings xviii. 17). It also receives illustration from the story of Nanarus, as told by Nicholas of Damascus, a writer whose Asiatic origin makes him a high authority upon the subject of Oriental habits. Nanarus, according to him, was one of the later Babylonian monarchs, a successor of the Belesis who appears to represent Nabopolassar. His court was one in which eunuchs held all the most important positions; and the head eunuch, Mitraphernes, was the chief counsellor of the king.[4]

The delight of the Babylonians in music, and the

---

[1] Herod., iii. 31.
[2] "Records of the Past," vol. vii., p. 120; vol. xi., p. 103.
[3] Ibid, vol. ix., p. 104; vol. xi., p. 103.
[4] See the "Fragm. Hist. Gr.," vol. iii., pp. 359—363.

advanced condition of the art among them, is confirmed and illustrated by the same story of Nanarus. Nanarus, according to Nicholas, maintained at his court no fewer than a hundred and fifty female musicians, of whom some sang, while others played upon instruments. Among the instruments indicated are three of those mentioned in Daniel—the flute, the cithern ("harp," A.V.), and the psaltery. Sculpture does not readily lend itself to the representation of so large a crowd, but we see in a bas-relief of a date a little anterior to Nebuchadnezzar a band of twenty-six performers.[1] At least eight or nine different instruments were known to the Assyrians;[2] and we can therefore feel no surprise that six were in use among the Babylonians of Nebuchadnezzar's time.

Considerable difficulty has been felt with respect to the names of several of the Babylonian instruments. These names have a Greek appearance; and it has been asked by critics of reputation, "How could Greek musical instruments have been used at Babylon late in the seventh, or early in the sixth century before our era?" A searching analysis of the words themselves has thrown a good deal of doubt on several of the supposed Greek etymologies. *Karna* and κέρας, *kitheros* and κιθάρις, *sabkah* and σαμβύκη are no doubt connected; but one of them is a root common to Semitic with Aryan, while the other two

---

[1] "Ancient Monarchies," vol. i., p. 542.
[2] Ibid., pp. 529—539.

passed probably from the Orientals to the Greeks. The Chaldee *karna* is Hebrew *keren*, and is at least as old in Hebrew as the Pentateuch ; *kitheros* is Persian *sitarch*, Greek κιθάρις, German *zither*, modern Arabic *koothir* ; *sabkah* is from *sabakh*, a well-known Semitic root, and is an appropriate name for a "harp" in Hebrew ;[1] whereas σαμβύκη is an unmeaning name in Greek. To derive *mashrokitha* from σύριγξ requires a very hardy etymologist. The two words may conceivably be derivatives from one root ; but neither can possibly have been the direct parent of the other. Even *pesanterin* and *sûmphonyah*, though so near to ψαλτήριον and συμφωνία, are not allowed by all critics to be of Greek origin.[2] Supposing, however, that they are, and that they imply the use by the Babylonians of Greek instruments, which brought their names with them from their native country, as "pianoforte" and "concertina" have done with us, there is nothing extraordinary in the circumstance. The Assyrians and the Greeks came into contact in Cyprus as early as the reign of Sargon,[3] whose effigy has been found at Idalium. Esar-Haddon obtained building materials from several Cyprian kings with Greek names.[4] As the inheritress of Assyrian luxury and magnificence, Babylon

---

[1] Pusey's "Daniel," p. 24, note 9.
[2] Ibid., pp. 27—30.
[3] "Ancient Monarchies," vol. ii., p. 150.
[4] "Records of the Past," vol. iii., p. 108.

would necessarily have some connection with Greeks. We hear of a Greek having served in Nebuchadnezzar's army, and won glory and reward under his banners.[1] Direct intercourse with Hellenes may thus have brought Hellenic instruments to Babylon. Or the intercourse may have been indirect. The Phœnicians were engaged in a carrying trade between Europe and Asia from a time anterior to Solomon; and their caravans were continually passing from Tyre and Sidon, by way of Tadmor and Thapsacus, to the Chaldæan capital. Nothing would be more natural than the importation into that city, at any time between B.C. 605 and B.C. 538, of articles manufactured in Greece, which the Babylonians were likely to appreciate.

The position of the king in the Babylonian court as absolute lord and master of the lives and liberties even of the greatest of his subjects, able to condemn to death, not only individuals (ch. iii. 19), but a whole class, and that class the highest in the state (ch. ii. 12—14), is thoroughly in accordance with all that profane history tells us of the Babylonian governmental system. In Oriental monarchies it was not always so. The writer of the Book of Daniel shows a just appreciation of the difference between the Babylonian and the Medo-Persian systems, when he makes Darius the Mede influenced by his nobles, and

---

[1] Strab. xiii. 3, § 2.

compelled to do things against his will by a "law of the Medes and Persians, which altered not" (ch. vi. 14—17); while Nebuchadnezzar the Babylonian is wholly untrammeled, and does not seem even to consult his lords on matters where the highest interests of the state are concerned. Babylonian and Assyrian monarchs were absolute in the fullest sense of the word. No traditional "law" restrained them. Their nobility was an official nobility, like that of Turkey at the present day. They themselves raised it to power; and it lay with them to degrade its members at their pleasure. Officers such as the tartan, or "commander-in-chief," the rab-shaketh, or "chief cup-bearer," and the rab-saris, or "chief eunuch," held the highest positions (2 Kings xviii. 17)—mere creatures of the king, whom a "breath had made," and a breath could as easily "unmake." The kings, moreover, claimed to be of Divine origin, and received Divine honours. "Merodach," says Nebuchadnezzar, "deposited my germ in my mother's womb."[1] Khammurabi claims to be the son of Merodach and Ri.[2] He was joined in inscriptions with the great gods, Sin, Shamas, and Merodach, during his lifetime, and people swore by his name.[3] Amar-agu and Naram-sin are also said to have been deified while

---

[1] "Records of the Past," vol. v., p. 113.
[2] Ibid., vol. i., p. 8.
[3] Ibid., vol. v., p. 100.

still living.[1] It was natural that those who claimed, and were thought to hold so exalted a position, should exercise a despotic authority, and be unresisted, even when they were most tyrannical.

---

[1] See note on Dan vi. 7, in the "Speaker's Commentary."

CHAPTER V.
NOTICES OF BABYLON IN DANIEL (continued).

CHAPTER V.

NOTICES OF BABYLON IN DANIEL (continued).

THE character of Nebuchadnezzar, as depicted in the Book of Daniel, is confirmed as fully as could be expected, considering the nature of the materials that have come down to us, from profane sources. These materials are scanty, and of a peculiar character. They consist of a very few brief notices in classical writers, and of some half-dozen inscriptions belonging to the reign of Nebuchadnezzar himself, and apparently either composed by him or, at least, put forth under his authority. These inscriptions are in some cases of considerable length,[1] and, so far, might seem ample for the purpose whereto we propose to apply them; but, unfortunately, they present scarcely any variety. With the exception of one, which is historical, but very short and much mutilated,[2] they are accounts of buildings,

---

[1] One of them consists of ten columns, with an average of sixty-two lines in each, and in the "Records of the Past" occupies twenty-three pages (vol. iii., pp. 113—135).

[2] See the "Transactions of the Society of Bibl. Archæology," vol. vii. pp. 218—222.

accompanied by religious invocations. It is evident that such records do not afford much opportunity for the display of more than a few points of character. They can tell us nothing of those qualities which are called forth in action, in the dealings of man with man, in war, in government, in domestic intercourse. Thus the confirmation which it is possible to adduce from this source can only be partial; and it is supplemented only to a very small extent from the notices of the classical writers.

The most striking features of Nebuchadnezzar's character, as pourtrayed for us in Scripture, and especially in the Book of Daniel, will probably be allowed to be the following: 1. His cruelty. Not only is he harsh and relentless in his treatment of the foreign enemies who have resisted him in arms, tearing thousands from their homes, and carrying them off into a miserable and hopeless captivity, massacring the chief men by scores (2 Kings xxv. 18—21), blinding rebel kings (ver. 7), or else condemning them to perpetual imprisonment (ver. 27), and even slaying their sons before their eyes (ver. 7); but at home among his subjects he can condemn to death a whole class of persons for no fault but inability to do what no one had ever been asked to do before (Dan. ii. 10—13), and can actually cast into a furnace of fire three of his best officers, because they decline to worship the image which he has set up (iii. 20—23).
2. His pride and boastfulness. The pride of Nebu-

chadnezzar first shows itself in Scripture in the contemptuous inquiry addressed to the "three children" (Dan. iii. 15), "Who is that God that shall deliver you out of my hands?" Evidently he believes that this is beyond the power of any god. He speaks as Sennacherib spoke by the mouth of Rab-shakeh: " Hearken not to Hezekiah, when he persuadeth you, saying, The Lord will deliver us. Hath any of the gods of the nations delivered at all his land out of the hand of the king of Assyria? Where are the gods of Hamath and of Arpad? Where are the gods of Sepharvaim, Hena, and Ivah? Have they delivered Samaria out of mine hand? Who are they among the gods of the countries, that have delivered their country out of mine hand, that the Lord should deliver Jerusalem out of mine hand?" (2 Kings xviii. 32—35). The event shows him that he is mistaken, and that there is a God who can deliver His servants, and "change the king's word" (Dan. iii. 38), and then for a time he humbles himself; but, later on, the besetting sin breaks out afresh; "his heart is lifted up, and his mind hardened in pride" (ch. v. 20), and he makes the boast which brings upon him so signal a punishment: "Is not this great Babylon that I have built for the house of my kingdom, *by the might of my power, and for the honour of my majesty?*" The punishment inflicted once more humbled him, and he confessed finally that there was one, "the King of heaven, all whose works were truth, and His ways judgment;" and that "those who walk in pride He was able to abase" (ch. iv. 37). 3. His religiousness. The spoils which Nebuchadnezzar carried off from the Temple at Jerusalem he did not convert to his own use, nor even bring into the national treasury; but "put them in his temple at Babylon" (2 Chron. xxxvi. 7), and "brought them into the treasure-house of his god" (Dan. i. 2). When Daniel revealed to him his dream and its interpretation (ch. ii. 27—45), he at once confessed, "Of a truth your God is a God of gods, and a Lord of kings, and a revealer of secrets, seeing thou couldst reveal this secret." The image which he made, and set up on the plain of Dura, was not his own image, but an image of a Babylonian god (ch. iii. 12, 14, 18), to whom he was anxious that all his subjects should do honour. His anger against Shadrach, Meshach, and Abednego was not so much because they resisted his will, as because they would not "serve his god." When the fiery furnace had no power on them, he accepted the fact as proving that there was another God, whom he had not known of previously, and at once commanded that this new God should be respected throughout his dominions (ch. iii. 29). But his religiousness culminates in the last scene of his life that is presented to us in Scripture. After his recovery from the severe affliction whereby his pride was punished, he at once "lifted up his eyes to heaven," and "blessed the Most High, and praised and honoured Him that liveth for ever" (ch. iv. 34), and made a proclamation, which he caused to be published throughout the length and breadth of his vast dominions (ver. 1), acknowledging his sin, and declaring that he "honoured and extolled the King of heaven" (ver. 37), and "thought it good to show the signs and wonders that the high God had wrought towards him" (ver. 2), since "His signs were great, and His wonders mighty, and His kingdom an everlasting kingdom, and His dominion from generation to generation" (ver. 3).

A fourth and special characteristic of Nebuchadnezzar, peculiar to him among the heathen monarchs brought under our notice in Scripture, is the mixed character of his religion, the curious combination which it presents of monotheism with polytheism, the worship of one God with that of many. Nebuchadnezzar's polytheism is apparent when he addresses Daniel as "one in whom is the spirit of the holy *gods*" (ch. iv. 8, 9, 18), and again when he calls the figure which he sees walking with the "three children" in the furnace "a son of the *gods*" (בַּר־אֱלָהִין *bar-elâhin*, ch. iii. 25), and still more plainly when he recognizes the God who has delivered the "children" as *a* God, "their God" (ver. 28), and declares his belief that "no *other god* can deliver *after this sort*" (ver. 29). His monotheism shows itself—though not made apparent in our version—

when he sets up a single image, and calls on the people to worship "his god" (ch. iii. 14), when he recognizes Daniel's God as "a Lord of kings and *God of gods*" (ch. ii. 47), and most conspicuously when in his last proclamation he acknowledges "the high God" (אֱלָהָא עִלָּיָא *ĕlâhâ 'illâyâ*, ch. iv. 2), "the Most High" (ver. 34), "the King of heaven" (ver. 37), Him that "liveth for ever" (ver. 34), and "*doeth according to His will in the army of heaven* and among the inhabitants of the earth," and "whose hand none can stay, nor can any say unto Him, What doest thou?" (ver. 35). Either he fluctuates between two beliefs, or else his polytheism is of that modified kind which has been called "Katheno-theism,"[1] where the worshipper, on turning his regards to any particular deity, "forgets for the time being that there is any other, and addresses the object of his adoration in terms of as absolute devotion as if he were the sole god whom he recognized, the one and only divine being in the entire universe."[2]

Limiting ourselves, for the present, to these four characteristics of the great Babylonian monarch—his cruelty, his boastful pride, his religiousness, and the curious mixture of two elements in his religion—let us inquire how far they are confirmed or illustrated

---

[1] Max Müller, "Chips from a German Workshop," vol. i., p. 28.
[2] See the author's "Religions of the Ancient World," p. 127.

by his own inscriptions, or by the accounts which profane writers have given of him.

And first, with respect to his cruelty. Here, it must be confessed, there is little, if any, confirmation. The one brief historical inscription of Nebuchadnezzar's time which we possess contains no notice of any severities, nor is the point touched in the few fragments concerning him which are all that classical literature furnishes. Berosus mentions the numerous captives whom he carried off to Babylonia in his first campaign,[1] but does not seem to regard their fate as exceptionally wretched. Josephus gives us in some detail the various cruelties recorded of him in Scripture, and adds others, as that he put to death a king of Egypt whom he conquered;[2] but Josephus is scarcely an unprejudiced witness. Abydenus, who tells us more about him than any other classical writer except Berosus, is bent on glorifying him, and would not be likely to mention what was to his discredit. If, however, we have no confirmation, we have abundant illustrations of Nebuchadnezzar's cruelties in the accounts given us of their own doings by the Assyrian monarchs to whose empire Nebuchadnezzar had succeeded. Assyrian monarchs transport entire nations to distant lands, massacre prisoners by scores or hundreds, put captive kings

---

[1] Ap. Joseph., "Ant. Jud.," x. 11, § 1.
[2] Ibid., x. 9, § 7.

to death, or mutilate them, cut men to pieces,[1] and even burn them to death in furnaces.[2] The recorded cruelties of Nebuchadnezzar pale before those which Asshur-bani-pal, the son of Esarhaddon, who lived less than a century earlier, mentions as commanded by himself, and executed under his orders.[3]

Nebuchadnezzar's pride and boastfulness were noted by Abydenus, who spoke of him as *superbia tumidus* and *fastu elatus.*[4] His own inscriptions not only accumulate on him titles of honour and terms of praise, but seem altogether composed with the object of glorifying himself rather than the deities whom they profess to eulogise. Among the titles which he assumes are those of "glorious prince," "the exalted," or "the exalted chief," "the possessor of intelligence," "he who is firm, and not to be overthrown," "the valiant son of Nabopolassar," "the devout and pious," "the lord of peace," "the noble king," and "the wise Mage."[5] Nebuchadnezzar declares that "the god Merodach deposited his germ in his mother's womb," that "Nebo gave into his hand the sceptre of righteousness," that Sin was "the strengthener of his hands," that Shamas "perfected

---

[1] "Records of the Past," vol. ix., p. 57.
[2] Ibid., vol. i., p. 77; vol. ix., p. 56, etc.
[3] Ibid., vol. i., pp. 57—102.
[4] "Fr. Hist. Græc.," vol. iv., p. 283, Fr. 8.
[5] "Records of the Past," vol. v., pp. 113, 114; vol. vii., pp. 71, 75.

good in his body," and Gula " beautified his person."[1]
He boasts that he is "the eldest son of Merodach,"
who has made him "the chosen of his heart;"[2] he,
for his part, is "the rejoicer of the heart of Merodach."[3]
"Merodach has made him a surpassing prince;" he
"has extended Merodach's power;"[4] owing his
own exaltation to Merodach and Nebo, he has exalted
them in turn; and the impression left is that they
have had rather the better of the bargain. Other
Babylonian kings are moderate in their self-praise
compared with Nebuchadnezzar, as may been seen
by his inscriptions and those of Neriglissar and
Nabonidus.

The religiousness of Nebuchadnezzar is even more
conspicuous in his inscriptions than his pride. Not
only was he, as a modern writer expresses it, "faithful to the orthodoxy of his day;"[5] but a real devotion
to his gods seems to have animated him. His own
name for himself is "the heaven-adoring king."[6] He
places some god, generally Merodach, in the forefront of every inscription; acknowledges that his
life and success were the fruit of the divine favour;
labours to show his gratitude by praises and invoca-

---

[1] "Records of the Past," vol. v., pp. 113, 114, 122, 123.
[2] Ibid., p. 125.
[3] Ibid., p. 134.
[4] Ibid., p. 134.
[5] G. Smith, "History of Babylonia," p. 167.
[6] "Records of the Past," vol. vii., p. 78.

tions, by the presentation of offerings, the building and repair of temples, the adornment of shrines, the institution of processions, and the proclamation of each god by his proper titles.[1] He speaks of Merodach "accepting the devotion of his heart;"[2] and there is no reason to doubt that he speaks sincerely. He looks to his deities for blessings, beseeches them to sustain his life, to keep reverence for them in his heart, to give him a long reign, a firm throne, abundant and vigorous offspring, success in war, and a record of his good deeds in their book.[3] He hopes that these good deeds are acceptable to them, and are regarded with satisfaction: whether he expects them to be rewarded in another life is not apparent.

The peculiar character of Nebuchadnezzar's religion —at one time polytheistic, at another monotheistic— is also evidenced by his inscriptions. The polytheism is seen in the distinct and separate acknowledgment of at least thirteen deities, to most of whom he builds temples, as well as in his mention of "the great gods,"[4] and the expressions "chief of the *gods*," "king of *gods*," and "god of *gods*," which are of frequent occurrence. The monotheism, or at least the "kathenotheism," discloses itself in the attitude

---

[1] "Records of the Past," vol., v., pp. 113, 114, etc.

[2] Ibid., p. 114.

[3] Ibid., vol. vii., pp. 72—77.

[4] Ibid., vol. v., p. 129; "Trans. of Bibl. Arch. Soc.," vol. vii., p. 219.

assumed towards Merodach, who is "the great Lord," "the God his maker," "the Lord of all beings," "the Prince of the lofty house," "the chief, the honourable, the Prince of the gods, the great Merodach," "the Divine Prince, the Deity of heaven and earth, the Lord God," "the King of gods and Lord of lords," "the chief of the gods," "the Lord of the gods," "the God of gods," and "the King of heaven and earth." Nebuchadnezzar assigns to Merodach a pre-eminence which places him on a pedestal apart from and above all the other deities of his pantheon. He does not worship him exclusively, but he worships him mainly; and when engaged in the contemplation of his greatness, scarcely takes into account the existence of any other deity. No other Babylonian king is so markedly the votary of one god as Nebuchadnezzar; though, no doubt, something of a similar spirit may be traced in the inscriptions of Khammurabi, of Neriglissar, and of Nabonidus.

Besides the main traits of character, of which we have hitherto spoken, there are certain minor features in the biblical portraiture which seem entitled to mention. Nebuchadnezzar is brave and energetic. He leads his armies in person (2 Kings xxiv. 1, 10, xxv. 1; Jer. xxi. 2, xxiv. 1, xxxiv. 1, etc.), presses his enterprises vigorously, is not easily discouraged or rebuffed, has the qualities of a good general, is brave, "bold in design, and resolute in action."[1] His own inscriptions so far agree, that they represent him as making war upon Egypt,[2] as desiring "the conquest of his enemies' land,"[3] and as looking forward to the accumulation at his great Babylonian temple of "the abundant tribute of the kings of nations and of all people."[4] Profane historians go far beyond this; they represent him as one of the greatest of conquerors. Berosus ascribes to him the conquest of Syria, Phœnicia, Egypt, *and Arabia!*[5] Abydenus says that he was "more valiant than Hercules," and not only reduced Egypt, but subdued all Libya, as far as the Straits of Gibraltar, and thence passing over into Spain, conquered the Iberians, whom he took with him to Asia, and settled in the country between Armenia and the Caucasus![6] Menander and Philostratus spoke of his thirteen-years-long siege of Tyre;[7] and Megasthenes put him on a par with Sesostris and Tirhakah.[8]

The religion of Nebuchadnezzar was, as might

---

[1] G. Smith, "History of Babylonia," p. 166.
[2] "Transactions of Society of Bibl. Archæology," vol. vii., p. 220.
[3] "Records of the Past," vol. vii., p. 77.
[4] Ibid., vol. v., p. 135.
[5] See the fragments of Berosus in the "Fr. Hist. Gr.," vol. ii., fr. 14.
[6] Ibid., vol. iv., p. 283, fr. 9.
[7] Ap. Joseph., "Ant. Jud.," x. 11, § 1, *sub fin.*
[8] Ap. Strab., xv. 1, § 6.

have been expected, tinged with superstition. We are told in Scripture that on one occasion a "king of Babylon," who can be no other than he, in one of his military expeditions, "stood at the parting of the way, at the head of two ways, to use divination. He made his arrows bright (or rather, 'he shook his arrows'); he consulted with images, he looked in the liver. At his right hand was the divination for Jerusalem" (Ezek. xxi. 21, 22). That is to say, having come to a certain point on his march, where the road parted, leading on the right hand towards Jerusalem, and on the left towards Rabbath of Ammon, instead of deciding on his course by military considerations, he employed divination, and allowed his campaign to be determined by a use of lots and a consultation of the entrails of victims. He showed an equal superstitiousness when, as we read on the Borsippa cylinder,[1] he could not allow himself to commence the work of restoration, which the great temple of the Seven Spheres so imperatively needed, until he had first waited for "a fortunate month," and in that fortunate month found an "auspicious day." Then, at length, "the bricks of its wall, and the slabs that covered it, the finest of them, he collected, and rebuilt the ruins firmly. Inscriptions written in his own name he placed within it, in the finest apartments (?), and of completing the upper part he

---

[1] Sir H. Rawlinson in the author's "Herodotus," vol. ii., p. 586.

made an end."[1] It has been said that all Babylonian kings were equally superstitious, and even that "the Babylonian kings never started on an expedition, or commenced any work, without consulting the omens;"[2] but no proof has been given of this assertion, and certainly neither Neriglissar nor Nabonidus relate that they waited for "fortunate days" to commence their works of restoration.

No doubt there are points in the character of Nebuchadnezzar with respect to which neither his own inscriptions nor the remains of classical antiquity furnish any illustration. His hasty and violent temper, quick to take offence, and rushing at once to the most extreme measures (Dan. ii. 9, 12, iii. 13, 19), is known to us only from the Book of Daniel, and the writers who follow that book in their account of him; e.g., Josephus. His readiness to relent, and his kindly impulse to make amends (ch. ii. 46, 49, iii. 26-30), are also traits unnoticed by profane authors, and not apparent in his inscriptions. But no surprise ought to be felt at this. We could only expect to find evidence of such qualities in inscriptions of a different character from those which have come down to us. Should the annals of Nebuchadnezzar ever be recovered, and should they be on the scale of those left by Asshurbani-pal, or even those of Sennacherib, Sargon,

---

[1] "Records of the Past," vol. vii., p. 77.
[2] Ibid., vol. v., p. 58.

and other earlier Assyrian kings, we might not improbably meet with indications of the great king's moods and temperament. The *one* historical inscription which we have is insufficient for the purpose. As originally written, it extended only to thirty lines, and of these there is not one which is not mutilated.[1] Nor are the remains of the profane historians who treat of his time such as naturally to supply the deficiency. Of the account which Berosus gave of him we possess but one considerable fragment : of Abydenus, we have two shorter ones : the remaining writers furnish only a few sentences or a few lines. It is unfortunate that this should be so ; but so it is. Had the Babylonian history of Berosus come down to us complete, or had kind fate permitted that Antimenides, the brother of Alcæus, should have written, and time have spared a record of his Babylonian experiences, the slighter details and more delicate shades of the monarch's character might have been laid open to us. At present we have to content ourselves with treating the broader features and more salient points of a character that was not without many minor tones and some curious complications.

---

[1] See "Transactions of Soc. of Bibl. Arch.," vol. vii., pp. 218—222.

CHAPTER. VI.

NOTICES OF BABYLON IN DANIEL (continued).

CHAPTER VI.

NOTICES OF BABYLON IN DANIEL (continued).

"THE king spake, and said, is not this great Babylon, that I have built for the house of the kingdom by the might of my power, and for the honour of my majesty?" (Dan. iv. 30).

When we think of the enormous size of Babylon, according to the most trustworthy accounts, it seems a most audacious boast on the part of any one man, that he had built the whole of it. According to Herodotus,[1] who represents himself as having visited the city about B.C. 450, the walls formed a circuit of 480 stades, or fifty-five miles, enclosing a square space, which was 120 stades, or nearly fourteen miles each way. Strabo reduced the circuit to 385 stades,[2] Quintus Curtius to 368,[3] Clitarchus to 365,[4] and Ctesias to 360.[5] If we accept the smallest of these estimates, it will give us a square of above

---

[1] Herod., i. 178.
[2] Strab., xvi., 1, § 5.
[3] "Vit. Alex. Magn.," v. 1.
[4] Ap Diod. Sic , ii. 7, § 3.
[5] Ibid.

ten miles each way, and consequently an area of above a hundred square miles. This is a space four times as great as that of Paris within the *enceinte*, and fully double that of London within the bills of mortality.

No doubt it is true that only a portion of this immense area was covered by buildings. "The district within the walls represented a vast entrenched camp, more than what we now mean by a city.[1] Aristotle remarks with respect to it: "It is not walls by themselves that make a town. Otherwise one would only have to surround the Peloponnese with a wall [in order to constitute it a city]. The case is the same with Babylon and all other towns, the walls of which enclose rather a nation than a body of citizens."[2] Large portions of the space enclosed were occupied by gardens, orchards, and palm groves; some part of it was even devoted to the cultivation of corn. It was calculated that, in case of a siege, the inhabitants might, by making the best use of all the unoccupied ground, raise grain sufficient for their own consumption.[3] Still, the area devoted to buildings was very large. The royal quarter, or palatial enclosure, as arranged by Nebuchadnezzar, seems to have extended some miles,

---

[1] Lenormant, "Manuel d'Histoire Ancienne," vol. ii., p 226.
[2] Aristot. "Pol.," iii. 1, *sub fin*.
[3] Q. Curt., l. s. c.

both in length and breadth. Outside this was the city proper, laid out on a regular plan, in streets cutting each other at right angles,[1] like Manheim and most American cities. The extent of this can only be guessed, for "the ninety stades" of Curtius is excessive as a diameter, insufficient as a circumference.

The height and massive character of the buildings was as remarkable as the area that they covered. Even the ordinary houses of the inhabitants were, in many instances, three or four storeys high.[2] The solidity and strength of the walls was most extraordinary. Herodotus estimates their width at fifty, their height at two hundred cubits.[3] He adds that the cubic of which he speaks is one of unusual length. Diodorus Siculus, who follows Ctesias, agrees almost exactly as to the height, which he makes fifty fathoms,[4] or three hundred ordinary feet. Pliny[5] and Solinus[6] reduce the three hundred feet of Diodorus to two hundred and thirty-five; while Strabo, who may be supposed to follow the historians of Alexander, makes a further and still greater reduction, estimating the height at no more than seventy-

---

[1] Herod., i. 180.
[2] Ibid.
[3] Ibid., i. 178.
[4] Diod. Sic., ii. 7, § 3.
[5] "Hist. Nat.," vi. 26.
[6] "Polyhist.," § 60.

five feet.[1] Even this low figure implies a mass of brickwork amounting to thirteen hundred and ninety millions (1,390,000,000) of square feet, and would have required for its construction at least three times that number of the largest bricks known to Babylonians. If we accept the estimate of height given by Pliny and Solinus, we must multiply these amounts by three; if we prefer that of Diodorus, by four; if that of Herodotus, by four and a-half. On the supposition that Herodotus has correctly reported the dimensions of the wall in his day, to build it would have required eighteen thousand seven hundred and sixty-five millions (18,765,000,000) of the largest Babylonian bricks known to us.

The royal quarter, or palatial enclosure, of Nebuchadnezzar's time, comprised three, or, according to some,[2] four principal buildings. These were the old palace, the new palace, the hanging gardens, and (if we allow it to have been a sort of adjunct to the palace) the great temple of Bel-Merodach. It was also guarded by a wall, which Herodotus declares to have been "very little inferior in strength" to the outer wall of the city;[3] and it contained further a vast artificial reservoir.[4] Some account must be

---

[1] Strab., xvi 1, § 5.
[2] Oppert, "Expédition Scientifique en Mésopotamie," vol. i., Plan of Babylon.
[3] Herod., i. 181.
[4] See the "Standard Inscription of Nebuchadnezzar" in the author's "Herodotus," vol. ii., p. 587.

given of these various buildings and constructions before we can appreciate fully Nebuchadnezzar's greatness as a builder.

The "old palace" seems to be represented by the modern "mound of Amram." This is a huge mass of ruins, almost triangular in its present shape, occupying the more southern portion of the ancient "royal city." It is about a thousand yards along its south western or principal side, which faced the river, and has perhaps been washed into its present receding line by water action. The northern face of the mound measures about seven hundred yards, and the eastern about eight hundred, the triangle being thus scalene, with its shortest side facing northwards.[1] The mound is deeply furrowed with ravines, worn by the rains in the friable soil; its elevation above the level of the plain is nowhere very considerable, but amounts in places to about fifty or sixty feet.[2] Excavators have driven galleries into it in various directions, but have found little to reward their labours; no walls or distinct traces of buildings of any kind have presented themselves. A few bricks, belonging to early kings of Babylon, are all that it has yielded,—enough, perhaps, to confirm the conjecture that it represents the site of the "old palace," but otherwise uninteresting. The huge

---

[1] See the author's "Ancient Monarchies," vol. ii., pp. 525, 526.

[2] Rich, "Memoir on the Ruins of Babylon," p. 61.

mass seems to be, in reality, less a palace than a palace mound—the basis or substratum on which once stood a royal edifice, which has now wholly disappeared. It was no doubt purely artificial; but whether originally constructed of unbaked bricks, or merely of the natural soil of the country, may be doubted. At present it consists wholly of a soft and friable mould, interspersed with a few fragments of bricks. The mound covers a space of about thirty-seven acres.[1]

If the "mound of Amram" represents the "old palace" of the Babylonian kings, the "new palace," which adjoined it,[2] can scarcely fail to be correctly identified with the "great mound" which immediately succeeds the Amram mound towards the north, and, according to some writers, is connected with it by a broad causeway.[3] The name *Kasr*, or "palace," still attaches to this mass of ruins. The "Kasr mound" is an oblong square, about seven hundred yards long by six hundred broad, with the sides facing the cardinal points.[4] Like the Amram hill, it is wholly of artificial origin, but is composed of somewhat better material, as loose bricks, tiles, and fragments of stone. It contains at least one subterranean passage, which is seven feet high, floored

---

[1] Oppert, "Expédition Scientifique," vol. i., p. 157.
[2] Berosus, ap. Joseph., "Ant. Jud.," x. 11, § 1.
[3] Rich, p. 62.
[4] "Ancient Monarchies," vol. ii., p. 524.

and walled with baked bricks, and roofed over with great blocks of sandstone, which reach from side to side. This passage may have been either a secret exit or a gigantic drain—more probably the latter. On the summit of the mound (which is seventy feet above the level of the plain), not very far from the centre, are the remains of the palace proper, from which the mound is named. This is a building of excellent brick masonry, in a wonderful state of preservation, consisting of walls, piers, and buttresses, and in places ornamented with pilasters, but of too fragmentary a character to furnish the modern inquirer with any clue to the original plan of the edifice. Probably it did not greatly differ from the palaces of the Assyrian monarchs at Nimrud, Koyunjik, and Khorsabad, consisting, like them, of a series of courts, great halls, galleries, and smaller apartments, ornamented throughout with sculptured or painted figures and with inscriptions in places. Fragments of the ornamentation have been found. One of these is a portion of a slab of stone, representing a frieze, where the abacus was supported by a series of figures of gods, sculptured in low relief, with their names attached to them.[1] The remainder are, for the most part, fragments of bricks, one side of which was painted in bright colours, and covered with a thick enamel or glaze. " The principal colours are a brilliant

---

[1] "Ancient Monarchies," vol. ii., p. 552.

blue, red, a deep yellow, white, and black"[1] Portions of the figures of men and animals have been detected upon these fragments, which are so numerous as fully to bear out the statement of Diodorus,[2] that the palace walls were artistically adorned with coloured representations of war scenes and hunting scenes, wherein the kings, and sometimes the queens, were depicted on horseback or on foot, contending with leopards or with lions, and with spear or javelin dealing them their death-stroke. Such were the "men pourtrayed upon the wall," which the Jewish captives saw at Babylon, and on which they doted; "the images of the Chaldeans pourtrayed with vermilion, girded with girdles upon their loins, exceeding in dyed attire upon their heads, all of them princes to look to, after the manner of the Babylonians of Chaldea, the land of their nativity" (Ezek. xxiii. 14, 15). The palace is said to have been further ornamented with statues;[3] and the figure of a colossal lion, which stands upon the mound, north-east of the Kasr building, may lend a certain support to this statement.

The "hanging gardens" were regarded as one of the seven wonders of the world.[4] They were said to have been constructed for the delectation of a

---

[1] Layard, "Nineveh and Babylon,' p. 507.
[2] Diod. Sic., ii. 8.
[3] Ibid.
[4] Abydenus, Fr. 9, *ad fin.*; Strab., xvi. 1, § 5.

Median princess, who disliked the flat monotony of the Babylonian plain, and longed for something that might remind her of the irregularities of nature in her own country.[1] The construction is described in terms which are somewhat difficult to understand; but, by comparing the several accounts,[2] we gather that the structure was a square, 400 feet each way, elevated to the height of at least 150 feet, and consisting of several tiers of arches, superimposed one upon another, after the manner employed by the Romans in the construction of their amphitheatres. The building was divided into as many storeys as there were tiers of arches, the number of these being uncertain, and was supported by internal walls of great thickness. In these storeys were many palatial apartments, where visitors rested on their way to the upper terrace; and in the uppermost storey was a room containing hydraulic machinery, whereby water was raised from the Euphrates to the level of the garden itself. This was superimposed on the uppermost tier of arches, and was a flat surface composed of four layers: first, one of reeds mixed with bitumen; next, one of brickwork, then one of lead, and finally a thick layer of earth, affording ample depth for the roots of the largest trees. The garden was planted with trees and shrubs of various kinds, and possibly

---

[1] Berosus, Fr. 14.
[2] Those of Diod. Sic. (ii. 10), Strabo (xvi. 1, § 5), and Q. Curtius (v. 1).

with flowers, though they are not mentioned. A spacious pleasure-ground was thus provided as an adjunct to the palace, where royalty was secure from observation, and where the delights of umbrageous foliage, flashing fountains, gay flower-beds, and secluded walks could be obtained at the cost of mounting a staircase somewhat longer than those of our great London and Paris hotels.

The great temple of Bel-Merodach is probably identified with the massive ruin which lies due north of the Kasr mound, at the distance of about a mile. This is a vast pile of brickwork, of an irregular quadrilateral shape, with precipitous sides furrowed by ravines, and with a nearly flat top.[1] Of the four faces of the ruin, the southern seems to be the most perfect. It extends a distance of two hundred yards, or almost exactly a stade, and runs nearly in a straight line from east to west. At its eastern extremity it forms a right angle with the east face, which runs nearly due north for about one hundred and eighty yards, also almost in a straight line. The other two faces are very much worn away, but probably in their original condition corresponded to those already described. The building was thus not an exact square, but a parallelogram, with the shorter sides proportioned to the longer as nine to ten. The ruin rises towards its centre, where it

---

[1] See "Ancient Monarchies," vol. ii., pp. 521—523.

attains an elevation of nearly one hundred and forty feet. It shows signs of having been enclosed within a precinct. Beyond a doubt, it is the edifice which Herodotus describes as follows:—" In the other division of the town was the sacred precinct of Jupiter Belus, a square enclosure two stades each way, with gates of solid brass; which was also remaining in my time. In the middle of the precinct there was a tower of solid masonry, a stade both in length and in breadth, upon which was raised a second tower, and upon that a third, and so on up to eight. The ascent to the top is on the outside, by a path which winds round all the towers. When one is about half-way up, one finds a resting-place and seats, where persons are wont to sit some tome on their way to the summit. On the topmost tower there is a spacious temple, and inside the temple stands a couch of unusual size, richly adorned, with a golden table by its side. The temple contains no image."[1] Herodotus adds: " Below, in the same precinct, there is a second temple, in which is a sitting figure of Jupiter, all of gold. Before the figure stands a large golden table; and the throne whereon it sits, and the base on which the throne is placed, are likewise of gold. The Chaldeans told me that all the gold together was eight hundred talents in weight. Outside this temple are two altars, one

---

[1] Herod., i. 181.

of solid gold, on which it is only lawful to offer sucklings; the other a common altar, but of great size, on which the full-grown animals are sacrificed."[1] The lower temple has disappeared, as have the altars and the upper stages of the Great Temple tower; but the massive basis remains, a solid piece of brickwork containing about four millions of square feet, and requiring for its construction at least twelve millions of the largest bricks made by the Babylonians. If the upper stages at all resembled those of the Great Temple of Borsippa, the bricks needed for the entire building must have been three times as many.

The artificial reservoir attached to the new palace is often mentioned in the inscriptions of Nebuchadnezzar.[2] It was called the *Yapur-Shapu*, and was probably of an oblong-square shape, with sides protected by a massive facing of burnt brick. If we accept the identification of its site suggested by Sir H. Rawlinson,[3] we must assign it a width of about a hundred yards, and a length of nearly a mile.

Among the other marvels of Babylon, according to the ancient writers, were a tunnel and a bridge. The tunnel was carried under the bed of the Euphrates, and was an arched passage, lined throughout with

---

[1] Herod., i. 183.
[2] "Records of the Past," vol. v., pp. 125, 126, 130, etc.
[3] See the author's "Herodotus," vol. iii., p. 580.

baked brick laid in bitumen, the lining having a thickness of twenty bricks. The width of the tunnel was fifteen feet, and its height, to the spring of the arch, twelve feet.[1] The length was about a thousand yards, or considerably more than half a mile.

The bridge was a structure composed of wood, metal, and stone. In the bed of the Euphrates were built a number of strong stone piers, at the distance of twelve feet apart, which presented to the current a sharp angle that passed gradually into a gentle curve. The stones were massive, and fastened together by clamps of iron and lead.[2] From pier to pier was stretched a platform of wood, composed of cedar and cypress beams, together with the stems of palms, each platform being thirty feet in width.[3] The length of the bridge, like that of the tunnel, was a thousand yards.[4]

We have now to consider to what extent these various constructions may be regarded as the work of Nebuchadnezzar, and how far, therefore, he may be viewed as justified in his famous boast. First, then, we have it distinctly stated, both by Berosus[5] and by himself,[6] that the new palace, which adjoined

---

[1] Diod. Sic. ii. 9.
[2] Herod., i. 186.
[3] Diod. Sic., ii. 8.
[4] Ibid.
[5] Ap. Joseph., "Ant. Jud.," x. 11, § 1.
[6] "Records of the Past," vol. v., pp. 130, 131.

the old, was completely and entirely built by him. The same is declared, both by Berosus[1] and Abydenus,[2] of the "hanging gardens." The former of these statements is confirmed by the fact that the bricks of the *Kasr* are, one and all of them, stamped with his name. The old palace he did not build; but, as he tells us, carefully repaired.[3] The *Yapur-Shapu* was also an ancient construction; but he seems to have excavated it afresh, and to have executed the entire lining of its banks.[4] With respect to the great Temple of Bel-Merodach, if we may believe his own account, it had gone completely to ruin before his day, and required a restoration that was equivalent to a rebuilding.[5] Here, again, we have the confirmation of actual fact, since the inscribed bricks from the Babil mound bear in every instance the name and titles of Nebuchadnezzar. Eight other Babylonian temples are also declared in his inscriptions to have been built or rebuilt by him.[6] But his greatest work was the reconstruction of the walls. We have seen their enormous length, breadth, and thickness, even according to the lowest estimates. Nebuchadnezzar found them dismantled and decayed

---

[1] Berosus, l. s. c.
[2] Abydenus, Fr. 9, *sub fin.*
[3] Sir H. Rawlinson in the author's "Herodotus," vol. ii., p. 588.
[4] Ibid., p. 587.
[5] "Records of the Past," vol. v., p. 119.
[6] Ibid., pp. 122, 123.

—probably mere lines of earthen rampart, such as inclose great part of the ruins to-day. He gave them the dimensions that they attained—dimensions that made them one of the world's wonders. It is this which is his great boast in his standard inscription: "Imgar-Bel and Nimiti-Bel, the great double wall of Babylon, I built. Buttresses for the embankment of its ditch I completed. Two long embankments with cement and brick I made, and with the embankment which my father had made I joined them. I strengthened the city. Across the river, westward, I built the wall of Babylon with brick."[1] And again, "The walls of the fortress of Babylon, its defence in war, I raised; and the circuit of the city of Babylon I have strengthened skilfully."[2]

Nebuchadnezzar, it may be further remarked, did not confine his constructive efforts to Babylon. Abydenus tells us, that, besides his great works at the capital, he excavated two large canals, the Nahr-Agane and the Nahr-Malcha;[3] the latter of which is known from later writers to have been a broad and deep channel connecting the Tigris with the Euphrates. He also, according to Abydenus, dug a huge reservoir near Sippara, which was one hundred and forty miles in circumference, and one hundred

---

[1] "Records of the Past," p. 125. Compare the author's "Herodotus," vol. ii., p. 587.
[2] Ibid., vol. v., pp. 133, 134.
[3] Abydenus, l. s. c.

and eighty feet deep, furnishing it with flood-gates, through which the water could be drawn off for purposes of irrigation. Abydenus adds, that he built quays and breakwaters along the shores of the Persian Gulf, and at the same time founded the city of Teredon, on the sea coast, as a defence against the incursions of the Arabs.

The inscribed bricks of this great monarch show a still more inexhaustible activity. They indicate him as the complete restorer of the temple of Nebo at Borsippa,[1] the mightiest of all the ruins in Mesopotamia, by some identified with the biblical "tower of Babel." They are widely spread over the entire country, occurring at Sippara, at Cutha, at Kalwadha (Chilmad ?), in the vicinity of Baghdad, and at scores of other sites. It is a calculation of Sir Henry Rawlinson's that *nine-tenths* of the bricks brought from Mesopotamia are inscribed with the name of Nebuchadnezzar, the son of Nabopolassar. "At least a hundred sites," says the same writer, " in the tract immediately about Babylon, give evidence, by bricks bearing his legend, of the marvellous activity and energy of this king."[2]

His inscriptions add, that, besides the great temple of Nebo, or of the Seven Spheres, at

---

[1] Compare his inscription, " Records of the Past," vol. vii., pp. 75—78.

[2] "Commentary on the Inscriptions of Babylonia and Assyria," p. 76.

Borsippa, he built there at least five others,[1] together with a temple to the Moon-god at Beth-Ziba,[2] and one to the Sun-God at Larsa, or Senkareh.[3] Altogether there is reason to believe that he was one of the most indefatigable of all the builders that have left their mark upon the world in which we live. He covered Babylonia with great works. He was the Augustus of Babylon. He found it a perishing city of unbaked clay; he left it one of durable burnt brick—unless it had been for human violence—capable of continuing, as the fragment of the *Kasr* has continued, to the present day.

---

[1] "Records of the Past," vol. v., p. 123.
[2] Ibid., p. 124.
[3] Ibid., vol. vii., pp. 71, 72.

VII.

NOTICES OF BABYLON IN JEREMIAH AND EZEKIEL.

CHAPTER VII.

NOTICES OF BABYLON IN JEREMIAH AND EZEKIEL.

THE Books of Jeremiah and Ezekiel contain numerous allusions, some prophetic, others historic, to the wars in which Nebuchadnezzar was engaged, or was to be engaged. A certain number of these notices refer to wars, which are also mentioned in Chronicles or Kings, and which have consequently already engaged our attention.[1] But others touch upon campaigns which Kings and Chronicles ignore, either on account of their lying outside the geographic range of the writer's vision, or from their being subsequent in point of time to the event which they view as constituting the close of their narratives. The campaigns in question are especially those against Tyre and Egypt, which are touched by both writers, but most emphatically dwelt upon by Ezekiel.

I. The war against Tyre. Ezekiel's description is as follows :—

"Thus saith the Lord God ; Behold I will bring

---

[1] See above, ch. iii., pp. 38—44.

upon Tyrus Nebuchadrezzar king of Babylon, a king of kings, from the north, with horses and with chariots, and with horsemen, and companies, and much people. He shall slay with the sword thy daughters in the field; and he shall make a fort against thee, and cast a mount against thee, and lift up the buckler against thee. And he ·shall set engines of war against thy walls, and with his axes he shall break down thy towers. By reason of the abundance of his horses, their dust shall cover thee; thy walls shall shake at the noise of the horsemen, and of the wheels, and of the chariots, when he shall enter into thy gates, as men enter into a city wherein is made a breach. With the hoofs of his horses shall he tread down all thy streets; he shall slay thy people by the sword, and thy strong garrisons shall go down to the ground. And they shall make a spoil of thy riches, and make a prey of thy merchandise; and they shall break down thy walls, and destroy thy pleasant houses; and they shall lay thy stones, and thy timber and thy dust in the midst of the water. And I will cause the noise of thy songs to cease; and the sound of thy harp shall be no more heard. And I will make thee like the top of a rock; thou shalt be a place to spread nets upon; thou shalt be built no more; for I the Lord have spoken it, saith the Lord God" (Ezek. xxvi. 7—14).

It is evident, from the entire character of the description, that the city attacked is—mainly, at any rate—not the island Tyre, but the ancient city upon the continent, Palætyrus, as the Greeks called it, which occupied a position directly opposite to the island, upon the sea-shore. Nebuchadrezzar, as he is correctly named,[1] fully established in his empire, not merely a "king of Babylon," but a "king of kings," comes with such an army as Polyhistor described him as bringing against Judæa,[2] to attack the Phœnician town. He brings "horses and chariots, and horsemen and companies, and much people." Polyhistor gives him, on the former occasion, ten thousand chariots, one hundred and twenty thousand horsemen, and one hundred and eighty thousand footmen. He proceeds to invest the city after the fashion commonly adopted by the Assyrian monarchs, and inherited from them by the Babylonians. Having constructed a movable fort or tower, such as we see in the Assyrian bas-reliefs,[3] he brings it against the walls, while at the same time he "raises a mount" against them, from which to work his engines and shoot his arrows with the better effect.[4] His men "lift up the buckler," as the Assyrians do while they mine the walls or fire the gates; while his "engines" ply their strokes, and his bravest soldiers, with "axes," or rather "swords"—

---

[1] Nebuchadrezzar exactly corresponds to the Nabu-kuduri-uzur of the inscriptions.
[2] Alex. Polyhist., Fr. 24.
[3] "Ancient Monarchies," vol. i., p. 471.
[4] Ibid., p. 473.

often used by the Assyrians for the purpose[1]—seek to "break down the towers." His efforts are successful, and a breach is made; the horsemen and chariots, as well as the footmen, enter the town; there is the usual carnage and plundering that accompany the storming of a stronghold; and, finally, there is a destruction or dismantling of the place, more or less complete.

It is remarkable that the siege and capture of the *island* city obtain no distinct mention. Some have supposed that it was not taken; but this is scarcely compatible with the words of the "Lament for Tyre," or with the "isles shaking at the sound of her fall" (Ezek. xxvi. 15, 18). Probably the two cities were so bound together that the conquest of the one involved the surrender of the other, and Nebuchadnezzar, master of the Old Tyre, experienced no resistance from the New.

The annalists of Tyre, though little disposed to dwell upon a passage of history so painful to patriotic men, were forced to admit the fact of the siege by Nebuchadnezzar, and even to give some account of it. They stated that it took place in the reign of a certain Ithobalus (Eth-Baal), and that the Tyrians offered a resistance almost without a parallel. They were besieged continuously for thirteen years.[1] The

---

[1] "Ancient Monarchies," vol. i., p. 473.

[2] Menand. Ephes. ap. Joseph. "Contr. Ap." i. 21; Philostrat. ap. Joseph. "Ant. Jud." x. 11, §. 1.

brief extracts from their works, which are all that we possess of them, do not say whether the siege was successful or the contrary; but it is scarcely conceivable that the great monarch would have allowed his efforts to be baffled, and it is certain that he carried a large number of Phœnician captives to Babylonia, whom he settled in various parts of the country.[1]

The fact of Nebuchadnezzar's siege of Tyre having lasted thirteen years, throws considerable light on another passage of Ezekiel. In the twenty-seventh year of the captivity of Jehoiachin (B.C. 573), the word of the Lord came to Ezekiel, saying:—

"Son of man, Nebuchadrezzar king of Babylon caused his army to serve a great service against Tyrus; *every head was made bald, and every shoulder was peeled;* yet had he no wages, nor his army, for Tyrus, for the service that he had served against it. Therefore thus saith the Lord God; Behold, I will give the land of Egypt unto Nebuchadrezzar, king of Babylon; and he shall take her multitude, and take her spoil, and take her prey; and it shall be the wages for his army. I have given him the land of Egypt for his labour wherewith he served against it, because they wrought for Me, saith the Lord God" (Ezek. xxix. 18–20).

---

[1] Berosus ap. Joseph, "Ant. Jud.," l.s.c.

The extraordinary length of the siege, in which men grew old and wore themselves out, explains the phrase,—" Every head was made bald, and every shoulder was peeled;" and at the same time accounts for the fact that Nebuchadnezzar was considered to have received no wages, *i.e.*, no sufficient wages, for his service, which had been very inadequately repaid by the plunder found in the exhausted city.

II. A great campaign in Egypt. In the year of the destruction of Jerusalem, Jeremiah prophesied as follows :—

"Then came the word of the Lord unto Jeremiah in Tahpanhes, saying, Take great stones in thine hand, and hide them in the clay in the brick-kiln, which is at the entry of Pharaoh's house in Tahpanhes, in the sight of the men of Judah; and say unto them, Thus saith the Lord of hosts, the God of Israel; Behold, I will send and take Nebuchadrezzar the king of Babylon, my servant, and will set his throne upon these stones that I have hid, and he shall spread his royal pavilion over them. And when he cometh, he shall smite the land of Egypt, and deliver such as are for death to death; and such as are for captivity to captivity; and such as are for the sword to the sword. And I will kindle a fire in the houses of the gods of Egypt, and he shall burn them, and carry them away captives: and he shall array himself with the land of Egypt, as a shepherd putteth on his garment ; and he shall go forth from thence in peace. He shall break also the images of Beth-shemesh, that is in the land of Egypt ; and the houses of the gods of the Egyptians shall he burn with fire " (Jer. xliii. 8—13).

Some time afterwards he delivered another prophecy (xlvi. 13—26) equally explicit, in which Migdol, Noph (Memphis), Tahpanhes (Daphnæ), and No-Ammon (Thebes) were threatened ; and the delivery of the entire country and people into the hand of Nebuchadrezzar, king of Babylon, and into the hand of his servants, was foretold.

Ezekiel delivered seven prophecies against Egypt, all of them having more or less reference to Babylon as the power which was to bring ruin upon the country, and two of them mentioning Nebuchadrezzar by name, as the monarch who was to inflict the chastisement (Ezek. xxix. 18, 19 ; xxx. 10). These prophecies are too long to quote in full. They are chiefly remarkable as declaring the complete desolation of Egypt, and as fixing a term of years during which her degradation should continue. In chap. xxx. we find among the places which are to suffer, Sin or Pelusium, Zoan or Tanis, On or Heliopolis, Noph or Memphis, Tahpanhes or Daphnæ, Pibeseth or Bubastis, and No-Ammon or Thebes. In chap. xxix. an even wider area is included. There we are told that the land of Egypt was to be "utterly waste and desolate from Migdol to Syene,[1] even unto the border of Ethiopia" (ver. 10). The time of Egypt's affliction is fixed at "forty years" (vers. 11—13), after which it is to recover, but to be a "base kingdom," "the basest of the kingdoms" (ver. 15), no more "exalted above the nations," no more a ruler over nations external to itself.

By the date of one of Ezekiel's prophecies (chap. xxix. 17—20), which is B.C. 573, it is evident that the great invasion prophesied had not then taken place, but was still impending. Nebuchadnezzar's attack must consequently be looked for towards the latter part of his long reign, which terminated in B.C. 562, according to the Canon of Ptolemy.

Until recently it would have been impossible to adduce any historical confirmation, or indeed illustration, of these prophecies. They were quoted by sceptical writers as prophecies that had been unfulfilled. Herodotus, it was remarked, knew nothing of any invasion of Egypt by the Asiatics during the reigns of either Apries or Amasis, with whom Nebuchadnezzar was contemporary, much less of any complete devastation of the entire territory by them. It was true that Josephus, anxious to save the reputation of his sacred books, spoke of an invasion of Egypt by Nebuchadnezzar later than the de-

---

[1] There is no doubt that this is the proper rendering, "From the tower of Syene even unto the border of Ethiopia" would have no meaning, since Syene bordered on Ethiopia.

struction of Jerusalem, and even made him kill one king and set up another.[1] But he placed these events in the fifth year after the fall of Jerusalem, that is in B.C. 581, whereas Ezekiel's date, in his twenty-ninth chapter, showed that they had not happened by B.C. 573. Moreover, he contradicted Egyptian history, which gave no change of sovereign till ten years after the time mentioned, or B.C. 571.

It was difficult to meet these objectors formerly. Within the last few years, however, light has been thrown on the subject from two inscriptions—one Egyptian, which had been long known, but not rightly understood; the other Babylonian, which was not discovered till 1878. The Egyptian inscription is on a statue in the Louvre, which was originally set up at Elephantiné by a certain Nes-Hor, an official of high rank, whom Apries, the Egyptian monarch called in Scripture "Pharaoh-Hophra," had made "Governor of the South." This officer, according to the latest and best interpretation of his inscription,[2] writes as follows:—"I have caused to be made ready my statue; my name will be perpetuated by means of it; it will not perish in this temple, inasmuch as I took care of the house, when it was injured by the foreign hordes of the Syrians, the people of the north, the Asiatics, and

---

[1] "Ant. Jud." x. 9, § 7.
[2] See Dr. Wiedemann's paper in the "Zeitschrift für Ægypt Sprache" for 1878, p. 4.

the profane [who intended evil] in their heart ; for it lay in their heart to rise up, to bring into subjection the upper country. But the fear of thy majesty was upon them ; they gave up what their heart had planned. I did not let them advance to Konosso, but I let them approach the place were thy majesty was. Then thy majesty made an [expedition] against them."

It results from this inscription, that, while Apries was still upon the throne, there was an invasion of Egypt from the north. A host of Asiatics, whom the writer calls *Amu, i.e.*, Syrians, or, at any rate, Semites from the direction of Syria, poured into the country, and, carrying all before them, advanced up the valley of the Nile, threatening the subjection of the " upper country." Memphis and Thebes must have fallen, since the invaders reached Elephantine. Apparently they were bent on subduing, not only Egypt, but Ethiopia. But Nes-Hor checked their advance ; he prevented them from proceeding further ; he even forced them to fall back towards the north, and brought them into contact with an army which Apries had collected against them, The result of the contact is not mentioned ; but the invaders must have retired, since Nes-Hor is able to embellish and repair the great temple of Kneph, which they have injured, and to set up his statue in it.

The other inscription is, unfortunately, very fragmentary. The tablet on which it was written

was of small size, and allowed space for only thirty
—not very long—lines. *All* the lines are more or
less mutilated. Of the first and second one word
only remains; of the twenty-fifth and twenty-eighth,
only one letter. The twenty-ninth is wholly obliterated. The termination alone remains of the
last seven. Some lacunæ occur in all the others.
Still, the general purport is plain. Nebuchadnezzar
addresses Merodach, and says,—" My enemies thou
usedst to destroy; thou causedst my heart to rejoice
. . . in those days thou madest my hands to capture;
thou gavest me rest; . . . thou causedst me to
construct; my kingdom thou madest to increase. . . .
Over them kings thou exaltedst; his warriors, his
princes, his paths, like . . . he made . . . to his army
he trusted . . . he hastened before the great gods.
[In the] thirty-seventh year of Nebuchadnezzar king
of the country [of Babylon, Nebuchadnezzar] to Egypt
to make war went. [His army Ama]sis, king of
Egypt, collected, and . . . [his soldiers] went, they
spread abroad. As for me (?) . . . . a remote
district, which is in the middle of the sea . . . .
many . . . from the midst of the country of Egypt
. . . . soldiers, horses, and chariots (?) . . . for his
help he assembled and . . . he looked before him
. . . . to his [army] he trusted and . . . fixed a
command."[1]

---

[1] "Transactions of Society of Biblical Archæology," vol.
vii., pp. 213—222.

Nebuchadnezzar, evidently, in this inscription, speaks of an expedition which he personally conducted into Egypt, as late as his thirty-seventh year, which was B.C. 568, five years later than the date of Ezekiel's dated prophecy. The king, however, against whom he made war, was not Apries, whose name in Egyptian was Ua-ap-ra, but apparently Amasis, his successor, since it ended in -*su*, probably in -*asu*.[1] This may seem to be an objection against referring the two inscriptions to the same events, since Apries was still king when that of Nes-Hor was set up. But a reference to Egyptian history removes this difficulty. Amasis, it appears, ascended the throne in B.C. 571; but Apries did not die until B.C. 565. For six years the two monarchs inhabited the same palace at Sais[2] and both bore the royal title. An Egyptian monument distinctly recognizes the double reign;[3] the expedition of Nebuchadnezzar, being in B.C. 568, falls exactly into this interval. It was natural that Nebuchadnezzar should mention the active young king, who had the real power, and was his actual antagonist; it was equally natural that Nes-Hor, an old *employé* under Apries, should ignore the upstart, and seek to do honour to his old master.

---

[1] See the inscription in the "Transactions of Bibl. Arch. Soc.," vol. vii., p. 220, reverse, line 1.

[2] Herod. ii. 169.

[3] Champollion, "Monuments de l'Egypte," vol. iv., p. 443, No. 1.

Other wars of Nebuchadnezzar are thought to be glanced at in Scripture, as one with Elam,[1] to which there may be allusion in Jer. xlix. 34—38, and Ezek. xxxii. 24; one with the Moabites, perhaps referred to in Ezek. xxv. 8—11; and one with Ammon, touched upon in Ezek. xxi. 20, 28—32, and xxv. 4—7. Josephus relates it as an historical fact, that he reduced both the Moabites and the Ammonites to subjection;[2] and there are some grounds for thinking that he also made himself master of Elam; but it cannot be said that these events are either confirmed or illustrated by profane writers, who make no distinct mention of any of his wars, except those with the Jews, the Phœnicians, and the Egyptians.

It was, however, widely recognised in antiquity that Nebuchadnezzar was a great general. His exploits were enormously exaggerated, since he was believed by some[3] to have conquered all North Africa and Spain, as well as the country between Armenia and the Caspian. But there was a basis of truth underlying the exaggerations. Nebuchadnezzar, at a comparatively early age, defeated Pharaoh-Necho at the great battle of Carchemish, conquered Cœle-syria, and reduced Judæa to vassalage. Somewhat later he engaged in the difficult enterprise of capturing Tyre, and exhibited a rare spirit of persistence

---

[1] G. Smith, "History of Babylonia," pp. 157—158.
[2] Joseph. "Ant. Jud.," x., 9. § 7.
[3] As Megasthenes and Abydenus.

and perseverance in his long siege of that town.
His capture of Jerusalem, after a siege of eighteen
months (2 Kings xxv. 1—4), was creditable to him,
since Samaria, a place of far less strength, was not
taken by the Assyrians until it had been besieged
for three years (2 Kings xvii. 5). The reduction of
Elam, if we may ascribe it to him, redounds still more
to his honour, since the Elamites were a numerous and
powerful nation, which had contended on almost
even terms with the Assyrians from the time of
Sargon to the close of the empire. The judgment
of a good general was shown in the subjugation of
Moab and Ammon, for it is essential to the security
of Syria and Palestine that the tribes occupying the
skirt of the great eastern desert shall be controlled
and their ravages prevented. In Egypt Nebuchadnezzar probably met his most powerful adversary,
since under the rule of the Psammetichi Egypt had
recovered almost her pristine vigour. Thus in this
quarter the struggle for supremacy was severe and
greatly prolonged. He contended with three successive Egyptian kings—Necho, Apries or Hophra,
and Amasis. From Necho he took the whole tract
between Carchemish and the Egyptian frontier.
Apries feared to meet him, and, after a futile demon-
stration, gave up the interference which he had
meditated (Jer. xxxvii. 7). Amasis, who had perhaps
provoked him by his expedition against Cyprus,[1]

---

[1] Herod. ii. 182.

which Nebuchadnezzar would naturally regard as his, he signally punished by ravaging his whole territory, injuring the temples, destroying or carrying off the images of the gods, and making prisoners of many of the inhabitants. It is possible that he did more than this. Egypt's degradation was to last for a long term of years.[1] It is not unlikely that Amasis became the vassal of Nebuchadnezzar, and his peaceful reign, and the material prosperity of his country[2] were the result of a compact by which he acknowledged the suzerainty of Babylon, and bowed his head to a foreign yoke.

---

[1] "Forty years" (Ezek. xxix. 11—13); but "forty years," in prophetic language, is not to be taken literally.

[2] Herod. ii. 177.

CHAPTER VIII.

NOTICES OF BABYLON IN EZEKIEL (continued).

CHAPTER VIII.

NOTICES OF BABYLON IN EZEKIEL (continued).

"A LAND of traffick . . . a city of merchants" (Ezek. xvii. 4). This allusion to the commercial character of Babylon does not stand alone and unsupported in Scripture. Isaiah speaks of the Babylonian "merchants" (Isa. xlvii. 15), and describes the Chaldæans as persons "whose cry is in their ships" (chap. xliii. 14). Ezekiel mentions Canneh (Calneh), and Chilmad, Babylonian towns, among the places that carried on commercial dealings with Tyre (Ezek. xxvii. 23). In the Revelation of St. John the Divine, Babylon is made the type of a city, which is represented as eminently commercial, as dealing in the "merchandise of gold, and silver, and precious stones, and of pearls, and fine linen, and purple, and silk, and scarlet, and all thyine wood, and all manner vessels of ivory, and all manner vessels of most precious wood, and of brass, and iron, and marble, and cinnamon, and odours, and ointments, and frankincense, and wine, and oil, and fine flour, and wheat, and beasts, and sheep, and horses, and chariots, and slaves, and the souls of men" (Rev. xviii. 12, 13).

The object of the present chapter will be to show that the notices of Babylon in profane writers and in the inscriptions fully bear out the character thus assigned to her, showing that she was the centre of an enormous land and sea commerce, which must have given occupation to thousands of merchants, and have necessitated the employment of numerous ships.

Nothing is more evident in the Babylonian inscriptions, and also in those of Assyria which treat of Babylonian affairs, than the large amount of curious woods, and the quantity of alabaster and other stone, which was employed in the great constructions of the Babylonians, and which must necessarily have been imported from foreign countries. Babylonia being entirely alluvial is wholly destitute of stone, and the only trees of any size that it produces are the cypress and the palm.[1] We find the Babylonian monarchs employing in their temples and palaces abundant pine and cedar trees, together with many other kinds of wood, which it is impossible to identify. Mention is made of "*Babil*-wood," "*umritgana*-wood," "*ummakana*-wood," "*ri*-wood," "*ikki*-wood," "*surman*-wood," "*asuhu*-wood,"

---

[1] See the author's "Ancient Monarchies," vol. iii. pp. 36, 38.

"*musritkanna*-wood," and "*mesukan*-wood."[1] Modern exploration has shown that among the building materials employed was teak,[2] but whether any one of these obscure names designates that species of wood is uncertain. What seems plain is that all these woods must have been imported. The teak must have come either from India, or possibly from one of the islands in the Persian Gulf;[3] there is evidence that the cedars and pines, together with the Babil-wood, were imported from Syria, being furnished by the forests that clothed the sides of Mounts Libanus and Amanus;[4] there is no evidence with respect to the remainder, but they may have been derived from either Armenia, Assyria, or Susiania.

Among the kinds of stone commonly used in building which must necessarily have been imported, were " alabaster blocks," " *zamat* stone," " *durmina-turda* and *kamina-turda* stone, *zamat-hati* stone, and lapis lazuli.[5] Xenophon speaks of the importation of " millstones " in his own day;[6] and, as Babylonia

---

[1] " Records of the Past," vol. v., pp. 117—133; vol. vii. p. 75.

[2] " Journal of the R. Asiat. Society," vol. xv. p. 264.

[3] As Heeren thinks, on the strength of a passage of Theophrastus (" As. Nat.," vol. ii. pp. 258, 259).

[4] " Records of the Past," vol. v., p. 119; vol. ix., p. 16; " Transactions of Bibl. Arch. Society," vol. vii., p. 154.

[5] " Records of the Past," vol. v., pp. 121, 125—127; vol. vii., p. 76, etc.

[6] Xen., " Anab.," i. 5, § 5.

could not furnish them, they must always have come in from without. Sandstone and basalt, which are found in some of the ruins, could have been obtained from the adjacent parts of Arabia ; but the alabaster, which has been also found, and the lapis lazuli, which was especially affected for adornment, must have been brought from a greater distance.

Stones of the rarer and more precious kinds were also largely imported, to serve either as seals or as ornaments of the person. Herodotus tells us that "every Babylonian carried a seal ;"[1] and the remains tend to confirm his testimony, since Babylonian seals, either in the shape of signet rings or of cylinders, exist by thousands in European museums, and are still found in large numbers by explorers. They are chiefly made of onyx, jasper, serpentine, meteoric stone, lapis lazuli, and chalcedony, all substances that must have been introduced from abroad, since no one of them is produced by Babylonia.

Babylonia must also have imported, or else carried off from foreign countries, the whole of its metals. Neither gold, nor silver, nor copper, nor tin, nor lead, nor iron are among the gifts which Nature has vouchsafed to the southern Mesopotamian region. No doubt her military successes enabled her to obtain from foreign lands, not by exchange but by plunder, considerable supplies of these commodities ; but besides this accidental and irregular mode of acquisi-

---

[1] Herod., i. 195.

tion, there must have been some normal and unceasing source of supply, to prevent disastrous fluctuations, and secure a due provision for the constant needs of the country. Every implement used in agriculture or in the mechanical trades had to be made of bronze,[1] the materials of which came from afar; copper perhaps from Armenia, which still produces it largely, tin from Further India, or from Cornwall, through the medium of the Phœnicians.[2] Every weapon of war had to be supplied similarly: all the gold and silver lavished on the doors and walls of the temples,[3] on images of the gods or the dresses in which the images were clothed,[4] on temple tables, altars, or couches,[5] on palace walls and roofs,[6] on thrones, sceptres, parasols, chariots, and the like,[7] or on bracelets, armlets, and other articles of personal adornment, had to be procured from some foreign land and to be conveyed hundreds or thousands of miles before the Babylonians could make use of them.

Another whole class of commodities which the Babylonians are believed to have obtained from

---

[1] Iron was not absolutely unknown in ancient Babylonia; but almost all the weapons and implements found are of bronze.
[2] Herod., iii. 115.
[3] "Records of the Past," vol. v., 117—120; vol. vii., p. 75.
[4] Ibid., vol. vii., pp. 5, 6.
[5] Herod., i. 181, 183; Diod. Sic. ii. 9.
[6] "Records of the Past," vol. v., pp. 131, 133.
[7] Ibid., vol. ix., p. 15.

foreign countries comprises the raw materials for their clothes, and for the greater part of their fabrics.[1] Babylonia was not a country suitable for the rearing of sheep, and, if it produced wool at all, produced it only in small quantities; yet the Babylonians wore ordinarily two woollen garments,[2] and some of their most famous fabrics were of the same material. Their other clothes were either linen or cotton; but, so far as is known, neither flax nor the cotton plant were cultivated by them.

Spices constituted another class of imports. In their religious ceremonies the Babylonians consumed frankincense[3] on an enormous scale; and they employed it likewise in purifications.[4] They also used aromatic reeds in their sacrifices,[5] as did the Jews who were brought into contact with them.[6] Whether they imported cinnamon from Ceylon or India,[7] may perhaps be doubted; but the spices of Arabia were certainly in request, and formed the material of a regular traffic.[8]

All the wine consumed in Babylonia, was imported from abroad. Babylonia was too hot, and probably

---

[1] Heeren, "Asiatic Nations," vol. ii., p. 199.
[2] Herod., i. 195.
[3] Ibid., i. 183.
[4] Ibid., i. 198.
[5] "Records of the Past," vol. vii., p. 140.
[6] Jer. vi. 20.
[7] As Heeren supposes ("As. Nat.," vol. ii., p. 240).
[8] Strabo, xvi. 3, § 3.

also too moist, for the vine, which was not cultivated in any part of the country.[1] A sort of spirit was distilled from dates, which the Greeks called "palm-wine,"[2] and this was drunk by the common people. But the wealthier classes could be content with nothing less than the juice of the grape ;[3] and hence there was a continuous importation of real wine into the country,[4] where there prevailed a general luxuriousness of living. The trade must consequently have been considerable, and is not likely to have been confined to a single channel. There were several vine-growing countries not very remote from Babylon ; and a brisk commerce was in all probability carried on with most of them.

Among other probable imports may be mentioned ivory and ebony, for the construction of rich furniture, pearls for personal adornment, rare woods for walking-sticks, dyes, Indian shawls, musical instruments, Phœnician asses, Indian dogs, and Persian greyhounds.

Ivory and ebony, which were brought to Solomon as early as B.C. 1000 (1 Kings x. 22), and which Tyre imported from Dedan, on the Persian Gulf, in the time of Ezekiel (Ezek. xxvii. 15), can scarcely have been unknown to the Babylonians, through

---

[1] Herod., i. 193.
[2] Ibid.
[3] Dan. i. 5, v. 1.
[4] Herod., i. 194.

whose territory the Phœnician trade with Dedan must have passed. Pearls, which were worn by the Assyrians,[1] and supplied to Western Asia generally from the famous fisheries of Bahrein and Karrak, in the Persian Gulf,[2] were doubtless as much appreciated by the Babylonians as by other Asiatics; and the pearl merchants can scarcely have been permitted to carry their precious wares into the interior without leaving a fair share of them to the country whereto they must have brought them first of all. Rare wood for walking-sticks is mentioned as grown in Tylos,[3] another island in the Gulf, and would naturally be transported to the neighbouring country, where walking-sticks were in universal use.[4] The dyes which gave to Babylonian fabrics their brilliant hues came probably from India or Kashmir, and were furnished by the Indian larva or the cochineal insect.[5] With their dyes the Indians would probably send their shawls, an early product of Hindoo industry, and one from time immemorial highly valued in the East.[6] The importation of musical instruments may be regarded as proved, if we allow any of the names used in Daniel to be derived from

---

[1] "Ancient Monarchies," vol. i., p. 559.
[2] Heeren, "As. Nat.," vol. ii., pp. 235—237.
[3] Theophrast., "Hist. Plant.," v. 6.
[4] Herod., i. 195.
[5] See Heeren, "As. Nat.," p. 200.
[6] Ibid., p. 209.

the Greek, since the Greek name could only reach Babylon together with the instrument whereto it belonged. Phœnician asses are expressly mentioned, as sold by one Babylonian to another, on one of the black contract stones found at Babylon,[1] as are "greyhounds from the East," which were most probably Persian. A large dog, most likely an Indian hound, is represented on a tablet brought by Sir H. Rawlinson from the same site,[2] and the representation is a fairly good proof of the importation of the animal pourtrayed.

It is impossible for a country to import largely unless it also exports largely, either its own products or those of other regions. In the long run exports and imports must balance each other. Babylonia seems to have exported chiefly its own manufactures. Large weaving establishments existed in various parts of the country;[3] and fabrics issued from the Babylonian looms which were highly esteemed by foreign nations. The texture was exquisite; the dyes were of remarkable brilliancy; and the workmanship was superior. The "Babylonian garment," found among the spoils of Jericho when the Israelites entered the Holy Land, and coveted by Achan,[4] is an evidence at once of the high esteem

---

[1] "Records of the Past," vol. ix., p. 105.
[2] See the author's "Herodotus," vol. i., p. 314.
[3] Strab., xvi. 1, § 7.
[4] Josh. vii. 21.

in which such fabrics were held, and of the distance to which, even thus early, they had been exported. Fringed and striped robes of seemingly delicate material appear on Babylonian cylinders[1] as far back as the Proto-Chaldæan period, or before B.C. 2000. We cannot fix their material; but perhaps they were of the class called "sindones," which appear to have been muslins of extreme fineness, and of brilliant hues, and which in later times were set apart for royal use.

The carpets of Babylon acquired a peculiar reputation.[3] Carpets are one of the principal objects of luxury in the East, where not only are the floors of the reception-rooms in all houses of a superior class covered with them, but they even form the coverlets of beds, couches, divans, and sofas, and are thus the main decoration of apartments. The carpets of Babylon were made of fine wool, skilfully woven, exquisite in their colours, and boasting patterns that gave them a character of piquancy and originality. They bore representations of griffins and other fabulous animals,[4] which excited the wonder and admiration of foreigners, who did not know whether they beheld mere freaks of fancy or portraits of the wonderful beasts of Lower Asia.

---

[1] "Ancient Monarchies," vol. i., p. 94.
[2] Theophrast., "Hist. Plant.," iv. 9.
[3] Arrian, "Exp. Alex.," vi. 29.
[4] Athen. "Deipn.," v., p. 197.

Besides their dresses, carpets, and other textile fabrics, it may be suspected that Babylonia exported rich furniture. When the Assyrian monarchs invaded a foreign territory, and obtained any considerable success, they almost universally carried off, on their return to their own land, great part of the furniture of any royal palace that fell into their hands, as the most valued portion of their booty. In their Babylonian expeditions alone, however, do they particularize the several objects. There we find mention of "the golden throne, the golden parasol, the golden sceptre, the silver chariot,"[1] and other articles that cannot be identified. There too we find that when a foreign prince needed persuading in order to make him render assistance, and a "propitiatory offering" had to be sent to him, "a throne in silver, a parasol in silver, a *pasur* in silver, and a *nirmaktu* in silver" were the objects sent.[2] It would only have been going a short step further to offer articles so highly appreciated to foreign customers generally.

It is uncertain whether the Babylonians exported grain, or dates, or any other produce of the palm.[3] Enormous quantities of wheat, barley, millet, and

---

[1] "Records of the Past," vol. ix., p. 15.

[2] Ibid., vol. vii., p. 45.

[3] The palm was said to furnish the Babylonians with bread, wine, vinegar, honey, groats, string and ropes of all kinds, and a mash for cattle (Strab., xvi. 1., §. 14).

sesame were raised in their country,[1] while the date palm grew so thickly in the lower parts of the territory as to form almost a continuous forest.[2] The natural wealth of the country consisted mainly in the abundance of these products, and it is scarcely possible that use was not made of the overplus beyond the wants of the inhabitants to maintain the balance of trade, which in so luxurious an empire must always have tended to declare itself against such great consumers. But ancient writers are rarely interested in such matters as trade and commerce, while the problems of political economy are wholly unknown to them. Hence they unfortunately leave us in the dark on numerous points which to us seem of primary importance, and force us to attempt to grope our way by reasonable conjecture.

We shall pass now from the consideration of the probable objects of traffic between Babylonia and other countries to that of the nature of the traffic, and the probable or certain direction of its various lines. Now the traffic was, beyond all doubt, carried on in part by land and in part by sea, the Babylonians not only having dealings with their continental neighbours, but also carrying on a commerce with islands and remote countries which were reached in ships.

---

[1] Herod., i. 193.
[2] Amm. Marc., xxiv. 3.

The land traffic itself was of two kinds. Caravans composed of large bodies of merchants, with their attendants and followers, proceeded from Babylon in various directions across the continent, carrying with them, on the backs of camels or asses, the native commodities which they desired to sell, and returning after a time with such foreign productions as were needed or desired by the Babylonians. Regular routes were established which these travelling companies pursued ; and it is not unlikely that stations or caravansaries, were provided for their accommodation at intervals.[1] The mass of the persons composing the caravans would travel on foot ; but the richer traders would be mounted on camels, or even sometimes on horses. It would be necessary to be well armed in order to resist the attacks of predatory tribes, or organized bands of robbers ;[2] and the caravans would require to be numerous for the same reason. There would be no great difference between these ancient companies and the caravans of the present day, except, to some extent, in the commodities conveyed, and in the absence of any other than a commercial motive.[3]

Other traders preferred to convey their goods along the courses of the great rivers, which, inter-

---

[1] See Herod., v. 52, who, however, speaks of Persian times.
[2] See Ezra viii. 22.
[3] The religious motive of pilgrimage to certain shrines swells the size of modern caravans.

secting Mesopotamia either as main streams or tributaries, form natural channels of commercial intercourse with the neighbouring countries, at any rate for a considerable distance. Boats and rafts readily descended the Tigris, the Euphrates, and their affluents,[1] and transported almost without effort the produce of Commagene, Armenia, and Media to the lower Mesopotamian territory. It was possible by the use of sails and by tacking to mount the rivers in certain seasons; and this we know to have been done on the Euphrates as high as Thapsacus.[2] Water-carriage was especially convenient for the conveyance of heavy goods, such as stone for building or for statuary, obelisks, and the like. Both the monuments and profane writers indicate that it was employed for these purposes.[3]

The principle lines of land traffic seem to have been five. One, which may be called the Western, was along the course of the Euphrates to about lat. 34° 30′, when it struck across due west to Tadmor, or Palmyra, and thence proceeded by way of Damascus to Tyre and Sidon. Traces of the employment of this route are found in Ezekiel (chap. xxvii. 18, 23, 24). Along it would be conveyed the whole of the Phœnician trade, including the important imports of tin, Tyrian purple,

---

[1] Herod., i. 194.
[2] Strab., xvi. 4, § 18.
[3] "Ancient Monarchies," vol. v., p. 338; Diod. Sic., ii. 11.

musical instruments, asses of superior quality, and possibly wine of Helbon, together with the exports of rich stuffs, dresses, and embroidery.

Another kept to the line of the Euphrates throughout, and may be called the North-Western route. It connected Babylon with Upper Mesopotamia and Armenia. Along this was conveyed wine, and probably copper; perhaps also other metals. It was a route used by Armenian merchants, who descended the stream in round boats, made of wicker-work covered with skins, and, having sold their wares, broke up the boats and returned on foot to their own country.[1] It was used also by the Babylonian colonists of the Persian Gulf, who mounted the stream as far as Thapsacus, and thence carried their goods by land in various directions.[2]

The third route was towards the North. It connected Babylon with Assyria, and probably followed mainly the line of the Tigris, which it may have struck in the vicinity of the great mart of Opis. The trade between the two countries of Babylonia and Assyria was, in the flourishing times of the latter country, highly valued ; and we find frequent provision made for its restoration or continuance in the treaties which from time to time were concluded between the two powers.[3] The alabaster blocks

---

[1] Herod., i. 194.
[2] Strab., l.s.c.
[3] "Records of the Past," vol. iii., pp. 34, 35 ; vol. v., p. 90.

which the Babylonians sometimes employed in their buildings came probably by this line, and the two countries no doubt interchanged various manufactured products.

A fourth line of land trade, and one of great importance, was that towards the North-east, which may be called the Medo-Bactrian. This line, after crossing Mount Zagros by the way of Holwan and Behistun, was directed upon the Median capital of Ecbatana, whence it was prolonged by way of Rhages and the Caspian Gates, to Balkh, Herat, and Cabul.[1] The lapis lazuli, which the Babylonians employed extensively, can only have come from Bactria,[2] and probably arrived by this route, along which may also have travelled much of the gold imported into Babylon, many of the gems, the fine wool, the shawls, the Indian dyes, and the Indian dogs.

The fifth line was towards the East and South-east. At first it ran nearly due east to Susa, but thence it was deflected, and continued on to the South-east, through Persepolis, to Kerman (Carmania). Wool was probably imported in large quantities by this route, together with onyxes from the Choaspes,[3] cotton, and the "greyhounds of the East."[4]

---

[1] Heeren, "Asiatic Nations," vol. ii., pp. 203, 209—211.
[2] Ibid., p. 206.
[3] Dionys. Perieg., ll. 1073—1077.
[4] See above, p. 135.

The sea trade of the Babylonians was primarily with the Persian Gulf. Here they had an important settlement on the southern coast, called Gerrha, which had a large land traffic with the interior of Arabia, and carried its merchandise to Babylon in ships.[1] The "ships of Ur" are often mentioned in the early inscriptions,[2] and the later ones show that numerous vessels were always to be found in the ports at the head of the gulf, and that the Babylonians readily crossed the gulf when occasion required.[3] It is uncertain whether they adventured themselves beyond its mouth into the Indian Ocean; but there is reason to believe that by some means or other they obtained Indian commodities which would have come most readily by this route. The teak found in their buildings, the ivory and ebony which they almost certainly used, the cinnamon and the cotton, in the large quantities in which they needed it, can only have come from the peninsula of Hindustan, and cannot be supposed to have travelled by the circuitous road of Cabul and Bactria. Arabian spices were conveyed by the Gerrhæans in their ships to Babylon itself, and the rest of the trade of the Gulf was probably chiefly in their hands. Perfumes of all kinds, pearls, wood for shipbuilding and

---

[1] Strab. xvi. 4, § 18; Agathemer, "De Mar. Erythr.," § 87.
[2] "Ancient Monarchies," vol. i., p. 16, note 1.
[3] "Records of the Past," vol. i., pp. 40, 43, 73; vol. vii, p. 63; vol. ix., p. 60.

walking-sticks, cotton, gems, gold, Indian fabrics, flowed into the Chaldæan capital from the sea, and were mostly brought to it in ships up the Euphrates, and deposited on the quays at the merchants' doors. Æschylus calls the Babylonians who served in the army of Xerxes "navigators of ships."[1] Commercial dealings among the dwellers in the city on a most extensive scale are disclosed by the Egibi tablets ;[2] "spice-merchants" appear among the witnesses to deeds.[3] Their own records and the accounts of the Greeks are thus in the completest agreement with the Prophet when he describes Babylon as "a land of traffick . . . a city of merchants."

---

[1] Æschyl. Pers., ll. 52—55.
[2] "Transactions of the Society of Biblical Archæology," vol. vii., pp. 1—78.
[3] "Records of the Past," vol. xi., p. 94.

CHAPTER IX.

NOTICES OF BABYLON IN DANIEL (resumed).

CHAPTER IX.

NOTICES OF BABYLON IN DANIEL (resumed).

"BELSHAZZAR the king made a great feast to a thousand of his lords, and drank wine before the thousand. Belshazzar, whiles he tasted the wine, commanded to bring the golden and silver vessels which his father, Nebuchadnezzar, had taken out of the temple which was in Jerusalem; that the king, and his princes, his wives, and his concubines, might drink therein. Then they brought the golden vessels that were taken out of the temple of the house of God that was at Jerusalem; and the king, and his princes, his wives, and his concubines, drank in them. They drank wine, and praised the gods of gold, and of silver, of brass, of iron, of wood, and of stone" (Dan. v. 1—4).

The main difficulties connected with the Book of Daniel open upon us with the commencement of chapter v. A new king makes his appearance—a king unknown to profane historians, and declared by some critics to be a purely fictitious personage.[1] We

---

[1] See De Wette, "Einleitung in das Alt. Test.," § 255a.

have to consider at the outset who this Belshazzar
can be. Does he represent any king known to us
under any other name in profane history? Can
we find a trace of him in the inscriptions? Or is
he altogether an obscure and mysterious personage,
of whose very existence we have no trace outside
Daniel, and who must therefore always constitute an
historical difficulty of no small magnitude?

Now, in the first place, he is represented as the
son of Nebuchadnezzar (vers. 2, 11, 13, 18, 22).
The only son of Nebuchadnezzar of whom we have
any mention in profane history is Evil-Merodach,[1]
who succeeded his father in B.C. 562, and reigned
somewhat less than two years, ascending the throne
in Tisri of B.C. 562, and ceasing to reign in Ab of
B.C. 560.[2] It has been suggested that the Belshazzar
of Daniel is this monarch.[3]

The following are the chief objections to this
theory:—(a) There is no reason to suppose that
Evil-Merodach ever bore any other name, or was
known to the Jews under one designation, to the
Babylonians under another. He appears in the
Book of Kings under his rightful name of Evil-
Merodach (2 Kings xxv. 27), and again in the

---

[1] Mentioned by Berosus, Fr. 14; Polyhistor (ap. Euseb., "Chron. Can." i. 5), and Abydenus (ap. Euseb. i. 10). He appears in the Babylonian dated tablets as Avil-Marduk.
[2] "Transactions of Bib. Arch. Soc.," vol. vi., pp. 25, 26.
[3] So Hupfeld and Hävernick.

Book of Jeremiah (Jer. lii. 31). Unless we have distinct evidence of a monarch having borne two names, it is to the last degree uncritical to presume it. (*b*) The third year of Belshazzar is mentioned in Daniel (ch. viii. 1). Evil-Merodach is assigned two years only by Ptolemy, Berosus, and Abydenus;[1] the latest date upon his tablets is his second year; he actually reigned no more than a year and ten months. (*c*) Evil-Merodach was put to death by his brother-in-law, Neriglissar, in B.C. 560. Babylon was at this time under no peril from the Medes and Persians, to whom the death of Belshazzar appears to be attributed (vers. 28—30). (*d*) The identification of Belshazzar with Evil-Merodach involves that of " Darius the Median " (ver. 31) with Neriglissar, who was not a Mede, and had a name as remote as possible from that of Darius.

If Belshazzar be not Evil-Merodach, can he be Neriglissar? Here the name is not so great a difficulty. For, in the first place, the two words have two elements in common. Neriglissar is in the Babylonian Nergal-shar-uzur, while Belshazzar is Bel-shar-uzur. Moreover, it was not an unknown thing in Babylonia and Assyria to substitute in a royal designation the name of one god for another.[2] But, *per contra*, (*a*) Nergal was a god so distinct

---

[1] Ptol., "Mag. Syntax.," v. 14; Beros., l s.c.; Abyden., l.s.c.

[2] "Transactions of Bib. Arch. Soc.," vol. vi., p. 28.

from Bel, that we can scarcely imagine such a substitution as Bel for Nergal having been allowable. (*b*) Neriglissar was the *son-in-law*, not the son, of Nebuchadnezzar. (*c*) He appears to have died peaceably, and to have been succeeded by his son, Labasi-Merodach (Labossoracus),[1] instead of being "slain" suddenly, and succeeded by a Darius. It seems therefore impossible that the Belshazzar of Daniel can be Neriglissar.

Is he, then, as Josephus supposed, Nabonidus?[2] Nabonidus, according to Ptolemy and Berosus, was the last native king. The Medes and Persians destroyed his kingdom, and made him prisoner; after which, in a little time, he died. On his capture the Medo-Persian rule was established, and continued thenceforth uninterruptedly except for one or two revolts. Here, again, (*a*) the name is an insuperable difficulty: nothing can well be more unlike Belshazzar than Nabu-nahid. But, further, (*b*) Nabu-nahid is distinctly said to have been in no way related to Nebuchadnezzar.[3] (*c*) Also his mother died in the ninth year of his reign,[4] eight years before his own capture and decease; but it is the mother of Belshazzar, probably, who comes into

---

[1] Berosus, l.s.c.
[2] Joseph., "Ant. Jud.," x. 11, § 2.
[3] Abydenus, l.s.c.
[4] See the "Nabonidus Tablet" in the "Transactions of the Bib. Arc. Soc.," vol. vii., p. 158.

the banquet house at the time of his feast.[1] (*d*) Nabonidus, again, did not die on the night that his kingdom passed to the Medes and Persians, as Belshazzar did (ver. 30). On the contrary, he survived eight months.[2] Thus the hypothesis that Belshazzar is Nabonidus, though embraced by many,[3] is as untenable as the others ; and we have still to seek an answer to the question, Who was the Belshazzar of Daniel ?

A discovery made by Sir H. Rawlinson in the year 1854 gave the first clue to what we incline to regard as the true answer. On cylinders placed by Nabonidus at the corners of the great temple of Ur, he mentioned by name " his eldest son, Bel-sharuzur," and prayed the moon-god to take him under his protection, " that his glory might endure." On reading this the learned decypherer at once declared it to be his opinion that Bel-shar-uzur had been associated in the government by his father, and possessed the kingly power. If this were so, it could scarcely be disputed that he was Daniel's Belshazzar. Sir H. Rawlinson's inference from the inscription has, however, been denied. Mr. Fox Talbot has maintained that the inscription does not

---

[1] See "Speaker's Commentary" on Dan. v. 10; and compare Pusey's " Daniel," p. 449.

[2] This is proved by the " Nabonidus Tablet " ("Transactions," etc., vol. vii., pp. 165—7).

[3] As Josephus, Heeren, Clinton, Winer, and others.

furnish "the slightest evidence" that Bel-shar-uzur was ever regarded as co-regent with his father. "He may," he says, "have been a mere child when it was written."[1] The controversy turns upon the question, What was Oriental practice in this matter? Sir H. Rawlinson holds that Oriental monarchs generally, and the Assyrian and Babylonian kings in particular, were so jealous of possible rivals in their own family, that they did not name even their sons upon public documents unless they had associated them. Kudur-mabuk mentions his son Rim-agu;[2] but he has made him King of Larsa. Sennacherib mentions Asshur-nadin-sum,[3] but on the occasion of his elevation to the throne of Babylon. Apart from these instances, and that of Bel-shar-uzur, there does not seem to be any mention made of their sons *by name* by the monarchs of either country.

The supposition that Bel-shar-uzur may have been "a mere child" when the inscription on which his name occurs was set up, is completely negatived by the newly-discovered tablet of Nabonidus, which shows him to have had a son—and Bel-shar-uzur was his "eldest son"—who held the command of his main army from his seventh year, B.C. 549, to his eleventh, B.C. 545.[4] It is a reasonable supposi-

---

[1] "Records of the Past," vol. v., p. 144.
[2] Ibid., vol. iii., p. 20.
[3] Ibid., vol. i., p. 40.
[4] "Transactions," vol. vii., pp 156—161.

tion that the prince mentioned upon this tablet was Bel-shar-uzur. He is called emphatically "the king's son," and is mentioned five times. While Cyrus is threatening Babylon both on the north and on the south, Nabonidus is shown to have remained sluggish and inert within the walls of the capital, the true kingly power being exercised by "the king's son," who is with the army and the officers in Akkad, or northern Babylonia, watching Cyrus and protecting Babylon. When the advance of the army of Cyrus is finally made, what "the king's son" did is not told us. Nabonidus must have roused himself from his lethargy and joined his troops; but as soon as he found himself in danger, he fled. Pursuit was made, and he was captured—possibly in Borsippa, as Berosus related.[1] The victorious Persians took him with them into Babylon. If at this time "the king's son" was still alive, any further resistance that was made must, almost certainly, have been made by him. Now *such resistance was made*. A body of "rebels," as they are called, threw themselves into Bit-Saggatu, or the fortified enclosure within which stood the Great Temple of Bel-Merodach and the Royal Palace, and shutting to the gates, defied the enemy. It is true our record says no preparations had been made previously for the defence of the place, and there was no store of weapons within it.

Berosus, Fr. 14.

But the soldiers would have their own weapons: the temple and the palace would probably be well supplied with wine and provisions; the defences would be strong; and the feeling of the defenders may well have been such as Herodotus ascribes to the mass of the Babylonians when they shut themselves within the walls of the town.[1] Bel-shar-uzur and his lords may have felt so secure that they could indulge in feasting and revelry. They may have maintained their position for months. It is at any rate most remarkable that the writer of the tablet, having launched his shaft of contempt against the foolish "rebels," interposes a break of *more than four months* between this and the next paragraph. It was at the end of Tammuz that the "rebels" closed the gates of Bit-Saggatu; it was not till the 3rd day of Marchesvan that "Cyrus to Babylon descended," and established peace there. It may have been on the night of his arrival with strong reinforcements that the final attack was made, and that Belshazzar, having provoked God by a wanton act of impiety, "was slain" (ver. 31). Nearly five months later, on the 27th of Adar, "the king (Nabonidus) died."

It is objected to the view, that the Belshazzar of Daniel is Bel-shar-uzur, the eldest son of Nabonidus:—1. That Belshazzar is called repeatedly the

---

[1] Herod i. 190.

son of Nebuchadnezzar,[1] while we have no evidence that Bel-shar-uzur was in any way related to that monarch. 2. That "the Book of Daniel gives not the least hint of Belshazzar as having a father still alive and on the throne."[2] The first of these objections has often been answered.[3] In Scripture, it has been observed, father stands for any male ancestor, "son" for any male descendant. Jehoshaphat is called "the son of Nimshi," though really his grandson; Jesus of Nazareth is "the son of David," who is "the son of Abraham" (Matt. i. 1); Ezra is "the son of Seraiah" (Ezra. vii. 1), the "chief priest" of the captivity (2 Kings xxv. 18), who died B.C. 586 (ver. 21), of whom Ezra therefore (B.C. 460—440) must have been really the grandson or great-grandson. Conversely, Abraham, Isaac, and Jacob are the "fathers" of the Israelites after they have been four hundred years in Egypt (Exod. iii. 15, 16); Jonadab, the son of Rechab, the friend of Jehu (2 Kings x. 15), is the "father" of the Rechabites, contemporary with Jeremiah (Jer. xxxv. 6), and Jehoram, king of Judah, is the father of Uzziah (Matt. i. 8), his fourth descendant. The *rationale* of the matter is as follows: Neither in Hebrew nor in Chaldee is there any word for "grandfather" or "grandson." To

---

[1] Fox Talbot, in "Records of the Past," vol. v., p. 144.
[2] Ibid.
[3] See the author's "Bampton Lectures," Lecture V., pp. 134, 135, and note.

express the relationship it would be necessary to say "father's father" and "son's son." But "father's father" and "son's son" are, by an idiom of the language, used with an idea of remoteness—to express distant ancestors or descendants. Consequently they are rendered by this usage unapt to express the near relationship of grandfather and grandson; and the result is that they are very rarely so used. As Dr. Pusey has well observed,[1] "A single grandfather, or forefather, is never called 'father's father,' always 'father' only." This is so, alike in early and in late Hebrew; and the Chaldee follows the idiom. Jacob says, "The God of my father, the God of Abraham, and the fear of Isaac" (Gen. xxxi. 42). God says to Aaron, "The tribe of Levi, the tribe of thy father" (Num. xviii. 2). The confession to be made at the offering of the first-fruits began, "a Syrian, ready to perish was my father" (Deut. xxvi. 5); and in the same sense, probably, Moses says, "the God of my father" (Exod. xviii. 4). David said to Mephibosheth, "I will surely show thee kindness for Jonathan thy father's sake, and will restore to thee all the land of Saul thy father" (2 Sam. ix. 7). And Asa is said to have "removed Maachah, his mother, from being queen," though it is said in the same chapter that she was the mother of Abijam, his

---

[1] See his "Lectures on Daniel," Lecture VII., pp. 405, 406.

father (1 Kings xv. 2, 13), Maachah herself, who is called "daughter of Abishalom" (1 Kings xv. 2), was really his granddaughter, he having left only one daughter, Tamar (2 Sam. xiv. 27), and her own father being Uriel (2 Chron. xiii. 2). Again it is said, "Asa did right in the eyes of the Lord, as did David his father" (1 Kings xv. 11), and in like way of Hezekiah (2 Kings xviii. 3). Contrariwise, it is said that "Ahaz did not right like David his father" (xvi. 2) ; that " Amaziah did right, yet not like David his father ; he did according to all things as Joash his father did " (xiv. 3). Here, in one verse, the actual father and the remote grandfather are alike called " his father ; " as before the father and grandfather of Mephibosheth were called, in the same verse, " his father." " Josiah," it is said, "walked in the ways of David his father ; he began to seek the God of David his father " (2 Chron. xxxiv. 2, 3). In Isaiah there occur "Jacob thy father" (Isa. lviii. 14) ; " thy first father " (xliii. 27)—*i.e.*, Adam ; and to Hezekiah he said, " Thus saith the Lord, the God of David thy father " (xxxviii. 5). So, on the other hand, there is no Hebrew or Chaldee word to express "grandson." In laws, if the relation has to be expressed, the idiom is " thy son's daughter " (Lev. xviii. 10), or thy " daughter's daughter " (Ibid.) ; or it is said, " Thou shalt tell it to thy son's son " (Exod. x. 2) ; " Rule thou over us, thou, and thy son, and thy son's son "

(Judg. viii. 22). The relation can be expressed in this way in the abstract, but there is no way in Hebrew or Chaldee to mark that one person was the grandson of another, except in the way of genealogy—"Jehu, the son of Jehoshaphat, the son of Nimshi." And so the name "son" stands for the "grandson," and a person is at times called the son of the more remarkable grandfather, the link of the father's name being omitted. Thus Jacob asked for "Laban, the son of Nahor" (Gen. xxix. 5), omitting the immediate father, Bethuel; Jehu is called "the son of Nimshi" (1 Kings xix. 16; 2 Kings ix. 20), omitting his own father, Jehoshaphat. The prophet Zechariah is called "the son of Iddo" (Ezra v. 1; vi. 14), his own father being Berachiah (Zech. i. 1). Hence the Rechabites said, as a matter of course, "Jonadab, the son of Rechab, our father, commanded us; we have obeyed in all things the voice of Jonadab, the son of Rechab, our father" (Jer. xxxv. 6, 8); although Jonadab lived some one hundred and eighty years before (2 Kings x. 15). And reciprocally God says, "The words of Jonadab, the son of Rechab, that he commanded his sons, are performed" (ver. 14); and "Because ye have obeyed the commandments of Jonadab your father, and kept all his precepts" (ver. 16).

But, it is objected, all this may be true; yet it proves nothing. Nabonidus *was not in any way* related to Nebuchadnezzar—he was "merely a

Babylonian nobleman."[1] How, then, should his son be even Nebuchadnezzar's grandson? This, too, has been answered,[2] and it is curious that the answer should be ignored. Belshazzar, it has been observed, may have been the grandson of Nebuchadnezzar *on the mother's side*. His father, Nabonidus, may have married one of Nebuchadnezzar's daughters.

It must be granted that we have no *proof* that he did. We have, however, some indications from which we should naturally have drawn the conclusion independently of the Book of Daniel. Two pretenders to the throne of Babylon started up during the reign of Darius Hystaspis, both of whom called themselves "Nebuchadnezzar, son of Nabonidus."[3] It is certain from this that Nabonidus must have had a son so called, for no pretender would assume the name of a person who never existed. How, then, are we to account for Nabonidus having given this name to one of his sons? Usurpers, as a rule, desire not to recall the memory of the family which they have dispossessed. The Sargonidæ discarded all the names in use among their predecessors. So did the Egyptian monarchs of the eighteenth and nineteenth dynasties. So, again, did those of the twenty-first, and the

---

[1] Fox Talbot, in " Records of the Past," vol. v., p. 144.
[2] See the author's " Bampton Lectures," Lecture V., note 41.
[3] See the " Behistun Inscription,' in the author's " Herodotus," vol. ii., pp. 596, 606.

Psammetichi. Nabonidus must have intended to claim a family connection with the preceding Babylonian monarchs when he thus named a son. And if he was indeed " no way related to Nebuchadnezzar," the connection could only have been by marriage. The probability, therefore, is that the principal wife of Nabonidus, the queen (or queen-mother) of Dan. v. 10, was a daughter of Nebuchadnezzar, and that through her Belshazzar was Nebuchadnezzar's grandson.

But further: it is objected that the " Book of Daniel gives not the slightest hint of Belshazzar having a father alive, and still upon the throne."[1] In reply it may be said, in the first place, that, were it so, no surprise need be felt; since, if the circumstances were as above supposed, if Nabonidus after a shameful flight was a prisoner in the hands of the enemy, and Belshazzar was conducting the defence alone, any distinct allusion to the captured king would be improbable. But secondly, it is not true that there is " no hint." Belshazzar makes proclamation that, if any one can read and interpret the writing miraculously inscribed upon the wall, " he shall be clothed with scarlet, and have a chain of gold about his neck, and shall be *the third ruler* in the kingdom" (v. 7); and when Daniel has read and interpreted the words, the acts promised are

---

[1] Fox Talbot, in " Records of the Past," l.s.c.

performed—" they clothed Daniel with scarlet, and put a chain of gold about his neck, and made a proclamation concerning him, that he should be *the third ruler* in the kingdom " (ver. 29). It has been suggested that to be the " third ruler " was to be one of the three presidents who were subsequently set over the satraps (vi. 2) ; but neither is this the plain force of the words, nor was the organization of chap. vi. 1, 2 as yet existing. To be " the third ruler in the kingdom " is to hold a position one degree lower than that of " second from the king," which was conferred upon Joseph (Gen. xli. 40—44), and upon Mordecai (Esth. x. 3) ; it is to hold a position in the kingdom inferior to two persons, and to two persons only. That the proclamation ran in this form is a " hint," and more than a hint, that the first and second places were occupied, that there were two kings upon the throne, and that therefore the highest position that could, under the circumstances, be granted to a subject was the third place, the place next to the two sovereigns. If we compare the two nearly parallel cases of Joseph and Mordecai—subjects whom their despotic master " delighted to honour "—with that of Daniel at this time, we shall find it scarcely possible to assign any other reason for his being promoted to the *third* place in the kingdom than the fact that the first and second places were already occupied by the son and father, Belshazzar and Nabonidus.

CHAPTER X.

NOTICES OF BABYLON IN DANIEL (continued).

CHAPTER X.

NOTICES OF BABYLON IN DANIEL (continued).

"DARIUS the Median took the kingdom, being about threescore and two years old. It pleased Darius to set over the kingdom an hundred and twenty princes, which should be over the whole kingdom" (Dan. v. 31 ; vi. 1).

The reign of "Darius the Median" over Babylon is the second great historical difficulty which the Book of Daniel presents to the modern inquirer. According to Herodotus,[1] Berosus,[2] and the Canon of Ptolemy, the immediate successor of Nabonidus (Labynetus) was Cyrus—no king intervened between them. The Babylonian records are in accord. Two contemporary documents[3] declare that Cyrus defeated Nabonidus, captured him, and took the direction of affairs into his own hands. One of

---

[1] Herod., i. 188, 191.
[2] Berosus, Fr. 14.
[3] See the "Cylinder Inscription of Cyrus," published in the "Journal of the Royal Asiatic Society," vol. xii., pp. 85—9; and "Transactions of Bibl. Archæol. Society," vol. vii., pp. 153—169.

them contains a proclamation, issued by Cyrus, as it would seem, immediately after his conquest,[1] in which he assumes the recognised titles of Babylonian sovereignty, calling himself "the great king, the powerful king, the king of Babylon, the king of Sumir and Akkad, the king of the four regions." Who, then, it has to be asked, is this "Darius the Median," who "took the kingdom," and made arrangements for its government, immediately after the fall of the native Babylonian power, and its supersession by that of the Medes and Persians?

All that Scripture tells us of "Darius the Median," besides the points already mentioned, is that he was the son of Ahasuerus, that he was an actual Mede by descent ("of the *seed* of the Medes," Dan. ix. 1), that he advanced Daniel to a high dignity (ch. vi. 2), and that afterwards he cast Daniel into the den of lions and released him. The first and second of these facts seem conclusive against a theory which has been of late years strongly advocated—viz., that he is really "Darius the son of Hystaspes,"[2] the great Darius, the only Darius mentioned in Scripture, except Codomannus, whose name occurs in one place (Neh. xii. 22.). We know not only the father, but the entire descent of Darius Hystaspes, up to

---

[1] "As. Soc. Journ.," vol. xii., p. 87.
[2] Particularly by Mr. Bosanquet ("Translations," etc., vol. vi., pp. 84, 100, 130).

Achæmenes, the founder of the Persian royal family;[1] and we find no "Ahasuerus"—the Hebrew form of the Persian *Khshayarsha*, the Greek Xerxes—in the list. There is the strongest evidence that he was of pure Persian race, and not an atom of evidence that he had any Median blood in his veins. It is among his proudest boasts that he is "an Aryan, of Aryan descent, a Persian, the son of a Persian."[2] He was a member of the Persian royal family, closely akin to Cyrus. The Medes revolted against him, and fought desperately to throw off his authority and place themselves under a real Mede, Frawartish, who claimed to be "of the race of Cyaxares."[3] Cyrus might with better reason be called a Mede than Darius, for some high authorities gave Cyrus a Median mother;[4] but there is no such tradition with respect to Darius, the son of Hystaspes.

Another extraordinary theory, recently broached, identifies "Darius the Mede" with Cyrus.[5] Darius, it is said, may be in Daniel, not a name, but a title. Etymologically the name would mean "holder," or "firm holder," and it may therefore have been a synonym for king or ruler. *Daryavesh Madaya* (in Dan. v. 31), may mean, not "Darius the Mede,"

---

[1] See the Author's "Herodotus," vol. iv., pp. 25—45.
[2] Ibid., p. 250.
[3] Ibid., vol. ii., pp. 598—602.
[4] Herod., i. 108; Xen. "Cyrop.," i. 2, § 1.
[5] "Transactions," etc., vol. vi., p. 29.

but only "the king or ruler of the Medes, a fit title for Cyrus"!

But how does this conjectural explanation suit the other passages of Daniel where the name of Darius occurs? We read in ch. vi. 28, "So this Daniel prospered in the reign of Darius, *and in the reign of Cyrus, the Persian.*" Does this mean, he prospered "in the reign of Cyrus, and in the reign of Cyrus"? Again, we read, in ch. ix. 1, of "Darius, the son of Ahasuerus." How can this apply to Cyrus, who was the son of Cambyses? Further, how are we to understand the expression "King Darius," which occurs in ch. vi. 6, 9, 25? Does it mean "king, king"? We will not insult our readers' intellects by continuing. We will only add one less obvious argument, an argument which may further our quest, and give us perhaps some help in determining, not only who "Darius the Median" was not, but who he was.

It is said, in ch. v. 31, that "Darius the Median *took* the kingdom," and in ch. ix. 1, that he "*was made king* over the realm of the Chaldeans." Neither of these two expressions is suitable to Cyrus. The word translated "took" means "received," "took from the hands of another;" and the other passage is yet more unmistakable. "Was made king" exactly expresses the original, which uses the Hophal of the verb, the Hiphel of which occurs when

David makes Solomon king over Israel (1 Chron. xxix. 20). No one would say of Alexander the Great, when he conquered Darius Codomannus, that he "*was made king* over Persia." The expression implies the reception of a kingly position by one man from the hands of another. Now, Babylon, while under the Assyrians, had been almost always governed by viceroys, who received their crown from the Assyrian monarchs.[1] It was not unnatural that Cyrus should follow the same system. He had necessarily to appoint a governor, and the "Nabonidus Tablet" tells us that he did so almost immediately after taking possession of the city. The first governor appointed was a certain Gobryas,[2] whose nationality is doubtful; but he appears to have been shortly afterwards sent to some other locality.[3] A different arrangement must have been then made. That Cyrus should have appointed a Mede, and allowed him to take the title of "king," is in no way improbable. He was fond of appointing Medes to high office, as we learn from Herodotus.[4] He was earnestly desirous of conciliating the Babylonians, as we find from his cylinder.[5] It was not many years before he

---

[1] "Ancient Monarchies," vol. iii., p. 42.
[2] So at least I understand the passage ("Transactions," etc., vol. vii. p. 166, l. 20).
[3] Ibid., p. 167, l. 22. The reading is uncertain.
[4] Herod., i. 159, 162.
[5] "Journal of Royal Asiatic Society," vol. xii., pp. 87—9

gave his son, Cambyses, the full royal power at Babylon, relinquishing it himself, as appears from a dated tablet.[1] The position of "Darius the Median" in Daniel is compatible with all that we know with any certainty from other sources. We have only to suppose that Cyrus, in the interval between the brief governorship of Gobryas and the sovereignty of Cambyses, placed Babylon under a Median noble named Darius, and allowed him a position intermediate between that of a mere ordinary "governor" and the full royal authority.

The position of Darius the Median, as a subject-king set up by Cyrus, has been widely accepted; but critics have not been content to rest at this point. Attempts have been made to identify him further with some person celebrated in history; and it has been suggested that he was either Astyages, the last Median monarch,[3] or his supposed son, Cyaxares.[3] Neither identification can be substantiated. The very existence of a second Cyaxares, the son of Astyages, is more than questionable.[4] The names are, in both cases, unsuitable. The age of Darius when he "took the kingdom" falls short of the probable age of Astyages. It seems best to acquiesce

---

[1] "Transactions," etc., vol. vi., p. 489.
[2] So Syncellus, Jackson, Marsham, and Winer.
[3] So Josephus, Prideaux, Hales, Hengstenberg, Von Lengerke, and others.
[4] Herodotus declares that Astyages had no male offspring (i., 109).

in the view of those who hold that "Darius the Mede is an historic character," but one "whose name has not yet been found except in Scripture."[1]

It is in no way surprising that, on being set over the realm of the Chaldees, Darius should have occupied himself in giving it a new organization. We are scarcely entitled to assume, from the expression used in Dan. vi. 1, that he called his new officers "satraps;" but still it is quite possible that he used the word, which had not yet received a technical sense, and only meant etymologically "supporters of the crown." The number, one hundred and twenty, is more than we should have expected, and can receive no support from the hundred and twenty-seven provinces of Ahasuerus (Esth. i. 1), who ruled from Ethiopia to India, whereas Darius reigned only over the realm of the Chaldees; we must view it either as resulting from Oriental ostentation, or as an anticipation of the maxim, *Divide et impera.* Each "satrap" must have ruled over a comparatively small district. They may have been the head men of tribes, and if so, it is pertinent to remark that the tribes of the Euphrates valley were exceedingly numerous. Twenty-four tribes of Lower Babylonia collected on one occasion to assist Susub;[2] in the middle region Tiglath-

---

[1] "Speaker's Commentary," on Dan. v. 31.
[2] "Records of the Past," vol. i., p. 47.

Pileser II. claims to have reduced thirty-four tribes;[1] the upper region had at least as many. An ancient geographical list seems to divide Babylonia proper into seventy-three districts.[2] If Cyrus intrusted to Darius the Euphrates valley up to Carchemish, and the regions of Cœlesyria and Phœnicia, we can quite understand the number of the "princes" (*i.e.*, satraps) being a hundred and twenty.

"Now, O king, establish the decree, and sign the writing, that it be not changed, according to the law of the Medes and Persians, which altereth not" (Dan. vi. 8).

"Know, O king, that the law of the Medes and Persians is, That no decree nor statute which the king establisheth may be changed" (ver. 15).

The inviolability of Medo-Persian law, and the moral impossibility that the king, having signed a decree, or in any way pledged his word to a matter, could afterwards retract, or alter it, which are so strongly asserted in these passages, and again so markedly implied in the Book of Esther, receive illustration from two narratives which have come down to us on the authority of Herodotus. "Cambyses," he tells us,[3] "the son of Cyrus, was anxious to marry one of his sisters; but, as he knew that it was an uncommon thing, and not the custom of the

---

[1] "Records of the Past," vol. v., p. 101.
[2] Ibid., vol. v., pp. 105—7.
[3] Herod., iii., 31.

Persians previously, he summoned a meeting of the royal judges, and put the question to them, whether there was any law which allowed a brother, if he wished it, to marry his sister? Now the royal judges," he remarks, "are certain picked men among the Persians, who hold their office for life, or until they are found guilty of some misconduct. By them justice is administered in Persia, and they are the interpreters of the old laws, all disputed cases of law being referred to their decision. When Cambyses, therefore, put his question to these judges, they gave him an answer which was at once true and safe— 'they did not find any law,' they said, 'allowing a brother to take his sister to wife ; but they found a law that the king of the Persians, might do whatever he pleased.' And so they neither warped the law through fear of Cambyses, nor ruined themselves by over-stiffly maintaining the law : but they brought another quite distinct law to the king's help, which allowed him to have his wish. Cambyses, therefore, married the object of his love ; and no long time afterwards he took to wife also another sister." Still more closely illustrative of the perplexity of Darius, and his inability to escape from the entanglement in which he found himself, is the following anecdote concerning Xerxes, one of the most self-willed and despotic of all the Persian monarchs : " Amestris, the wife of Xerxes, having a cause of quarrel, as she thought, against the wife of a Persian prince named

Masistes, determined to compass her death. She waited, therefore, till her husband gave the great royal banquet—a feast which took place once every year—in celebration of the king's birthday, and then made request of Xerxes that he would please to give her, as her present, the wife of Masistes. But he at first refused; for it seemed to him shocking and monstrous to give into the power of another a woman who was not only his brother's wife, but was likewise wholly guiltless in the matter which had enraged Amestris; and he was the more unwilling inasmuch as he well knew the intention with which his wife had preferred her request. After a time, however, he was wearied by her importunity, and, *feeling constrained by the law of the feast*, which required that no one who asked a boon that day at the king's board should be denied his request, he yielded, but with a very ill will, and gave the woman into her power."[1] Amestris, as he had expected, caused the woman to be put to death, first mutilating her in a most barbarous manner.

It is indicative of the complete knowledge that the writer has of the change which Babylon underwent when she passed from the uncontrolled despotism of the old native kings to the comparatively limited monarchy of Persia that he exhibits to us Nebuchadnezzar and Belshazzar as wholly unre-

---

[1] Herod., ix. 110, 111.

strained by those about them, or admitting, at the most, domestic counsels, while he represents Darius as trammelled by Medo-Persian law, a passive instrument in the hands of his councillors, forced to do an act against which his soul revolted, and only venturing upon a vindication of his own authority when he had been the witness of a stupendous miracle (ch. vi. 14—24).

"The king spake and said unto Daniel, O Daniel, servant of the living God, is thy God, whom thou servest continually, able to deliver thee from the lions?" (Dan. vi. 20).

"Then King Darius wrote unto all people, nations, and languages, that dwell in all the earth: Peace be multiplied unto you. I make a decree, That in every dominion of my kingdom men tremble and fear before the God of Daniel: for He is the living God, and steadfast for ever, and His kingdom that which shall not be destroyed, and His dominion shall be even unto the end. He delivereth and rescueth, and He worketh signs and wonders in heaven and in earth, who hath delivered Daniel from the power of the lions" (Dan. vi. 25—27).

As the Medo-Persic kings introduced some novelty into the political situation when they became the rulers of Babylon, so they further introduced a more considerable religious change. The ordinary Babylonian system is sufficiently indicated in the account of Belshazzar's feast. It was grossly polytheistic and idolatrous. It recognised a hierarchy of gods as ruling in the heavenly sphere,[1] and it worshipped them under the form of images[2] in gold, and silver, and brass, and iron, and wood, and stone (ch. vi. 4, 23). The religion of the Medo-Persians was very different. It admitted of no use of images.[3] It did not absolutely reject the employment of the word god in the plural;[4] but it acknowledged one god as infinitely superior to all others, and viewed him as alone truly "living," as alone the fount and origin of all life, whether earthly or spiritual. The Ahura-Mazda of the Medes and Persians was a god of a very spiritual and exalted character. He had made the celestial bodies, earth, water, and trees, all good creatures, and all good, true things. He was good, holy, pure, true, the holy god, the holiest, the essence of truth, the father of all truth, the best being of all, the master of purity. He was supremely happy, possessing every blessing—health, wealth, virtue, wisdom, immortality.[5]

These facts, which are known to us especially through the Zendavesta, the sacred book of the ancient Medes and Persians, throw considerable light

---

[1] "Ancient Monarchies," vol. i., pp. 110—142; vol. iii., pp. 25—33.
[2] Ibid., vol. iii., p. 28.
[3] Herod., i. 131.
[4] See Pusey's "Lectures on Daniel," pp. 529—539.
[5] "Ancient Monarchies," vol. ii., pp. 324—5.

on the picture drawn of the religion of the Babylonian court under Darius the Mede, compared with that of the same court almost immediately before, under Belshazzar. Belshazzar allowed that "the spirit of *the holy gods*" might be in Daniel, and that therefore his words might be deserving of attention. He praised "the gods," and recognised the duty of worshipping them as embodied in their images of wood and stone and metal. In the account given of Darius the Mede, idolatry has, on the other hand, no place. Polytheism *of a kind* just makes its appearance in the expression, "Whosoever shall ask a petition of *any god*" (ch. vi. 7, 12); but monotheism is predominant. Darius, before knowing if a miracle has been performed or no, recognises Daniel as a "servant of *the living God*" (ver. 20); and afterwards, when assured of Daniel's deliverance, praises and exalts "the living God" as one "who is steadfast for ever and ever," whose "kingdom shall not be destroyed," but shall continue "even unto the end;" "who delivereth and rescueth," and "worketh signs and wonders in heaven and earth" (vers. 26, 27). These words, which would seem strange in the mouth of most heathens, are natural enough in those of a Zoroastrian, who, while allowing a certain qualified worship of the sun, and of the gods presiding over his own family,[1] would recognise as infinitely above

---

[1] "Behist. Inscript.," col. iv., par. 12, 13; Pusey's "Daniel," p. 531, note 8.

these, placed in a category apart and by himself, the great giver of life, Ahura-Mazda, the true "living God," the Creator, the Preserver, the Deliverer from evil, the Supreme Spirit, to whom all others were subordinate, the one and only ruler of heaven and earth.

It does not interfere with this view that Cyrus, and as his vice-gerent, Darius, tolerated—nay, even patronized to some extent—the Babylonian religion.[1] This they did as politic rulers over subjects likely to be disaffected. But in their court, among their privy-councillors, they would act differently. There they would show their true feelings. Even in a proclamation addressed to all their subjects, as that of Darius was (ver. 25), they would not scruple to show their own feelings—as Darius Hystaspes and his successors all did in their rock-inscriptions—so long as they abstained from any direct disparagement of their subjects' gods, and merely required the acknowledgment of an additional deity besides those of the popular Pantheon.

---

[1] "Journal of the Royal Asiatic Society," vol. xii., pp. 88—9.

CHAPTER XI.

FURTHER NOTICES OF BABYLON IN DANIEL, ISAIAH, JEREMIAH, AND EZEKIEL.

CHAPTER XI.

FURTHER NOTICES OF BABYLON IN DANIEL, ISAIAH, JEREMIAH, AND EZEKIEL.

IT is proposed in the present paper to bring together the scattered notices in Scripture bearing upon the general condition of Babylon, the character of its government, and the manners and customs of its people; and to inquire how far profane history confirms or illustrates what Scripture tells us on these matters. A certain number of the points have necessarily been touched in some of the earlier chapters of the present volume, and thus it will be impossible to avoid a certain amount of repetition; but the endeavour will be made to pass lightly over such topics as have been already put before the reader, and thus to reduce the repetition to a minimum.

We have noticed indirectly, in connection with its commerce, the great wealth of Babylon. Isaiah calls it emphatically, "the *golden* city" (Isa. xiv. 4), or "the exactress of gold," as the passage may be rendered literally. Jeremiah compares Babylon to "a *golden* cup in the hand of the Lord" (Jer. li. 7), and calls her "abundant in treasures" (ib. ver. 13), declaring moreover that, at her fall, all those who partook of her spoil should be "satisfied" (ib. l. 10). In Daniel the Babylonian kingdom is typified by the "head of gold" (Dan. ii. 38), and the opulence of the monarch is shown by the enormous size of the image, or rather pillar, of gold which he set up, a pillar ninety feet high by nine feet wide (ib. iii. 1). The inscriptions are in accordance. Nebuchadnezzar tells us that he brought into the treasury of Merodach at Babylon "wares and ornaments for the women, silver, molten gold, precious stones, metal, *umritgana* and cedar wood, a splendid abundance, riches and sources of joy."[1] The temple of Merodach he "made conspicuous with fine linen, and covered its seats with splendid gold, with lapis lazuli, and blocks of alabaster."[2] Its portico, "with brilliant gold he caused men to cover; the lower threshold, the cedar awnings with gold and precious stones he embellished."[3] And the rest of his sacred buildings were adorned similarly.[4]

The primary source of the wealth of Babylon was its agriculture. Herodotus tells us that the yield of grain was commonly two hundred-fold, and in some

---

[1] "Records of the Past," vol. v., pp. 116-7.
[2] Ibid., p. 117.
[3] Ibid., pp. 119—20.
[4] Ibid., vol. vii., pp. 72, 75—6.

instances three hundred-fold.[1] Pliny asserts that the wheat-crop was reaped twice, and afterwards afforded good keep for beasts.[2] When Babylonia became a province of the Persian Empire, it paid a tribute of a thousand talents of silver,[3] and at the same time furnished the entire provision of the court during one-third of the year.[4] Notwithstanding these calls upon them, its satraps became enormously wealthy.[5] To the wealth obtained by agriculture is to be added that derived from commerce, and from conquest. Both of these points have already engaged our attention, and we have seen reason to believe that the gains made were in each case very great. Scripture makes allusion to the agricultural wealth of the country, when it enumerates among the chief calamities of the final invasion, the "cutting off of the sower, and of him that handled the sickle in the time of harvest" (Jer. l. 16) ; and again when it makes special mention of the "opening of the granaries" as a feature in the sack of the city (ib. ver. 26). The commercial wealth is implied in the description of Babylon as "a city of merchants" (Ezek. xvii. 4), and of Babylonia as "a land of traffick" (ib.). The wealth derived from conquest receives notice in the statement

---

[1] Herod., i. 193.
[2] Plin. "Hist. Nat." xviii. 17.
[3] Herod., iii. 92.
[4] Ibid., i. 192.
[5] Ibid.

of Habakkuk, "Because thou has spoilt many nations, all the remnant of the people shall spoil thee" (Hab. ii. 8), and is illustrated by the narrative of Kings (2 Kings xxv. 13—17). Nebuchadnezzar alludes to it when he says, "A palace for my royalty in the midst of the city of Babylon I built . . . tall cedars for its porticoes I fitted . . . with silver, gold, and precious stones I overlaid its gates . . . *I valiantly collected spoils*; as an adornment of the house were they arranged and collected within it; trophies, abundance, royal treasures, I accumulated and gathered together;"[1] and again, "*Gatherings from great lands I made;* and, like the hills, I upraised its head."[2]

Among the spoil which was regarded as of especial value were scented woods, more particularly cedars, and perhaps pines, from Lebanon and Amanus. Isaiah, in describing the general rejoicing at the fall of the Babylonian Empire, remarks, "The whole earth is at rest and is quiet; they break forth into singing: yea, the fir trees rejoice at thee, and the cedars of Lebanon, saying, Since thou art laid down, no feller is come up against us" (Isa. xiv. 7, 8). The cuneiform inscriptions show that the practice of cutting timber in the Syrian mountains and conveying it to Mesopotamia, which had been begun by the Assyrian monarchs (2 Kings xix. 23), was

---

[1] "Records of the Past," vol. v., p. 131.
[2] Ibid., p. 133.

continued by the Babylonians. Nebuchadnezzar expressly states that "the best of his pine-trees *from Lebanon*, with tall babil-wood, he brought;"[1] and Nabonidus tells us that, in his third year, he went to "Amananu, a mountainous country, where tall pines grew, and brought a part of them to the midst of Babylon."[2]

The great size of Babylon, and the immense height and thickness of its walls, have been dwelt upon at some length in a former chapter.[3] Jeremiah is particularly clear upon these points, though, naturally, he enters into no details. "Though Babylon should *mount up to heaven,*" he says, "and though she should *fortify the height of her strength*, yet from me shall spoilers come unto her, saith the Lord" (Jer. li. 53); and again, "The *broad* walls of Babylon shall be utterly broken, and her *high* gates shall be burned with fire" (ib. ver. 58); and, with respect to the size of the city, "One post shall run to meet another, and one messenger to meet another, to show the king of Babylon that his city is taken at one end" (ib. ver. 31).

The government of Babylon by a despotic monarch, the sole source of all power and authority, and the absolute master of the lives and liberties of

---

[1] Ibid., vol. v., p. 119.
[2] "Transactions of the Bibl. Archæolog. Society," vol. vii., p. 154.
[3] See above, ch. vi., pp. 91, 92.

his subjects, which the Babylonian notices in Scripture set before us consistently, and which appears most markedly in Daniel (ch. ii, 12, 48, 49; iii. 6, 15, 29), is in complete accordance with all that profane history teaches on the subject. Nebuchadnezzar claims in his inscription to rule by Divine right. "The sceptre of righteousness is delivered into his hand that therewith he may sustain men."[1] From him alone commands issue; by him alone all works are accomplished. No subject obtains any mention as even helping him. The inscriptions of Neriglissar and Nabonidus are of nearly the same character. And the classical accounts agree. It is clear that in Semitic Babylon, prior to the Medo-Persic conquest, there was no noble class possessing independent power, or any right of controlling the king.

There was, however, a learned class, which possessed a certain distinction, which furnished priests to the chief temples, and claimed to interpret dreams and omens, and to foretell the future by means of astrology. Herodotus[2] and Diodorus[3] give this class the name of "Chaldæans," a nomenclature with which the Book of Daniel may be said to agree, if we accept the identification of "Chaldæans" with *Casdim*. At any rate, the book testifies to the

---

[1] "Records of the Past," vol. v., p. 114.
[2] Herod., i. 181, 183.
[3] Diod. Sic., ii. 29.

existence of the class, and to the functions which belonged to it, as also does Isaiah, when he says of Babylon, "Let now the astrologers, the star-gazers, the monthly prognosticators, stand up and save thee from these things which shall come upon thee" (Isa. xlvii. 13). The title Rab-Mag, which may be suspected to have belonged to the chief of the Chaldæan order, is found both in Scripture (Jer. xxxix. 3, 13) and in the inscriptions. It has been translated "chief of the Magi;"[1] but there seems to be no reason to believe that Magianism was in any way recognised by the Babylonians of the independent empire.

There was also in Babylonia a numerous class of officials—a "bureaucracy," as it has been called—whereby the government of the country was actually carried on. In some places, the native sovereigns were indeed allowed to retain their authority for a time (2 Kings xxiv. 1, 17), and the Babylonian monarch could thus be called with propriety a "king of kings" (Dan. ii. 37; Ezek. xxvi. 7); but the general system was to replace kings by "governors" (2 Kings xxv. 22, 23; Berosus, Fr. 14) or "princes" (Dan. ii. 2), and to employ under these last a great variety of subordinates. The Babylonian contract tablets show at least eight or ten names of officers under government, of different

---

[1] Speaker's Commentary on Jeremiah, xxxix. 3.

ranks and gradations,[1] correspondent (in a general way) to the "princes, governors, captains, judges, treasurers, counsellors, sheriffs, and rulers of provinces" of the Book of Daniel, and thus indicate sufficiently the bureaucratic character of the government.

The general character of the Babylonian court as depicted in Daniel, and its agreement with what we know from other sources, has been already noticed. But the following illustrations may be added to those already given. The high position of the queen-mother at the court of Belshazzar receives illustration from the mention of "the mother of the king" in the tablet of Nabonidus, and from the fact that at her death there was a court mourning of three days' duration.[2] The polygamy of the monarchs (Dan. v. 2, 3) accords with what we hear of the "concubines" of Saul-Mugina.[3] The employment of eunuchs (2 Kings xx. 10 ; Dan. i. 3) agrees with Herod. iii. 92 ; that of music (Isa. xiv. 11 ; Dan. iii. 5, 7) with passages in the Assyrian inscriptions, which speak of musicians and musical instruments as in vogue at the courts of other neighbouring kings ;[4] that of "sweet odours" in

---

[1] "Records of the Past," vol. ix., pp. 91—108; vol. xi., pp. 91—8.
[2] "Transactions of the Bibl. Archæolog. Society," vol. vii., pp. 158—9.
[3] "Records of the Past," vol. i., p. 77.
[4] Ibid., vol. ix., pp. 54—55.

the way of religious service (Dan. ii. 46) with what Herodotus relates of the burning of frankincense on sacrificial occasions.[1] The long detention in prison of offenders against the dignity of the crown, of which Isaiah speaks, when he says of the Babylonian monarch that he "opened not the door of his prisoners" (Isa. xiv. 17), and which is exemplified by the confinement of Jehoiachin by Nebuchadnezzar for the extraordinary term of thirty-seven years (2 Kings xxv. 27), receives illustration from the story of Parsondas, as told by Nicholas of Damascus. Parsondas was a Mede, who desired to become king of Babylon under Artæus, and obtained from him the promise of the kingdom. Nannarus, the actual monarch, hearing of it, got Parsondas into his power, and kept him a prisoner at his court for seven years, even then releasing him, not of his own free-will, but on the application of Artæus, and under the apprehension that, if he refused, Artæus would make war upon him, and deprive him of his sovereignty.[2]

One of the most surprising points in the representation of Babylonian customs which the Scriptural account of the people brings before us is the severity and abnormal character of the punishments which were in use among them. To burn men to death in a furnace of fire, as Nebuchadnezzar proposed to do with Shadrach, Meshach, and Abednego

---
[1] Herod, i. 183. [2] Nic. Dam., Fr. 11.

(Dan. iii. 15—23), is so extraordinary a proceeding as to seem, at first sight, well-nigh incredible. To have men "cut to pieces," which was the threat held out by the same monarch on two occasions (Dan. ii. 5; iii. 29), is almost as remarkable a mode of executing them. It might mitigate, perhaps, the feeling of incredulity with which the ordinary European hears of such terrible punishments to call attention to the punitive systems of other Oriental kingdoms. Take, for instance, the practice of the Persians:—

"We may notice as a blot upon the Persian system and character" (I have elsewhere observed) "the cruelty and barbarity which was exhibited in the regular and legal punishments which were assigned to crimes and offences. The criminal code was exceedingly severe. The modes of execution were also, for the most part, unnecessarily cruel. Prisoners were punished by having their heads placed upon a broad stone, and then having their faces crushed, and their brains beaten out by repeated blows with another stone. Ravishers and rebels were put to death by crucifixion. The horrible punishment of 'the boat' seems to have been no individual tyrant's conception, but a recognised and legal form of execution. The same may be said also of burying alive. And the Persian secondary punishments were also, for the most part, exceedingly barbarous."[1]

---

[1] "Ancient Monarchies," vol. iii., pp. 246—7.

But, besides this, there is direct evidence that the actual punishments mentioned as in use among the Babylonians of Nebuchadnezzar's time were known to the Mesopotamians of the period, and were upon occasions applied to criminals. Asshur-bani-pal, the son of Esar-haddon, declares, with respect to Saul-Mugina, his own brother, whom he had made king of Babylon, but who had revolted against him—" Saul-Mugina, my rebellious brother, who made war with me, *in the fierce burning fire they threw him*, and destroyed his life."[1] Of another rebel, Dunanu, chief of the Gambulu, he also states—" Dunanu in Nineveh, *over a furnace they placed him, and consumed him entirely.*"[2] Nay, so natural does he consider it that rebels should, when taken, suffer death in this way, that when he has to notice the escape of a certain number of Saul-Mugina's adherents, who had betaken themselves to flight, he expresses himself thus—" The people, whom Saul-Mugina, my rebellious brother, had caused to join him, and who, for their evil deeds, deserved death . . . they *did not burn in the fire* with Saul-Mugina their lord "[3] —implying that, if they had been caught, this would have been the mode of their execution. Again, of other rebels, kept apparently in some stone-quarries from the time of Sennacherib, his grandfather,

---

[1] " Records of the Past," vol. i., p. 77.
[2] Ibid., vol. ix., p. 56.
[3] Ibid., vol. i., l.s.c.

Asshur-bani-pal tells us, "I threw those men again into that pit; *I cut off their limbs*, and caused them to be eaten by dogs, bears, eagles, vultures, birds of heaven, and fishes of the deep."[1]

The liberty and publicity allowed to women in Babylonia, so contrary to usual Oriental custom, which appears in the Book of Daniel (ch. v. 2, 3, 10), is illustrated by the traditions concerning Semiramis and Nitocris, and also by the account, which Herodotus gives, of certain Babylonian customs of a very unusual character. "Once a year," Herodotus tells us, "the marriageable maidens of every village in the country were required to assemble together into one place, while all the men stood round them in a circle. Then a herald (cf. Dan. iii. 4) called up the damsels one by one and offered them for sale ... All who liked might come even from distant villages and bid for the women."[2] Again he says, "The Babylonians have one most shameful custom. Every woman born in the country must, once in her life, go and sit down in the precinct of Venus and there consort with a stranger. Many of the wealthier sort, who are too proud to mix with the others, drive in covered carriages to the precinct, followed by a goodly train of attendants, and there take their station. Where they sit there is always a great crowd, some coming and others going. Lines of

---

[1] "Records of the Past," p. 78.
[2] Herod., i. 196.

cord mark out paths in all directions; and the strangers pass along them to make their choice ... Some women have remained three or four years in the precinct."[1] The statements of Herodotus on these points are confirmed by other writers; and there is ample reason to believe that the seclusion of the sex, so general in other parts of the East, was abhorrent to Babylonian ideas.[2]

The free use of wine in Babylonia, not only at royal banquets (Dan. v. 1-4), but in the ordinary diet of the upper classes (ib. i. 5—16), is what we should scarcely have expected in so hot a region, and one wholly unsuited for the cultivation of the vine. Yet it is quite certain from profane sources that the fact was as represented in Scripture. Herodotus tells us of a regular trade between Armenia and Babylon down the course of the Euphrates, in which the boats used were sometimes of as much as five thousand talents burden.[3] He declares that the staple of the trade was wine, which, not being produced in the country, was regularly imported from abroad year after year. In the story of Parsondas we find Nannarus abundantly supplied with wine, and liberal in its use.[4] The Chaldæan account of the Deluge represents Hasis-adra as collecting it "in receptacles, like the waters of a

---

[1] Herod., i. 199.
[2] See the author's "Ancient Monarchies," vol. iii., p. 22.
[3] Herod., i. 194.   See Nic. Dam., Fr. 11.

river," for the benefit of those who were about to enter the ark,[1] and as pouring "seven jugs" of it in libation, when, on the subsidence of the waters, he quitted his shelter.[2] Quintus Curtius relates that the Babylonians of Alexander's time were fond of drinking wine to excess; their banquets were magnificent, and generally ended in drunkenness.[3]

The employment of war-chariots by the Babylonians, which is asserted by Jeremiah (Jer. iv. 13; l. 37), in marked contrast with his descriptions of the Medo-Persians, who are represented as "riders upon horses" (ib. ver. 42; compare ch. li. 27): receives confirmation from the Assyrian inscriptions, which repeatedly mention the chariot force as an important part of the Babylonian army,[4] and is also noticed by Polyhistor.[5] Their skill with the bow, also noted by the same prophet (ch. iv. 29; v. 16; vi. 23; li. 3), has the support of Æschylus;[6] and is in accordance with the monuments, which show us the bow as the favourite weapon of the monarchs.[7]

The pronounced idolatry prevalent in Babylon under the later kings, which Scripture sets forth in such strong terms (Jer. l. 2, 38; li. 17, 47, 52;

---

[1] "Records of the Past," vol. vii., p. 137.
[2] Ibid., p. 140.
[3] Q. Curt., v. 1.
[4] "Records of the Past," vol. i., p. 22; vol. vii., p. 59; vol. xi., p. 55.
[5] See the "Fragm. Hist. Græc." of C. Müller, vol. iii., p. 320.
[6] Æschyl., "Pers.," l. 55.
[7] See "Ancient Monarchies," vol. ii., p. 560; vol. iii., p. 7.

Dan. v. 4), scarcely requires the confirmation which is lent to it by the inscriptions and by profane writers. Idolatrous systems had possession of all Western Asia at the time; and the Babylonian idolatry was not of a much grosser type than the Assyrian, the Syrian, or the Phœnician. But it is perhaps worthy of remark that the particular phase of the religion, which the great Hebrew prophets set forth, is exactly that found by the remains to have characterized the later empire. In the works of these writers three Babylonian gods only are particularised by name—Bel, Nebo, Merodach—and in the monuments of the period these three deities are exactly those which obtain the most frequent mention and hold the most prominent place. The kings of the later empire, with a single exception, had names which placed them under the protection of one or other of these three; and their inscriptions show that to these three they paid, at any rate, especial honour. Merodach holds the first place in the memorials of their reigns left by Nebuchadnezzar and Neriglissar; Bel and Nebo bear off the palm in the inscriptions of Nabonidus. While "the great gods" obtain occasional but scanty notice, as "the holy gods" do in the Book of Daniel (Dan. iv. 8, 9), Bel, Nebo, and Merodach alone occur frequently, alone seem to be viewed, not as local, but as great national deities, alone engage the thoughts and receive the adoration of the nation.

CHAPTER XII.

FURTHER NOTICES OF BABYLON IN ISAIAH AND JEREMIAH.

CHAPTER XII.

FURTHER NOTICES OF BABYLON IN ISAIAH AND JEREMIAH.

THE complete destruction of Babylon, and her desolation through long ages, is prophesied in Scripture repeatedly, and with a distinctness and minuteness that are very remarkable. The most striking of the prophecies are the following :—

"Babylon, the glory of kingdoms, the beauty of the Chaldees' excellency, shall be as when God overthrew Sodom and Gomorrah. It shall *never be inhabited*, neither shall it be dwelt in from generation to generation ; *neither shall the Arabian pitch tent there*, neither shall the shepherds make their fold there. But *wild beasts of the desert shall lie there ;* and their houses shall be full of doleful creatures ; and *owls shall dwell there*, and satyrs shall dance there. And the wild beasts of the islands shall cry in their desolate houses, and dragons in their pleasant palaces ; and her time is near to come ; and her days shall not be prolonged" (Isa. xiii. 19—22).

"I will rise up against them, saith the Lord of hosts, and cut off from Babylon the name, and remnant, and son, and nephew, saith the Lord. I will also *make it a possession for the bittern, and pools of water;* and I will sweep it with the besom of destruction, saith the Lord of hosts" (Isa. xiv. 22, 23).

"Chaldea shall be a spoil; all that spoil her shall be satisfied, saith the Lord. Because ye were glad, because ye rejoiced, O ye destroyers of My heritage; because ye are grown fat, as the heifer at grass, and bellow as bulls; your mother shall be sore confounded, she that bare you shall be ashamed; behold, the hindermost of the nations *shall be a wilderness, a dry land, and a desert.* Because of the wrath of the Lord *it shall not be inhabited, but it shall be wholly desolate; every one that goeth by Babylon shall be astonished,* and hiss at all her plagues. Put yourselves in array against Babylon round about; all ye that bend the bow, shoot at her, spare no arrows; for she hath sinned against the Lord. Shout against her round about; she hath given her hand; *her foundations are fallen, her walls are thrown down;* for it is the vengeance of the Lord: take vengeance upon her: as she hath done, do unto her" (Jer. l. 10—15).

"*A drought is upon her waters; and they shall be dried up;* for it is the land of graven images, and they are mad upon their idols. Therefore *the wild beasts of the desert*, with the wild beasts of the islands, shall dwell there, and *the owls shall dwell therein; and it shall be no more inhabited for ever;* neither shall it be dwelt in from generation to generation. As God overthrew Sodom and Gomorrah and the neighbour cities thereof, saith the Lord, *so shall no man abide there, neither shall any son of man dwell therein*" (vers. 38—40).

"Thus saith the Lord; Behold, I will plead thy cause, and take vengeance for thee; and *I will dry up her sea*, and make her springs dry. And *Babylon shall become heaps, a dwelling-place for dragons, an astonishment and a hissing, without an inhabitant.* They shall roar together like lions; they shall yell as lions' whelps. In their heat I will make their feasts, and I will make them drunken, that they may rejoice, and sleep a perpetual sleep, and not wake, saith the Lord. I will bring them down like lambs to the slaughter, like rams with he-goats. How is Sheshach taken! And how is the praise of the whole earth surprised! How is Babylon become an astonishment among the nations! *The sea is come up upon Babylon;* she is covered with the multitude of the waves thereof. *Her cities are a desolation, a dry land, and a wilderness, a land wherein no man dwelleth, neither doth any son of man pass thereby*" (Jer. li. 36-43).

The extraordinary accuracy of these descriptions has been frequently noticed, scarcely a traveller from the time of Pietro della Valle to the present day having failed to be struck by it. But it seems worth while to consider, somewhat in detail, the principal points on which the prophetical writers insist, and to adduce upon each of them the testimony of modern observers.

First, then, the foundations of Babylon were to fall, her lofty and broad walls were to be thrown down (Jer. l. 15), and she was not to present the appearance of a ruined city at all, but simply to "become heaps" (ch. li. 37). It is the constant remark of travellers that what are called the ruins of Babylon are simply a succession of unsightly mounds, some smaller, some larger—" shapeless heaps of rubbish,"[1] "immense tumuli,"[2] elevations that might easily be mistaken for natural hills, and that only after careful examination convince the beholder that they are human constructions.[3] The complete disappearance of the walls is particularly noticed;[4] and the visitor,[5] who has alone attempted to conjecture the position which they occupied, can mark no more than some half-dozen mounds along the line which he ventures to assign to them. One main portion of the ruins is known to the Arabs as the Mujellibé, or, "the Overturned," from the utter

---

[1] Layard, "Nineveh and Babylon," p. 491.

[2] Ker Porter, "Travels," vol. ii., p. 294.

[3] Ker Porter speaks of the ruins as "ancient foundations, *more resembling natural hills in appearance*, than mounds covering the remains of former great and splendid edifices" ("Travels," vol. ii., p. 297).

[4] Layard, "Nineveh and Babylon," pp. 493, 494.

[5] Oppert, "Expédition Scientifique en Mésopotamie," vol. i., p. 220—234.

confusion that reigns among the broken walls and blocked passages and deranged bricks of its interior. Only a single fragment of a building still erects itself above the mass of rubbish whereof the mounds are chiefly composed,[1] to show that human habitations really once stood where all is now ruin, decay, and desolation.

When Babylon was standing in all its glory, with its great rampart walls from two hundred to three hundred feet high, with its lofty palaces and temple-towers, with its " hanging gardens," reckoned one of the world's wonders, and even its ordinary houses from three to four storeys high,[2] it was a bold prophecy that the whole would one day disappear—that the edifices would all crumble into ruin, and the decomposed material cover up and conceal the massive towers and walls, presenting nothing to the eye but rounded hillocks, huge unsightly "heaps." It may be that such a fate had already befallen the great cities of Assyria, which had been destroyed nearly a century earlier, and which, from the nature of their materials, must have gone rapidly to decay. But the lessons of the past do not readily impress themselves on men; and it must have required a deep conviction of God's absolute foreknowledge on the part of the Hebrew prophets to publish it abroad,

---

[1] Layard, "Nineveh and Babylon," p. 484; Rich, "First Memoir," p. 25.

[2] Herod., i. 180.

on the strength of a spiritual communication, that such a fate would overtake the greatest city of their day—"the glory of kingdoms, the beauty of the Chaldees' excellency" (Isa. xiii. 19)—the city "given to pleasure, that dwelt carelessly, that said in her heart, I am, and none else beside me; I shall not sit as a widow, neither shall I know the loss of children" (ch. xlvii. 8).

The second point specially to be noted in the prophecies concerning Babylon is the prediction of absolute loss of inhabitants. The positions of important cities are usually so well chosen, so rich in natural advantages, that population clings to them; dwindle and decay as they may, decline as they may from their high estate, some town, some village, some collection of human dwellings still occupies a portion of the original site; their ruins echo to the sound of the human voice; they are not absolute solitudes. Clusters of Arab huts cling about the pillars of the great temples at Luxor and Karnac; the village of Nebbi Yunus crowns the hill formed by the ruins of Sennacherib's palace at Nineveh; Memphis hears the hum of the great city of Cairo; Tanis, the capital of Rameses II. and his successor, the Pharaoh of the Exodus, lives on in the mud hovels of San; Damascus, Athens, Rome, Antioch, Byzantium, Alexandria, have remained continuously from the time of their foundation towns of consequence. But Babylon soon became, and has for ages been, an absolute desert.

Strabo, writing in the reign of Augustus, could say of it that "the great city had become a great solitude."[1] Jerome tells us that the Persian kings had made it into one of their "paradises," or hunting parks.[2] Seleucia, Ctesiphon, Bagdad, successively took its place, and were built out of its ruins. There was no healing of its bruise." When European travellers began to make their way to the far East, the report which they brought home was as follows:—"Babylon is in the grete desertes of Arabye, upon the way as men gone towards the kyngdome of Caldee. But it is fulle longe sithe ony man neyhe to the towne; for *it is alle deserte*, and full of dragons and grete serpentes."[3] The accounts of modern explorers are similar. They tell us that "the site of Babylon is a naked and a hideous waste."[4] "All around," says one of the latest, "is a blank waste, recalling the words of Jeremiah—'Her cities are a desolation, a dry land, and a wilderness, a land wherein no man dwelleth, neither doth any son of man pass thereby.'"[5] No village crowns any of the great mounds which mark the situations of the principal buildings; no huts nestle among the lower eminences. A single modern build-

---

[1] Strab., xvi. 1, § 5:—Ἡ μεγάλη πόλις μεγάλη 'στιν ἐρημία.

[2] "Comment. in Esaiam," vol. v., p. 25, C.

[3] Maundeville's Travels (1322), quoted by Ker Porter, vol. ii. p. 336.

[4] Layard, l.s.c.

Loftus, "Chaldæa and Susiania," p. 20.

ing shows itself on the summit of the largest tumulus; it is a tomb, empty and silent.

Isaiah intensifies his description of the solitude by the statement, "Neither shall the Arabian pitch tent there, neither shall the shepherds make their fold there" (ch. xiii. 20). If the entire space contained within the circuit of the ancient walls be viewed as "Babylon," the words of the prophet will not be literally true. The black tents of the Zobeide Arabs are often seen dotting the plain—green in spring, yellow in autumn—which encircles the great mounds, stretching from their base to the far horizon. Much of this space was no doubt included within the walls of the ancient city; and this is traversed by the Arabian from time to time—flocks are pastured there, and tents pitched there. But if the term "Babylon" be restricted to the mass of ruins to which the name still attaches, and which must have constituted the heart of the ancient town, then Isaiah's words will be strictly true in their most literal sense. On the actual ruins of Babylon the Arabian neither pitches his tent nor pastures his flocks—in the first place, because the nitrous soil produces no pasture to tempt him; and secondly, because an evil reputation attaches to the entire site, which is thought to be the haunt of evil spirits.[1]

---

[1] "All the people of the country," says Mr. Rich, "assert that it is extremely dangerous to approach this mound (the

A curious feature in the prophecies, and one worthy of special notice, is the apparent contradiction that exists between two sets of statements contained in them, one of which attributes the desolation of Babylon to the action of water, while the other represents the water as "dried up," and the site as cursed with drought and barrenness. To the former class belong the statements of Isaiah, "I will also make it *a possession for the bittern, and pools of water*" (ch. xiv. 23); and "The cormorant (pelican?) *and the bittern shall possess it*" (ch. xxxiv. 11); together with the following passage of Jeremiah, "The *sea is come up upon Babylon; she is covered with the multitude of the waves thereof*" (ch. li. 42); to the latter such declarations as the subjoined, "*A drought* is upon her waters, and they shall be "*dried up*" (Jer. l. 38); "I will *dry up* her sea" (ch. li. 36); "Her cities are a desolation, *a dry land*, and a wilderness" (ver. 43); "the hindermost of the nations shall be a wilderness, *a dry land, and a desert*" (ch. l. 12); "Come down and *sit in the dust*, O virgin daughter of Babylon" (Isa. xlvii. 1).

But this antithesis, this paradox, is exactly in accordance with the condition of things which travellers note as to this day attaching to the site. The dry, arid aspect of the ruins, of the vast mounds

---

Kasr) after nightfall, on account of the multitude of evil spirits by which it is haunted" ("First Memoir," p. 27). Compare Ker Porter's "Travels," vol. ii., p. 371.

which cover the greater buildings, and even of the lesser elevations which spread far into the plain at their base, receives continual notice. "The whole surface of the mounds appears to the eye," says Ker Porter, "nothing but *vast irregular hills of earth*, mixed with fragments of brick, pottery, vitrifications, mortar, bitumen, etc., while the foot at every step sinks into *the loose dust and rubbish.*"[1] And again, "*Every spot of ground in sight was totally barren*, and on several tracks appeared the common marks of former building. It is an old adage that 'where a curse has fallen grass will never grow.' In like manner *the decomposing materials of a Babylonian structure doom the earth on which they perish to an everlasting sterility.*"[2] "On all sides," says Sir Austen Layard, "fragments of glass, marble, pottery, and inscribed brick are mingled with *that peculiar nitrous and blanched soil* which, bred from the remains of ancient habitations, checks or destroys vegetation, and *renders the site of Babylon a naked and hideous waste.*"[3]

On the other hand, the neglect of the embankments and canals which anciently controlled the waters of the Euphrates, and made them a defence to the city and not a danger, has consigned great part of what was anciently Babylon to the continual

---

[1] Ker Porter, "Travels," vol. ii., p. 372.
[2] Ibid., p. 391.
[3] Layard, "Nineveh and Babylon," p. 484.

invasion of floods, which, stagnating in the lower grounds, have converted large tracts once included within the walls of the city into lakes, pools, and marshes. " The country to the westward of Babylon," writes Ker Porter, " seemed very low and swampy. . . . On turning to the north, similar morasses and ponds tracked the land in various parts. Indeed, for a long time after the annual overflowing of the Euphrates, not only great part of the plain is little better than a swamp, but large deposits of the waters are left stagnant in the hollows between the ruins."[1] "From the summit of the Birs Nimroud," observes Layard, " I gazed over a vast marsh, for Babylon is made 'a possession for the bittern, and pools of water.'"[2] Of the space immediately about the chief ruins, Ker Porter notes, " This spot contains some cultivation, but *more water*, which sapping element may well account for the abrupt disappearance of the two parallel ridges at its *most swampy* point."[3]

Even some of the minor features of the picture, which one might naturally have regarded as the mere artistic filling up of the scene of desolation, which he had to depict, by the imagination of the prophet, are found to be in strict and literal accordance with the actual fact. " The daughters of the owl shall dwell there," says Isaiah (ch. xiii. 21), and

---

[1] Ker Porter, " Travels," vol. ii., p. 389.
[2] " Nineveh and Babylon," p. 300.
[3] Ker Porter, " Travels," vol. ii., p. 351.

Jeremiah, "The owls shall dwell therein" (ch. l. 39). "In most of the cavities of the Babil mound," remarks Mr. Rich, "there are numbers of bats and *owls*."[1] Sir Austen Layard goes further into particulars. "A large grey owl," he tells us, "is found in great numbers—frequently in flocks of nearly a hundred—in the low shrubs among the ruins of Babylon."[2] The "owl" of the prophets is thus not a mere flourish of rhetoric, but a historical reality—an actual feature of the scene, as it presents itself to the traveller at the present day.

"Wild beasts of the desert shall lie there" (Isa. xiii. 21); "the wild beasts of the desert, with the wild beasts of the islands, shall dwell there" (Jer. l. 39). So it was prophesied, and so it is. Speaking of the Babil mound, Mr. Rich observes, "There are many dens of wild beasts in various parts, in one of which I found the bones of sheep and other animals, and perceived a strong smell, like that of a lion."[3] "There are several deep excavations into the sides of the mound," remarks Ker Porter. "These souterrains are now the refuge of jackals and other savage animals. The mouths of their entrances are strewn with the bones of sheep and goats; and the loathsome smell that issues from most of them is sufficient

---

[1] Rich, "First Memoir," p. 30.
[2] Layard, "Nineveh and Babylon," p. 484, note.
[3] Rich, "First Memoir," pp. 29, 30.

warning not to proceed into the den."[1] On a visit to the Birs Nimroud, the same traveller observed through his glass several lions on the summit of the great mound, and afterwards found their footprints in the soft soil of the desert at its base.[2] This feature of the prophecies also is therefore literally fulfilled. The solitude, deserted by man, is sought the more on that account by the wild beasts of the country; and the lion, the jackal, and probably the leopard, have their lairs in the substructions of the temple of Belus, and the palace of Nebuchadnezzar.

No doubt there are also features of the prophetic announcements which have not at present been authenticated. It is impossible to say what exactly was intended by the "doleful creatures" and the "satyrs" of Isaiah, which were to haunt the ruins, and to have their habitation among them. Literally, the "satyrs" are "hairy ones,"[3] — a descriptive epithet, which is applicable to beasts of the field generally. The "dragons" of Isaiah (ch. xiii. 22) and Jeremiah (ch. li. 37) should be serpents, which have not been noted recently as lurking among the "heaps." Sir J. Maundeville,[4] however, tells us that in his day—the early part of the fourteenth century —the site of Babylon was "fulle of dragons and

---

[1] Ker Porter, "Travels," vol. ii., p. 342.
[2] Ibid., pp. 387—8.
[3] שְׂעִירִים from שָׂעִיר, "hairy, rough."
[4] Quoted by Ker Porter ("Travels," vol. ii., p. 336).

grete serpentes," as well as of "dyverse other veneymouse bestes alle abouten." It is possible that the breed of serpents has died out in Lower Mesopotamia; it is equally possible that it exists, but has been hitherto overlooked by travellers.[1]

On the whole, it is submitted to the reader's judgment whether the prophetic announcements of Holy Scripture, as to what was to befall Babylon, are not almost as important evidence of the truth of the Scripture record as the historical descriptions. The historical descriptions have to be compared with the statements of profane writers, which may or may not be true statements. The prophetical declarations can be placed side by side with actual tangible facts, facts which it is impossible to gainsay, facts whereto each fresh observer who penetrates into Lower Mesopotamia is an additional witness. Travellers to the site of Babylon, even when in no respect religious men, are, if they have the most moderate acquaintance with Scripture, penetrated with a deep feeling of astonishment at the exactness of the agreement between the announcements made two thousand five hundred years ago and the actual state of things which they see with their eyes. The fate denounced against Babylon has been accomplished, not only in all essential points, but even in various minute

---

[1] If the true interpretation of the word used be (as some think) "jackals," the statement made would be one of those fulfilled most clearly.

particulars. The facts cannot be disputed—there they are. While historical evidence loses force the further we are removed from the events recorded, the evidence of fulfilled prophecy continually gains in strength as the ages roll on in their unceasing course: and the modern searcher after truth possesses proofs of the trustworthiness of the Word of God which were denied to those who lived at an earlier period.

PART II.
BIBLICAL NOTICES OF EGYPT.

CHAPTER I.
THE BIBLICAL NOTICES OF EGYPT IN GENESIS.

CHAPTER I.

THE NOTICES OF EGYPT IN GENESIS.

"THE sons of Ham: Cush, and Mizraim, and Phut, and Canaan" (Gen. x. 6). "And Mizraim begat Ludim, and Ananim, and Lehabim, and Naphtuhim, and Pathrusim, and Casluhim (out of whom came Philistim), and Caphtorim" (Gen. x. 13, 14).

These are the first notices of Egypt which occur in Holy Scripture. The word Mizraim, which is here simply transliterated from the Hebrew (מִצְרַיִם), is elsewhere, except in 1 Chron. i. 8, uniformly translated by "Egypt," or "the Egyptians." It undoubtedly designates the country still known to us as Egypt; but the origin of the name is obscure. There is no term corresponding to it in the hieroglyphical inscriptions, where Egypt is called "Kam," or "Khem," "the Black (land)," or "Ta Mera," "the inundation country." The Assyrians, however, are found to have denominated the region "Muzur," or "Musr," and the Persians "Mudr," or "Mudraya," a manifest corruption. The present Arabic name is

"Misr"; and it is quite possible that these various forms represent some ancient Egyptian word, which was in use among the people, though not found in the hieroglyphics. The Hebrew "Mizraim" is a dual word, and signifies "the two Mizrs," or "the two Egypts," an expression readily intelligible from the physical conformation of the country, which naturally divides itself into "Upper" and "Lower Egypt," the long narrow valley of the Nile, and the broad tract, known as the Delta, on the Mediterranean.

We learn from the former of the two passages quoted above that the Egyptian people was closely allied to three others, viz., the Cushite or Ethiopian race, the people known to the Hebrews as "Phut," and the primitive inhabitants of Canaan. The ethnic connection of ancient races is a matter rarely touched on by profane writers; but the connection of the Egyptians with the Canaanites was asserted by Eupolemus,[1] and a large body of classical tradition tends to unite them with the Ethiopians. The readiness with which Ethiopia received Egyptian civilization[2] lends support to the theory of a primitive identity of race; and linguistic research, so far as it has been pursued hitherto, is in harmony with the supposed close connection.

---

[1] See a fragment of Eupolemus quoted by Polyhistor in C. Müller's "Fr. Hist. Græc.," vol. iii., p. 212, Fr. 3.
[2] Herod. ii. 30.

From the other passage (Gen. x. 13, 14) we learn that the Egyptians themselves were ethnically separated into a number of distinct tribes, or subordinate races, of whom the writer enumerates no fewer than seven. The names point to a geographic separation of the races, since they have their representatives in different portions of the Egyptian territory. Now this separation accords with, and explains, the strongly marked division of Egypt into "nomes," having conflicting usages and competing religious systems. It suggests the idea that the "nome" was the original territory of a tribe, and that the Egyptian monarchy grew up by an aggregation of nomes, which were not originally divisions of a kingdom, like counties, but distinct states, like the kingdoms of the Heptarchy. This is a view taken by many of the historians of ancient Egypt, derived from the facts as they existed in later times. It receives confirmation and explanation from the enumeration of Egyptian races—not a complete one, probably—which is made in this passage.

"Abram went down into Egypt, to sojourn there . . . And it came to pass, when he was come into Egypt, the Egyptians beheld the woman (Sarai) that she was very fair. The princes also of Pharaoh saw her, and commended her before Pharaoh; and the woman was taken into Pharaoh's house. And he entreated Abram well for her sake: and he had sheep, and oxen, and he-asses, and men-servants, and

maid-servants, and she-asses, and camels. And the
LORD plagued Pharaoh and his house with great
plagues, because of Sarai, Abram's wife. And
Pharaoh called Abram, and said, What is this that
thou hast done unto me? Why didst thou not tell
me that she was thy wife? Why saidst thou, She
is my sister? So I might have taken her to me to
wife: now therefore behold thy wife, take her, and
go thy way. And Pharaoh commanded his men
concerning him; and they sent him away, and his
wife, and all that he had" (Gen. xii. 10—20).

The early date of this notice makes it peculiarly
interesting. Whether we take the date of Abraham's
visit as *circ.* B.C. 1920, with Usher, or, with others,[1] as
a hundred and sixty years earlier, it seems almost
certain that it must have fallen into the time of that
"old Egyptian Empire" which preceded the great
Hyksôs invasion, and developed at that remote date
the original Egyptian civilization. Does then the
portraiture of the Egypt of this period resemble
that of the ancient empire, as revealed to us by the
monuments? No doubt the portraiture is exceedingly slight, the main object of the writer, apparently, being to record an incident in the life of
Abraham wherein he fell into sin. Still certain
points are sufficiently marked, as the following:—
1. Egypt is a settled monarchy under a Pharaoh,
who has princes (*sarim*) under him, at a time when

---

[1] As Mr. Stuart Poole ("Dict. of the Bible," vol. i., p. 508).

the neighbouring countries are occupied mainly by nomadic tribes under petty chiefs. 2. Reports are brought to the Pharaoh by his princes with respect to foreigners who enter his country. 3. Egypt is already known as a land of plenty, where there will be corn and forage when famine has fallen upon Syria. 4. Domesticated animals are abundant there, and include sheep, oxen, asses, and camels, but (apparently) no horses. What has profane history to say on these four points?

First, then, profane history lays it down that a settled government was established in Egypt, and monarchical institutions set up, at an earlier date than in any other country. On this point Herodotus, Diodorus, and the Greek writers generally, are agreed, while the existing remains, assisted by the interpretation of Manetho, point to the same result. It is not now questioned by any historian of repute but that the Egyptian monarchy dates from a time anterior to B.C. 2000, while there are writers who carry it back to B.C. 5004.[1] The title of the monarch, from a very remote antiquity,[2] was "Per-ao," or "the Great House,"[3] which the Hebrews would naturally represent by Pharaoh (פַּרְעֹה). He was,

---

[1] So Lenormant, following Mariette ("Manuel d'Histoire Ancienne," vol. i., p. 321).

[2] See Canon Cook in the "Speaker's Commentary," vol. i., p. 478.

[3] Compare the phrase "the Ottoman Porte."

from the earliest times to which the monuments go back, supported by powerful nobles, or "princes," who were hereditary landed proprietors of great wealth.[1]

Secondly, a scene in a tomb at Beni Hassan clearly shows that, under the Old Empire, foreigners on their arrival in the country, especially if they came with a train of attendants, as Abraham would (Gen. xiv. 14), were received at the frontier by the governor of the province, whose secretary took down in writing their number, and probably their description, doubtless for the purpose of forwarding a "report" to the court. Reports of this character, belonging to later times, have been found, and are among the most interesting of the ancient documents. It was regarded as especially important to apprise the monarch of all that happened upon his north-eastern frontier, where Egypt abutted upon tribes of some considerable strength, whose proceedings had to be watched with care.

Thirdly, there is abundant evidence that, under the Old Empire, Egypt was largely productive, and kept in its granaries a great store of corn, which was available either for home consumption, or for the relief of foreigners on occasions of scarcity. In the time of the twelfth dynasty state-granaries existed, which were under the control of overseers appointed by the crown, who were officials of a high

---

[1] Birch, "Egypt from the Earliest Times," pp. 44, 64, etc.

dignity, and had many scribes, or clerks, employed in carrying out the details of their business.[1] Even private persons laid up large quantities of grain, and were able in bad seasons to prevent any severe distress, either by gratuitous distributions, or by selling their accumulations at a moderate price.[2]

Fourthly, the domesticated animals mentioned on the monuments of the early times include all those mentioned as given to Abraham by the Pharaoh with whom he came into contact, except the camel, while they do not include the horse. It was once denied[3] that the Egypt of Abraham's time possessed asses; but the tombs of Ghizeh have shown that they were the ordinary beasts of burden during the pyramid period, and that sometimes an individual possessed as many as seven or eight hundred. No trace has been found of camels in the Egyptian monuments, and it is quite possible that they were only employed upon the north-eastern frontier; but the traffic between Egypt and the Sinaitic peninsula, which was certainly carried on by the Pharaohs of the fourth, fifth, sixth, and twelfth dynasties, can scarcely have been conducted in any other way.[4] For Abraham, a temporary sojourner in the land, about to return

---

[1] Birch, "Egypt from the Earliest Times," p. 63.
[2] "Records of the Past," vol. xii., pp. 63, 64.
[3] By Von Bohlen in his work entitled "Die Genesis erlautert."
[4] Compare Gen. xxxvii. 25.

through the desert into Palestine, camels would be a most appropriate present, and thus their inclusion in the list of animals given is open to no reasonable objection, though certainly without confirmation from the remains hitherto discovered in Egypt. The omission from the list of the horse is, on the contrary, a most significant fact, since horses, so abundant in Egypt at the date of the Exodus (Exod. ix. 3; xiv. 9, 23; xv. 1, 21), were unknown under the early monarchy,[1] having been first introduced by the Hyksôs, and first largely used by the kings of the eighteenth dynasty.

"They lifted up their eyes, and looked, and, behold, a company of Ishmeelites came from Gilead, with their camels, bearing spicery, and balm, and myrrh, going to carry it down to Egypt . . . and they sold Joseph to the Ishmeelites for twenty pieces of silver: and they brought Joseph into Egypt . . . and sold him into Egypt unto Potiphar, an officer of Pharaoh's, and captain of the guard" (Gen. xxxvii. 25—36).

The first thing here especially noticeable is that Egypt requires for its consumption large quantities of spices, and is supplied with them, not by direct commerce with Arabia across the Red Sea, as we might have expected, but by caravans of merchants, who reach Egypt through Gilead and Southern

---

[1] Birch, pp. 42, 82; Chabas, "Etudes sur l'Antiquité Historique," p. 421.

Palestine. Now the large consumption of spices by the Egyptians is witnessed by Herodotus, who tells us that, in the best method of embalming, which was employed by all the wealthier classes of the Egyptians, a large quantity of aromatics, especially myrrh and cassia, was necessary, the abdomen being not only washed out with an infusion of them, but afterwards filled up with the bruised spices themselves.[1] The Egyptian monuments show that aromatics were also required for the worship of the gods, especially Ammon. Not only do we continually see the priests with censers in their hands, in which incense is being burnt, but we read of an expedition made to the land of Punt for the express purpose of bringing frankincense and frankincense trees "for the majesty of the god Ammon," to "honour him with resin from the incense-trees, and by vases full of fresh incense."[2] It is observable, however, that on this particular occasion, the spicery imported came from Arabia, and reached Egypt by sea, which may seem at first sight to be an objection to the existence of a caravan spice trade. But a consideration of the dates deprives this objection of all force. The expedition to Punt, which is spoken of as the first that ever took place,[3] was sent by Queen Hatasu, and belongs to the eighteenth dynasty—the first of the New Empire. Joseph was sold into Egypt

---

[1] Herod. ii. 86. "Records of the Past," vol. x., pp. 18, 19.
[3] Though this assertion is made in the inscription, it is not strictly true. There had been one previous expedition in the

under the Middle Empire, and, according to tradition,[1] was prime minister of Apepi, the "shepherd" king. The sea-trade with Punt for spices not having been at that time opened, the spices of Arabia could only be obtained by land traffic.

The passage further implies the existence in Egypt at this time of a traffic in slaves, who were foreigners, and valued at no very high rate. The monuments prove slaves to have been exceedingly numerous under the Ancient Empire. The king had a vast number; the estates of the nobles were cultivated by them; and a large body of *hieroduli*, or "sacred slaves," was attached to most of the temples. Foreign slaves seem to have been preferred to native ones, and wars were sometimes undertaken less with the object of conquest or subjugation than with that of obtaining a profit by selling those who were taken prisoners in the slave market.[2] We have no direct information as to the value of slaves at this period from Egyptian sources, but from their abundance they were likely to be low-priced, and "twenty shekels" is very much the rate at which, judging from analogy, we should have been inclined to estimate them.

"The Lord was with Joseph, and he was a

---

reign of Sankara, the last monarch of the eleventh dynasty. It appears, however, to have been an isolated fact, and not to have opened the trade.

[1] Syncellus, "Chronograph," p. 62, B.
[2] Brugsch, "Hist. of Egypt," vol. i., p. 161.

prosperous man; and he was in the house of his master, the Egyptian. And his master saw that the Lord was with him, and that the Lord made all that he did to prosper in his hand. And Joseph found grace in his sight, and he served him; and he made him overseer over his house, and all that he had he put into his hand. And it came to pass from the time that he had made him overseer in his house, and over all that he had, that the Lord blessed the Egyptian's house for Joseph's sake; and the blessing of the Lord was upon all that he had in the house, and in the field. And he left all that he had in Joseph's hand, and he knew not aught he had, save the bread which he did eat. And Joseph was a goodly person and well-favoured. And it came to pass after these things that his master's wife cast her eyes upon Joseph; and she said, Lie with me. But he refused, and said unto his master's wife, Behold, my master wotteth not what is with me in the house, and he hath committed all that he hath to my hand; there is none greater in this house than I; neither hath he kept back anything from me but thee, because thou art his wife; how then can I do this great wickedness, and sin against God? And it came to pass, as she spake to Joseph day by day, that he hearkened not unto her, to lie by her, or to be with her. And it came to pass about this time that Joseph went into the house to do his business, and there was none of the men of the house there within.

And she caught him by his garment, saying, Lie with me; and he left his garment in her hand, and fled, and got him out. And it came to pass when she saw that he had left his garment in her hand, and was fled forth, that she called unto the men of her house, and spake unto them saying, See, he hath brought in an Hebrew unto us to mock us; he came in unto me to lie with me, and I cried with a loud voice ; and it came to pass, when he heard that I lifted up my voice and cried, that he left his garment with me, and fled, and got him out. And she laid up his garment by her until his lord came home. And she spoke unto him according to these words, saying, The Hebrew servant which thou hast brought unto us came in unto me to mock me; and it came to pass, as I lifted up my voice and cried, that he left his garment with me and fled out. And it came to pass, when his master heard the words of his wife, which she spake unto him, saying, After this manner did thy servant to me, that his wrath was kindled. And Joseph's master took him and put him into the prison " Gen. xxxix. (2—20).

It has often been observed that this picture is in remarkable harmony with the general tone of Egyptian manners and customs. The licentiousness of the women provoked the strictures of the Greek historians, Herodotus and Diodorus.[1] The liberty which they enjoyed of intermixing and conversing with men, so

---

[1] Herod. ii. 111 ; Diod. Sic. i. 59.

contrary to the general Oriental practice, is fully borne out, both by the tales of the Egyptian novelists, and by the scenes represented upon the monuments. The life of an Egyptian noble, at once a royal official and a landed proprietor, with much to manage "in the field" (ver. 5) as well as in his house, is graphically sketched. The *one* garment of the slave is casually indicated by the expression, so often repeated, "he left *his garment* in her hand." The extraordinary dependence placed upon "overseers," or stewards, who had the entire management of the household, the accounts, and the farm or estate—a very peculiar feature of Egyptian life—is set forth with great force. But, besides these isolated points, the whole narrative receives most curious illustration from one of the tales most popular among the Egyptians, which has fortunately descended to our day. In the story of "The Two Brothers," written by the illustrious scribe Anna, or Enna, for the delectation of Seti II., when heir-apparent to the throne, we have a narrative which contains a passage so nearly parallel to this portion of Joseph's history, that it seems worth while quoting it *in extenso.*

"There were two brothers," says the writer, "children of one mother and of one father—the name of the elder was Anepu, the name of the younger Bata. Anepu had a house and a wife; and his younger brother was like a son to him. He it was who provided Anepu with clothes, he it was who attended upon his cattle, he who managed the ploughing, he who did all the labours of the fields; indeed, his younger brother was so good a labourer, that there was not his equal in the whole land.

"And when the days were multiplied after this, it was the wont of the younger brother to be with the cattle day by day, and to take them home to the house every evening; he came laden with all the herbs of the field. The elder brother sat with his wife, and ate and drank, while the younger was in the stable with the cattle. The younger, when the day dawned, rose before his elder brother, took bread to the field, and called the labourers together to eat bread in the field. Then he followed after his cattle, and they told him where all the best grasses grew, for he understood all that they said; and he took them to the place where was the goodly herbage which they desired. And the cattle which he followed after became exceedingly beautiful. And they multiplied exceedingly.

"Now when the time for ploughing came his elder brother said to him, 'Let us take our teams for ploughing, because the land has now made its appearance [*i.e.*, the inundation has subsided], and the time is excellent for ploughing it. Come thou then with the seed, and we shall accomplish the ploughing.' Thus he spake. And the younger brother proceeded to do all that his elder brother told him; and when the day dawned they went to the field with their [teams?], and worked at their tillage, and enjoyed themselves exceedingly at their work.

"But when the days were multiplied after this, they were in the field together, and the elder brother sent the younger, saying, 'Go and fetch seed for us from the village.' And the younger brother found the wife of the elder one sitting at her toilet; and he said to her, 'Arise, and give me seed, that I may go back with it to the field, because my elder brother wishes me to return without any delay.' And she said to him, 'Go, open the bin, and take, thyself, as much as thou wilt, since my hair would fall by the way.' So the youth entered the stable, and took a large vessel, for he wished to take back a great deal of seed; and he loaded himself with grain and went out with it. And she said to him, 'How much have you [on your arm]?' And he answered, 'Two measures of barley, and three measures of wheat—in all, I have five measures on my arm.' Then she spake to him, saying, 'What great strength is there in thee! Indeed, I notice thy vigour every day' . . . Then she seized upon him, and said to him, 'Come and let us lie down for an instant' . . . The youth became as a panther with fury, on account of the shameful words which she had addressed to him. And she herself was alarmed exceedingly. He spake to her, saying, 'Verily, I have looked upon thee in the light of a mother, and on thy husband in the light of a father. What great abomination is this which thou hast mentioned to me! Do not repeat it again, and I will not speak of it to any one. Verily, I will not permit a word of it to escape my mouth to any man.'

"He took up his load, and went forth to the field. He rejoined his elder brother, and they accomplished the task of their labour. And when the time of evening arrived, the elder brother returned to his house. His younger brother [tarried] behind his cattle, laden with all the things of the field. He drove his cattle before him, that they might lie down in their stable.

"Behold, the wife of the elder brother was alarmed at the discourse which she had held. She made herself as one who had suffered violence from a man; for she designed to say to her husband, 'It is thy younger brother who has done me violence.'

"Her husband returned home at evening, according to his daily wont. He came to his house, and he found his wife lying as if murdered by a ruffian. She did not pour water on his hands, according to her wont; she did not light the lamp before him, his house was in darkness. She was lying there all uncovered. Her husband said to her, 'Who is it that has been conversing with thee?' She replied, 'No one has been conversing with me except thy younger brother. When he came to fetch seed for thee he found me sitting alone, and he said to me, 'Come and let us lie down for an instant.'

That is what he said to me. But I did not listen to him. 'Behold, am I not thy mother; and thy elder brother, is he not as a father to thee?'—that is what I said to him. Then he became alarmed, and did me violence, that I might not be able to report the matter to thee. But if thou lettest him live, I shall kill myself' . . . Then the elder brother became like a panther; he made his dagger sharp, and took it in his hand. And he put himself behind the door of his stable, in order to kill his younger brother, when he returned at even to bring the cattle to their stalls.'[1]

It is unnecessary to pursue the story further. Anepu is bent on killing his brother, but is prevented. Potiphar, with a moderation which seems to argue some distrust of his wife's story, is content to imprison Joseph. Innocence in both cases suffers, and then triumphs; but the triumph in the Egyptian tale is effected by repeated metempsychosis, and therefore diverges altogether from the Mosaic *history*. Still, it is conceivable that the Egyptian novel, written several centuries after Joseph's death, was based upon some traditional knowledge of the ordeal through which he had passed unscathed, and the ultimate glory to which he had attained as ruler of Egypt.[2]

---

[1] See "Records of the Past," vol. ii., pp. 139—142.

[2] Bata, after his many transmigrations, is finally re-born as the child of an Egyptian princess, and rules Egypt for thirty years (ib., p. 151).

CHAPTER II.

NOTICES OF EGYPT IN GENESIS (continued).

CHAPTER II.

NOTICES OF EGYPT IN GENESIS (continued).

THE history of Joseph in Egypt after he was thrown into prison by Potiphar, which occupies the last eleven chapters of Genesis, is delivered to us at too great length to be conveniently made the subject of illustration by means of comment on a series of passages. We propose therefore to view it in the mass, as a picture of Egypt at a certain period of its history, to be determined by chronological considerations, and then to inquire how far the portraiture given corresponds to what is known to us of the Egypt of that time from profane sources.

The time of Joseph's visit to Egypt is variously given by chronologers. Archbishop Usher, whose dates are followed in the margin of the English Bible, as published by authority, regards him as having resided in the country from B.C. 1729 to B.C. 1635. Most other chronologers place his sojourn earlier: Stuart Poole[1] from B.C. 1867 to

---

[1] "Dictionary of the Bible," vol. i., p. 508.

B.C. 1772; Clinton[1] from B.C. 1862 to B.C. 1770; Hales[2] from B.C. 1886 to B.C. 1792. Even the latest of these dates would make his arrival anterior to the commencement of the New Empire, which was certainly not earlier than B.C. 1700. If we add to this the statement of George the Syncellus,[3] that all writers agreed in making him the prime minister of one of the shepherd kings, we seem to have sufficient grounds for the belief that the Egypt of his time was that of the Middle Empire or Hyksôs, an Asiatic people who held Egypt in subjection for some centuries before the great rising under Aahmes, which re-established a native dynasty upon the old throne of the Pharaohs.

Does then the Egypt of the later chapters of Genesis correspond to this time? It has been argued that it does not, because, on the whole, it is so like the Egypt of other times. We have the king depicted in all his state, with his signet ring upon his finger (Gen. xli. 42), with chariots to ride in (ib. 43), and gold chains to give away, possessed of a "chief butler" and a "chief baker" (ch. xl. 9, 16), able to imprison and execute whom he will (ib. 3, 22), with "magicians" and "wise men" for counsellors (ch. xli. 8), rich in flocks and herds (ch. xlvii. 6), despotic over the people (ch. xli. 34;

---

[1] "Fasti Hellenici," vol. i., pp. 300, 320.
[2] "Ancient Chronology," vol. i, p. 104, et seq.
[3] "Chronographia," p. 62, B.

xlvii. 21), with no fear or regard for any class of his subjects but the priests (ch. xlvii. 22, 26). We have the priests as a distinctly privileged class, supported by the monarch in a time of famine, possessed of lands, and not compelled to cede to the king any right over their lands. We have mention of the "priest of On," or Heliopolis, as a magnate of the first class, with whom Joseph did not disdain to ally himself after he had become grand vizier, and was the next person in the kingdom to the king (ch. xli. 45, 50). We have the Egyptian contempt for foreigners noted in the statement that "the Egyptians might not eat bread with the Hebrews" (ch. xliii. 32), and their special aversion to herdsmen touched on in the observation that "every shepherd is an abomination unto the Egyptians" (ch. xlvi. 34). We see agriculture the main occupation of the people, yet pasturing of cattle carried on upon a large scale in the Delta (ch. xlvii. 1—6). We find embalming practised, and a special class of embalmers (ch. l. 2), and it appears that embalmed bodies are placed within coffins (ib. 26). Chariots and horses are tolerably common, for when Joseph goes from Egypt to Canaan to bury his father, there goes up with him "a very great company, both chariots and horsemen" (ib. 9), while "horses," no less than cattle and asses, are among the domesticated animals exchanged by the Egyptians generally for corn (ch. xlvii. 17). But, though horses are in use among the people, especially the official classes and the rich, asses are still the main beasts of burden, and are alone employed in the conveyance of commodities between Egypt and Canaan (ch. xlv. 23). Wheeled vehicles are known, and are used for the conveyance of women and children (ib. 19—21). Such are the leading features of the Egypt depicted by the writer of Genesis in these chapters. It is said to be too thoroughly Egyptian to be a true representation of a time when a foreign dynasty was in possession, and the nation was groaning under the yoke of a conqueror.[1]

The general answer to this objection seems to be that, as so often happens when a race of superior is overpowered by one of inferior civilization, the conquerors rapidly assimilated themselves in most respects to the conquered, affected their customs, and even to some extent adopted their prejudices. M. Chabas remarks that the Hyksôs, or shepherd kings, after a time became "Egyptianised."[2] "The science and the usages of Egypt introduced themselves among them. They surrounded themselves with learned men, built temples, encouraged statuary, while at the same time they inscribed their own names on the statues of the Old Empire, which were still standing, in the place of those of the Pharaohs who had erected them. It is this period of civiliza-

---

[1] Canon Cook in the "Speaker's Commentary," vol. i., p. 449.
[2] "Les Pasteurs en Égypte," p. 30.

tion which alone has left us the sphinxes, the statues, and the inscriptions which recall the art of Egypt; the manners of the foreign conquerors had by this time been sensibly softened."[1] And again, "Apepi, the last shepherd king, was an enlightened prince, who maintained a college of men skilled in sacred lore, after the example of the Pharaohs of every age, and submitted all matters of importance to them for examination before he formed any decision."[2] The Pharaoh of Joseph, according to the Syncellus,[3] was this very Apepi, the last shepherd king, the predecessor of the Aahmes, who, after a long and severe struggle, expelled the Hyksôs, and re-established in Egypt the rule of a native dynasty.

Thus, it was to have been expected that, if Joseph lived under Apepi, or indeed under any one of the later shepherd kings, a description of the Egypt of his day would greatly resemble any true description of that country either in earlier or later times, and possess but few distinctive features. Still *some* such distinctive features might have been expected to show themselves, and it must be our object now to inquire, first, what they would be; and secondly, how far, if at all, they appear in the narrative.

First, then, what distinctive features would there

---

[1] "Les Pasteurs en Egypte," p. 33.
[2] Ibid., p. 31. Brugsch and Lenormant take the same view.
[3] "Chronographia," p. 62, B.

there be separating and marking off the Second Empire from the First, the Hyksôs rule from that of the old Pharaohs who built the Pyramids, set up the first obelisks, and accomplished the great works in the Fayoum? In the first place, their residence would be different. The pyramid kings lived at Memphis, above the apex of the Delta, in the (comparatively speaking) narrow valley of the Nile, before the river enters on the broad tract which it must have gradually formed by its own deposits. The great monarchs of the obelisk and Fayoum period—those assigned by Manetho to his eleventh, twelfth, and thirteenth dynasties—lived at Thebes, more than three hundred miles further up the course of the Nile, in a region from which the Delta could only be reached by a lengthy and toilsome journey along the river bank, or by a voyage down its channel. The Hyksôs monarchs, on the other hand, fixed their residence in the Delta itself; they selected Tanis—an ancient Egyptian town of considerable importance—for the main seat of their court.[1] While maintaining a great fortified camp at Avaris, on their eastern frontier, where they lived sometimes, they still more favoured the quiet Egyptian city on the Tanitic branch of the Nile, where they could pass their time away from the sound of arms, amid ancient temples and sanctuaries dedicated to various Egyptian gods,

---

[1] Brugsch, "History of Egypt," vol. i., pp. 236—7, 1st edition

which they allowed to stand, if they did not even use them for their own worship. The Delta had never previously been the residence of Egyptian kings, and it did not again become their residence until the time of the nineteenth dynasty, shortly before the Exodus.

A second peculiarity of the Hyksôs period, belonging especially to its later portion, is to be found in the religious views professed, proclaimed, and enjoined upon subject princes. Apepi, according to the MS. known as "the First Sallier papyrus," made a great movement in Lower Egypt in favour of monotheism. Whereas previously the shepherd kings had allowed among their subjects, if they had not even practised themselves, the worship of a multitude of gods, Apepi "took to himself" a single god "for lord, refusing to serve any other god in the whole land."[1] According to the Egyptian writer of the MS., the name under which he worshipped his god was "Sutech"; and some critics have supposed that he chose this god out of the existing Egyptian Pantheon, because he was the god of the North, where his own dominion especially lay.[2] But Sutech, though undoubtedly he had a place in the Egyptian Pantheon from very ancient times,[3] seems to have

---

[1] See "Records of the Past," vol. viii., p. 3.

[2] Chabas, "Les Pasteurs en Egypte," p. 35.

[3] Mariette, "Lettre à M. le Vicomte de Rougé," in the *Revue Archéologique*, vol. v., p. 303.

been essentially an Asiatic god, the special deity of the Hittite nation,[1] with which there is reason to believe that the shepherd kings were closely connected. Apepi, moved by a monotheistic impulse, selected Sutech, we should suppose, rather out of his own gods than out of the Egyptian deities, and determined that, whatever had been the case previously, henceforth he would renounce polytheism, and worship one only lord and god, the god long known to his nation, and to his own ancestors,[2] under the name above mentioned. There is reason to believe that he did not identify him with the Egyptian god, Set, or Sutech, but rather with some form or other of the Egyptian sun-god, or else with their sun-gods generally, since he appointed sacrifice to be made to Sutech, "with all the rites that are performed in the temple of Ra-Harmachis,"[3] who was one of these gods, and required the vassal king of Thebes, Ra-Sekenen, to neglect the worship of all the other gods honoured in his part of Egypt, excepting Ammon-Ra, who was another of them. Sutech, among the Hittites, seems to have been equivalent to Baal, and was certainly a sun-god,[4] probably identified with the material sun itself, but viewed as having also a spiritual nature, and as the creator and sustainer of

---

[1] "Records of the Past," vol. iv., p. 31.
[2] Ibid., p 36.
[3] Ibid., vol. viii., p. 3.
[4] Ibid., vol. iv., p. 28, par. 8.

the universe. Apepi's great temple of Sutech at Tanis was the natural outcome of his exclusive worship of this god, and showed forth in a tangible and conspicuous form the earnestness of his piety.

Among the changes in manners and customs belonging to the Middle Empire, there is one which cannot be gainsaid—the introduction of the horse. The horse, which is wholly absent from the remains, written or sculptured, of the Old Empire, appears as well known and constantly employed in the very earliest records of the New, and must consequently have made its appearance in the interval. Hence it has been argued by those best acquainted with the ancient remains that the military successes of the Hyksôs, and especially their conquest of Egypt, were probably the result to a considerable extent of their invading the country with a chariot force and with cavalry at a time when the Egyptians fought wholly on foot. Neither horses nor chariots, nor even carts, were known under the Pharaohs of the Old Empire ; they were employed largely from the very beginning of the New Empire, the change having been effected by the empire which occupied the intervening space.

Before proceeding further, let us consider how these characteristics suit the Egypt of Joseph. First, then, the indications of Genesis, though not very precise, decidedly favour the view that the king is residing in the Delta. He receives in person the brethren of Joseph on their arrival in the land, and even has an interview with the aged Jacob himself (Gen. xlvii. 7—10), whom his son would certainly not have presented to him if the court had not been near at hand. Goshen, the eastern portion of the Delta, is chosen for the residence of the family, especially because, dwelling there, they will be "near to Joseph" (ch. xlv. 10), who must have been in constant attendance on the monarch. "All the servants of Pharaoh, the elders of his house, and all the elders of the land of Egypt (ch. l. 7) would scarcely have accompanied the body of Jacob to the cave of Machpelah unless the court had been residing in Lower Egypt. Bishop Harold Browne, who writes as a common-sense critic, and not as an Egyptologist, well observes, "Joseph placed his brethren naturally on the confines of Egypt nearest to Palestine, *and yet near himself. It is probable that Memphis or Tanis was then the metropolis of Egypt.*"[1] But both before and after the shepherd kings the capital for many hundred years was Thebes.

Secondly, there are indications in the later chapters of Genesis that the Pharaoh of the time was a monotheist. Not only does he make no protest against the pronounced monotheism of Joseph (ch. xli. 16, 25, 32), as Nebuchadnezzar does against that of Shadrach, Meshach, and Abednego, when he draws the conclusion from their escape, that "no

---

[1] "Speaker's Commentary," vol. i., p. 215.

other god can deliver *after this sort*," but he uses himself the most decidedly monotheistic language when he says to his nobles, "Can we find such a one as this is—*a man in whom the spirit of God is?*" (ib. 38), and again when he addresses Joseph as follows : "*Forasmuch as God hath showed thee all this*, there is none so discreet and wise as thou art" (ib. 39). No such distinct recognition of the unity of God is ascribed either to the Pharaoh of the Old Empire who received Abraham (ch. xii. 15—20), or to those of the New Empire who came into contact with Moses (Exod. i.—xiv.)

The contrast between the Egypt of Abraham's time and that of the time of Joseph in respect of horses has often been noticed. As the absence of horses from the list of the presents made to Abraham (ch. xii. 16) indicates with sufficient clearness the time of the Old Empire, so the mention of horses, chariots, and wagons in connection with Joseph (ch. xli. 43 ; xlv. 19 ; xlvi. 29 ; xlvii. 17 ; l. 9) makes his time either that of the Middle Empire or of the New. The fact that the possession of horses does not seem to be as yet very common, points to the Middle Empire as the more probable of the two.

Certain leading features, moreover, of the narrative, which have been reckoned among its main difficulties, either cease to be difficulties at all, or are reduced to comparative insignificance, if, in accordance with tradition and with the most probable chronology, we regard Joseph as the minister of a shepherd king.

The native Egyptian monarchs had an extreme jealousy of their Eastern neighbours. The East was the quarter from which Egypt lay most open to invasion, and from the later times of the Old Empire down to the twentieth dynasty in the New there was continual fear, when a native dynasty sat upon the throne, lest immigrants from these parts should by degrees filch away from Egypt the possession of the Delta. Small bodies of Asiatics, like those who came with Abraham, or the thirty-seven Amu under Abusha,[1] might occasionally be received with favour, to sojourn or to dwell in the land; but larger settlements would have been very distasteful. An early king of the twelfth dynasty, built a wall "to keep off the Sakti," as the Asiatics of these parts were called,[2] and such powerful monarchs as Seti I. and Rameses II. followed his example. The only kings who were friendly to the Asiatics, and likely to receive a large body of settlers with favour, were the Hyksôs, Asiatics themselves, whom every such settlement strengthened against the revolt, which always threatened, of their Egyptian subjects. Now the family and dependants of Jacob were a large body of settlers. Abraham had three hundred and

---

[1] Brugsch, "History of Egypt," vol. i., p. 157.
[2] "Records of the Past," vol. vi., p. 135.

eighteen adult male servants born in his house (Gen. xiv. 14). Jacob's attendants, when he returned from serving Laban, formed "two bands" (Gen. xxxii. 10), literally "two armies." The number of those who entered Egypt with Jacob has been reasonably calculated at "several thousands."[1] To place such a body of foreigners "in the best of the land" (ch. xlvii. 6, 11), on the eastern frontier, where they could readily give admission to others, is what no king of either the Old or the New Empire would have been likely to have done; but it is exactly what might have been expected of one of the Hyksôs.

Again, the sudden elevation of a foreigner from the slave condition to the second place in the kingdom, the putting him above all the Egyptians and making them bow down to him (ch. xli. 43), and the giving him in marriage the daughter of the high-priest of Heliopolis (ib. 45), though perhaps within the prerogative of any Egyptian king, who, as a god upon earth,—"son of the Sun,"—could do no wrong, are yet exceedingly unlikely things, if Egypt were in its normal condition. It is far from paralleled by the "story of Saneha," even if that story is a true one, and not a novelette; for Saneha's rise is very gradual; he is a courtier in his youth; he commits

---

[1] Kurtz, "History of the Old Covenant," vol. ii., p. 149, E.T.

an offence, and flies to a foreign land, where he passes the greater part of his life; it is not until he is an old man that his pardon reaches him, and he returns, and is restored to favour; nor does he rise even then to a rank at all equal to that of Joseph.[1] Joseph's history would have been "incredible" if Egypt had never had foreign rulers.[2] But a Hyksôs monarch would be trammelled by none of the feelings or restraints natural to an Egyptian. A foreigner himself, he would be glad to advance a foreigner, would not be very careful of offending a high-priest, and would feel more confidence in committing important affairs to a stranger wholly dependent upon himself than to a native who might at any time turn traitor.

The limits of a work like the present will not allow us to treat this point at greater length. We proceed, therefore, to notice briefly two objections which Genesis is supposed to offer to the traditional view of Joseph's place in Egyptian history. The first is the designation of Goshen in one passage (ch. xlvii. 11) as "the land of Rameses." Now Rameses is a name which first appears in Egypt under the New Empire, and a "land of Rameses" is not likely to have existed until there had been a monarch of the name, which first happened under the nineteenth dynasty. But it is quite possible, as Bishop Harold Browne suggests, that the writer of

---
[1] "Records of the Past," vol. vi., pp. 135, 150.
[2] Stuart Poole in Smith's "Dict. of the Bible," vol. i., p. 509.

Genesis may have used the phrase, "land of Rameses," by anticipation,[1] to designate the tract so called in his day. This would be merely as if a modern writer were to say that the Romans under Julius Cæsar invaded *England*, or that Pontius Pilate, when recalled from Judæa, was banished to *France*.

The other objection is drawn from the statement that in Joseph's time "every shepherd was an abomination to the Egyptians" (ch. xlvi. 34). This is said to be "quite conclusive" against the view that the Pharaoh of Joseph was a shepherd king.[2] But it is admitted that the prejudice was anterior to the invasion of the Hyksôs, and appears on the monuments of the Old Empire. It would certainly not have been lessened by the Hyksôs conquest, nor can the shepherd kings be supposed to have been ignorant of it. If it was a caste prejudice, it would have been quite beyond their power to put down; and nothing would have been left for them but to bear with it, and make the best of it. This is what they seem to have done. When men of the nomadic races were feasted at the Hyksôs court, they were feasted separately from the Egyptians (ch. xliii. 32); and when a nomad tribe had to be located on Egyptian territory, it was placed in a position which brought it as little as possible into contact with the natives. Pharaoh had already put his own herdsmen

---

[1] "Speaker's Commentary," vol. i., p. 221.
[2] Ibid. vol. i., p. 449, note 33.

in Goshen (ch. xlvii. 6), with the view of isolating them. In planting the Israelite settlers there, he did but follow the same principle. Like a wise ruler, he arranged to keep apart those diverse elements in the population of his country which were sure not to amalgamate.

CHAPTER III.

NOTICES OF EGYPT IN EXODUS.

CHAPTER III.

NOTICES OF EGYPT IN EXODUS.

"NOW there arose up a new king over Egypt, which knew not Joseph. And he said unto his people, Behold, the people of the children of Israel are more and mightier than we; come on, let us deal wisely with them, lest they multiply, and it come to pass that, when there falleth out any war, they join also unto our enemies, and fight against us, and so get them up out of the land. Therefore they did set over them taskmasters, to afflict them with their burdens. And they built for Pharaoh treasure-cities, Pithom and Raamses" (Exod. i. 8—11).

The question of the period of Egyptian history into which the severe oppression of the Israelites, and their "exodus" from Egypt, are to be regarded as falling, is one of no little interest, and at the same time of no little difficulty. In the last chapter we saw reason for accepting the view that the Pharaoh whom Joseph served was Apepi, the last king of the seventeenth (shepherd) dynasty. In order, however, to obtain from this fact any guidance as to the dynasty, and still more as to the kings, under whom the events took place which are related in the first section of the Book of Exodus (chs. i.— xiv.), we have to determine, first of all, what was the length of the Egyptian sojourn. But here we find ourselves in the jaws of a great controversy. Taking the Authorised Version as our sole guide, we should indeed think the matter plain enough, for there we are told (ch. xii. 40, 41) that "the sojourning of the children of Israel, who dwelt in Egypt, was *four hundred and thirty years;* and it came to pass *at the end of the four hundred and thirty years*, even the selfsame day it came to pass, that all the hosts of the Lord went out from the land of Egypt." If we consult the Hebrew original, the plainness and certainty seems increased, for there we find that the words run thus:—" The sojourning of the children of Israel, *which they sojourned in Egypt,* was *four hundred and thirty years,"* which seems to leave no loophole of escape from the conclusion that the four hundred and thirty years mentioned are those of Israel's *stay in Egypt.* And it is quite admitted that thus far—if this were all the evidence—there could be no controversy upon the subject. Doubt arises from the fact that in the two most ancient versions of Exodus that we possess the passage runs differently. We read in the Septuagint, " The sojourning of the children of Israel, which they sojourned in Egypt *and in the land of Canaan*, was four hundred and thirty years;" and in the Samaritan version, "The sojourning of the children of Israel *and of their fathers*, which they sojourned *in the land of Canaan and in Egypt*, was four hundred and thirty years." Nor is this the whole. St. Paul, it is observed, writing to the Galatians (ch. iii. 17), makes the giving of the law from Mount Sinai "four hundred and thirty years after," not the going down into Egypt, but the entering into covenant with Abraham. And it is further argued that the genealogies for the time of the stay in Egypt are incompatible with the long period of four hundred and thirty years, and require the cutting down of the time to the dimensions implied by the Septuagint and Samaritan translations. This time is two hundred and fifteen years, or exactly half the other, since it was two hundred and fifteen years from the promise made to Abraham until the entering of the Israelites into Egypt.

Now, if the Exodus was but two hundred and fifteen years after any date in the reign of Apepi, it must have fallen within the period assigned by Manetho and the monuments to the eighteenth dynasty. But if we are to substitute four hundred and thirty years for two hundred and fifteen, it must have belonged rather to the later part of the nineteenth. Let us consider, therefore, whether on the whole the weight of argument is in favour of the shorter or the longer term of years.

First, then, with regard to the versions. The Hebrew text must always be considered of paramount authority, unless there is reason to suspect that it has been tampered with. But, in this case, there is no such reason. Had the clause inserted by the LXX. existed in the Hebrew original, there is no assignable ground on which we can imagine it left out. There is, on the other hand, a readily conceivable ground for the insertion of the clause by the LXX. in their anxiety to harmonise their chronology with the Egyptian system prevalent in their day. Further, the clause has the appearance of an insertion, being irrelevant to the narrative, which is naturally concerned at this point with Egypt, and with Egypt only. The Samaritan version may appear at first sight to lend the Septuagint confirmation; but a little examination shows the contrary. The Samaritan translator has the Septuagint before him, but is dissatisfied with the way in which his Greek predecessor has amended the Hebrew text. His version is an amendment of the Greek text in two points. First, he sees that the name "children of *Israel*" could not properly be given to any but the descendants of Jacob, and therefore he inserts the clause "and of their fathers." Secondly, he observes that the LXX. have inverted the historical order of the sojourns in Egypt and in Canaan, placing that in Egypt first. This he corrects by a transposition. No one can suppose that he derived his emendations from the Hebrew. He evolved them from his inner consciousness. He gave his readers, not what Moses had said, but what, in his opinion, he ought to have said.

Secondly, with respect to St. Paul's statement to the Galatians, it is to be borne in mind that he wrote to Greek-speaking Jews, whose only Bible was the Septuagint Version, and that he could not but follow it unless he was prepared to intrude on them a chronological discussion, which would in no way have advanced his argument. His argument is that the law, having been given long after the covenant made with Abraham, could not disannul it; *how long* after was of no consequence, whether four hundred and thirty or six hundred and forty-five years.

Thirdly, the genealogies of the period, as given in the Pentateuch, contain undoubtedly no more than six names—in fact, vary between four and six —which, taken by itself, is doubtless an argument for the shorter period. But (*a*) the Jews constantly abbreviated genealogies by the omission of a portion of the names (Ezra vii. 1—5; Matt. i. 2—16; comp. 1 Chron. ix. 4—19 with Neh. xi. 4—22); and (*b*) there is one genealogy belonging to the period, given in 1 Chron. vii. 22—27, that of Joshua, which contains ten names. The Hebrews, at this portion of their history, and indeed to a considerably later date, reckoned a generation at forty years, so that the ten generations from Jacob to Joshua, who was fully grown up at the time of the Exodus (Exod. xvii. 9—13), would cover four hundred years, or not improbably a little more.

Another argument in favour of the longer date is derivable from the terms of the announcement made to Abraham with respect to the Egyptian servitude :—" Know of a surety, that thy seed shall be a stranger in *a land* that is *not theirs*, and shall serve *them*, and *they* shall afflict them four hundred years ; and also *that nation whom they shall serve*, will I judge ; and *afterward* shall they come out with great substance" (Gen. xv. 13, 14). In this prophecy but one land is spoken of, and but one people ; this people is to afflict Israel for four hundred years ; it is then to be judged ; and, after the judgment, Israel is to " come out,"—to come out, moreover, with great substance. Nothing is said that can by any possibility allude to the Canaanites, or the land of Canaan. One continuous affliction in one country, and by one people, lasting—in round numbers—four hundred years, is announced with the utmost plainness.

But the crowning argument of all, which ought to be regarded as completely settling the question, is that derivable from the numbers of the Israelites on entering and on quitting Egypt. Their numbers, indeed, on entering, cannot be definitely fixed, since they went down to Egypt " with their households "

(Exod. i. 1), and these, to judge by that of Abraham (Gen. xiv. 14), were very numerous. Still no writer has supposed that altogether the settlers exceeded more than a few—say two or three—thousands.¹ On quitting Egypt, they were, at the lowest estimate, two millions. What time, then, is required, under favourable circumstances, for the expansion of a body (say) of two thousand persons into one a thousand times that number?

There are writers who have argued that population may double itself in the space of fifteen, nay, in that of thirteen years.² But I know of no proved instance of the kind where there has not been a large influx through immigration. No increase, or at any rate, no important increase, of the Israelites in Egypt can be assigned to this cause. They multiplied, as it is distinctly implied in the narrative, in the ordinary way, without foreign accretion. It is reasonable, therefore, to apply to them Mr. Malthus's law for the *natural* increase of population *by descent* under favourable circumstances. Now this is a doubling of the population, not every thirteen, or every fifteen, but every twenty-five years.³ By

---

¹ Kurtz ("History of the Old Covenant," vol. ii., p. 149) used the vague expression, "several thousands." Dean Payne Smith, in his "Bampton Lectures" (p. 89), suggests three thousand.

² Clinton. "Fasti Hellenici," vol. i., p. 294.

³ "Essay on Population," vol. i., p. 8; "Encyclopædia Britannica," vol. xviii., p. 340.

this law two thousand persons would, in two hundred and fifteen years, have multiplied to the extent, not of two millions, but of less than one million. The law, moreover, only acts where population is scanty, where the sanitary circumstances are favourable, and where the means of subsistence are wholesome, and readily obtained. Long before the time that the Israelites reached a quarter of a million, most of the artificial checks which tend to keep down the natural increase of population would have begun to operate among them. The territory assigned them was not a very large one, and they were not its sole inhabitants (Gen. xlvii. 6; Exod. iii. 22, xii. 31—36). It would soon be pretty densely peopled. The tasks in which they were employed by their Egyptian lords, from the time that the severe oppression began (Exod. i. 13, 14), could not be favourable to health. They were no doubt sufficiently well fed, as slaves usually are, but not on a very wholesome dietary (Num. xi. 5). The rate of increase would naturally fall under these circumstances, and it may ere long have taken them fifty years to double their numbers, which is about the rate now existing among ourselves. Supposing them to have been two thousand at the first, and to have doubled their numbers at the end of the first twenty-five years, but to have required five years longer for each successive duplication until the full term of fifty years was reached, it would have taken them four hundred and twenty-five years to reach the amount of two millions.

Altogether it is perfectly clear that an increase which is abnormal, and requires some explanation, if it be regarded as occupying the space of four hundred and thirty years, must be most unlikely, if not impossible, to have occurred in half that time.

If then we take four hundred and thirty years from the early part of Apepi's reign, and follow the line of the Egyptian kings, as we find it in Manetho or in the monuments, we are carried on beyond the time of the eighteenth dynasty into that of the nineteenth, and have to look for the monarchs mentioned in Exodus among those who reigned in Egypt between the close of the eighteenth dynasty and the commencement of the twentieth.

Before proceeding, however, with this inquiry, it seems natural to ask, Is there no tradition with respect to the time of the Exodus in Egyptian history, as we found that there was with respect to the time of Joseph; and if there is any such tradition, what is it?

The Egyptian tradition was delivered at great length by Manetho, whose account is preserved to us in Josephus.[1] It was also reported more briefly by Chæremon.[2] It placed the Exodus in the reign of an "Amenophis," who was the son of a

---
[1] Joseph., "Contra Apion.," i. § 26.
[2] Ibid., § 32.

"Rameses," and the father of a "Sethos." Each of these two facts belongs to one "Amenophis" only out of the four or five in Manetho's lists, and we have thus a double certainty that he intended the monarch of the nineteenth dynasty, who was the son and successor of Rameses II., commonly called "Rameses the Great," and was himself succeeded on the throne by his son, Seti-Menephthah, or Seti II.;- about B.C. 1300, or a little earlier. There is no other Egyptian tradition, excepting one reported by George the Syncellus,[1] which is wholly incompatible with the generally allowed synchronism of Joseph with Apepi, and quite unworthy of consideration; viz., that the Exodus took place under Amasis (Aahmes), the first king of the eighteenth dynasty, who was probably contemporary with the later years of Joseph himself.

Manetho's tradition, then, harmonising, as it does, with the chronological considerations above adduced, which would place the Exodus *towards* the end of the nineteenth dynasty, seems to deserve our acceptance, and indeed has been accepted by the great bulk of modern Egyptologists, as by Brugsch, Birch, Lenormant, Chabas, and others.[2] Allowing it, we

---

[1] "Chronographia," p. 62, B.

[2] See Brugsch, "History of Egypt," vol. ii., p. 125; Birch, "Egypt from the Earliest Times," p. 133; Lenormant, "Manuel d'Histoire Ancienne de l'Orient," vol. ii., p. 292, edition of 1882; Chabas, "Recherches pour servir à l'histoire de la Xix^{me} Dynastie, p. 157.

are able to fix definitively on the three Pharaohs especially concerned in the severe oppression of the Israelites, and thus to give a vividness and realism to our conception of the period of history treated of in Exod. i.—xiv., which add greatly to the interest of the narrative.

If Menephthah I., the son and successor of Rameses II., was the Pharaoh of the Exodus, it follows necessarily that his father, the *great* Rameses, was the king of Exod. ii., from whom Moses fled, and after whose death he was directed to quit Midian and return into Egypt for the purpose of delivering his brethren (ch. ii. 23 ; iv. 19). But as Moses was eighty years old at this time (ch. vii. 7), it is evident that the Pharaoh from whom he fled cannot be the same with the one who, more than eighty years previously, gave the order for the destruction of the Hebrew male children (ch. i. 22). The narrative of Exodus must speak of three Pharaohs, of the first in ch. i., of the second in ch. ii., and of the third in chs. v—xiv. If the second of these is Rameses II., the father of Menephthah I., the first must be Seti I., the father of Rameses II.

Now, it happens that Seti I. and Rameses II. are among the most distinguished of all the Egyptian monarchs, great warriors, great builders, setters-up of numerous inscriptions. We know them almost better than any other Egyptian kings, are familiar with their very countenances, have ample means of forming an estimate of their characters from their own words. Seti I. may well be the " new king, which knew not Joseph." He was the second king of a new dynasty, unconnected with either of the dynasties with which Joseph had been contemporary. He came to the throne at the time when a new danger to Egypt had sprung up on the north-eastern frontier, and when consequently it was natural that fear should be felt by the Egyptian ruler lest, "when any war fell out, the people of Israel should join unto Egypt's enemies, and fight against the Egyptians, and so get them up out of the land" (ver. 10). The Hittites had become masters of Syria, and were dominant over the whole region from Mount Taurus to Philistia. " Scarcely was Seti settled upon the throne, when he found himself menaced on the north-east by a formidable combination of Semitic with Turanian races, which boded ill for the tranquility of his kingdom."[1] He was occupied in a war with them for some years. At its close he engaged in the construction, or reparation, of a great wall for the defence of the eastern frontier. It would be natural that, in connection with this wall, and as a part of his general system for the protection of the frontier, he should build "treasure-cities" (ver. 11), or more properly " store-cities," *i.e.*, arsenals and magazines. That he should name one of these after a god

---

[1] Rawlinson, "History of Ancient Egypt," vol. ii., p. 287.

whom he was in the habit of honouring,[1] and the other after his father or after his son, whom he early associated, is not surprising. The ardour for building which characterised him would account for his employing the Israelites so largely "in mortar and in brick" (ver. 14), and in the construction of edifices. The severity of his oppression is quite in accordance with the cruelty which he exhibited in his wars, and of which he boasts in his inscriptions.[2]

Rameses II. was associated on the throne by his father when he was ten or eleven years of age. The two kings then reigned conjointly for about twenty years. Rameses outlived his father forty-seven years, and probably had the real direction of the government for about sixty years. There is no other reign in the New Empire which reaches nearly to the length of his. He was less of a warrior than his father, and more of a builder. Among his principal works was the completion of the city of Rameses (Pi-Ramesu), begun by his father, and made by Rameses the residence of the court, and one of the chief cities of the empire. He appears also to have completed Pithom (Pi-Tum), and to have entirely built many other important towns. All his works were raised by means of forced labour; and for the purpose of their construc-

---

[1] Birch, "Egypt from the Earliest Times," p. 119.
[2] "History of Ancient Egypt," vol. ii., pp. 289—291.

tion he required an enormous mass of human material, which had to be constantly employed under taskmasters in the most severe and exhausting toil, under a burning sun, and with few sanitary precautions. M. Lenormant says of him and his "great works"[1] :—" Ce n'est qu'avec un véritable sentiment d'horreur que l'on peut songer aux milliers de captifs qui durent mourir sous le bâton des gardes-chiourmes, ou bien victimes des fatigues excessives et des privations de toute nature, en élevant en qualité de forçats les gigantesques constructions auxquelles se plaisait l'insatiable orgueil du monarque égyptien. Dans les monuments du règne de Ramsès il n'y a pas une pierre, pour ainsi dire, qui n'ait coûté une vie humaine." Such was the character of the monarch under whom the Israelites are said to have "sighed by reason of their bondage," and to have "cried" so that "their cry came up to God by reason of their bondage; and God heard their groaning, and God remembered His covenant with Abraham, with Isaac, and with Jacob; and God looked upon the children of Israel, and God had respect unto them" (Exod. ii. 23—25).

Besides his suitability in character to be the Pharaoh who continued the severe oppression begun by Seti I., Rameses II., by the great length of his reign, exactly fits into the requirements of the Biblical narrative. That narrative requires for its

---

[1] "Manuel d'Histoire Ancienne," vol. i. 423.

second Pharaoh a king, who reigned at least forty years, probably longer. The New Empire furnishes only three reigns of the necessary duration,—those of Thothmes III. (fifty-four years), Rameses II. (sixty-seven years), and Psammetichus I. (fifty-four years). Psammetichus, who reigned from B.C. 667 to 613, is greatly too late; Thothmes III. is very much too early; Rameses II. alone verges upon the time at which the severe oppression must necessarily be placed. It can scarcely be a coincidence that Egyptian tradition should point out Menephthah I. as the Pharaoh of the Exodus, and that, the Biblical narrative assigning to his predecessor an exceptionally long reign, the monuments and Manetho should agree in giving to that predecessor the exceptionally long reign of sixty-six or sixty-seven years.

CHAPTER IV.

NOTICES OF EGYPT IN EXODUS (continued).

CHAPTER IV.

NOTICES OF EGYPT IN EXODUS (continued).

THE portraits of the first and second Pharaohs mentioned in the Book of Exodus are only faintly and slightly sketched. That of the third monarch—"the Pharaoh of the Exodus," as he is commonly termed—is, on the contrary, presented to us with much clearness and distinctness, though without effort or conscious elaboration. He is an oppressor as merciless as either of his predecessors, as deaf to pity, as determined to crush the aspirations of the Hebrews by hard labour. To him belongs the ingenious device for aggravating suffering, which has passed into the proverbial phraseology of modern Europe, the requirement of "bricks without straw" (ch. v. 7—19). He disregards the afflictions of his own countrymen as completely as those of his foreign slaves, and continues fixed in his determination not to "let Israel go," until he suffers the loss of his own first-born (ch. xii. 29—32). When finally he has been induced to allow the Hebrews to withdraw themselves from his land, he suddenly repents of his concession, pursues after them, and seeks, not so much to prevent their escape, as to destroy them to the last man (ch. xv. 9). To this harshness and cruelty of temper he adds a remarkable weakness and vacillation—he will and he will not; he makes promises and retracts them; he "thrusts the Israelites out" (ch. xi. 1; xii. 31), and then rushes after them at the head of all the troops that he can muster (ch. xiv. 5—9). Further—and this is most remarkable — unlike the generality of Egyptian monarchs, he seems to be deficient in personal courage; at any rate, there is no appearance of his having imperilled himself in the attack made on the Israelites at the Red Sea,—" the Egyptians pursued, and went in after them to the midst of the sea, even all Pharaoh's horses, his chariots, and his horsemen" (ch. xiv. 23); but not, so far as appears, Pharaoh himself. This, indeed, has been disputed, and Ps. cxxxvi. 15 has been quoted as a positive proof to the contrary;[1] but the expression of a poet who wrote some centuries after the event would be very weak evidence with respect to the fact, besides which his statement is, not that the Pharaoh was killed, but that he was "overthrown." Neither the narrative in Exod. xiv. nor the song of rejoicing in the following chapter contains the slightest allusion to the Pharaoh's death, an omission almost

---

[1] Canon Cook in the "Speaker's Commentary," vol. i., p. 309.

inconceivable if he really perished with his warriors.[1] Further, the Pharaoh of the Exodus seems to have been grossly and abnormally superstitious: one who put real trust in magicians and sorcerers, and turned to them in times of difficulty rather than to statesmen and persons of experience in affairs.

What, then, does profane history tell us of the Menephthah whom we have shown to be at once the traditional " Pharaoh of the Exodus " and the king pointed out by chronological considerations as the ruler of Egypt at the period ? M. Lenormant begins his account of him by observing,[2] " Moreover, he was neither a soldier nor an administrator, but one whose mind was turned almost exclusively towards the chimeras of sorcery and magic, resembling in this respect his brother, Kha-m-uas." " The Book of Exodus," he adds, " is in the most exact agreement with historical truth when it depicts him as surrounded by priest-magicians, with whom Moses contends in working prodigies, in order to affect the mind of the Pharaoh."[3]

Later on in his history of Menephthah, M. Lenor-

---

[1] That the Pharaoh did not perish is maintained by Wilkinson ("Ancient Egyptians," vol. i., p. 54), Chabas (Recherches pour servir à l'Histoire de l'Egypte," pp. 152, 161), Lenormant ("Manuel d'Histoire Ancienne," vol. ii., p. 292, edition of 1883), and others.

[2] "Manuel d'Histoire Ancienne," vol. ii., p. 281 (edition of 1883).

[3] Ibid.

mant has the following passage.[1] He is describing the great invasion of Libyans and others which Menephthah repulsed in his fifth year. "The barbarians advanced without meeting any serious resistance. The terrified population either fled before them, or made its submission, but attempted nothing like a struggle. Already had the invading army reached the neighbourhood of Pa-ari-sheps, the Prosopis of the Greeks; On (Heliopolis) and Mannofri (Memphis) were seriously threatened. Menephthah assembled his army in front of these two towns, in order to cover them; he drew from Asia a number of mercenaries, to supply the lack of Egyptian soldiers of sufficient experience; at the same time he fortified the banks of the middle branch of the Nile, to prevent the enemy from crossing it, and to place in safety, at any rate, the eastern half of the Delta. Sending forward in advance, first of all, his chariot-force and his light-armed auxiliaries, the Pharaoh *promised to join the battle array* with the bulk of his troops *at the end of fourteen days. But he was not personally fond of actual fight, and disliked exposing himself to the chance of defeat.* An apparition of the god Phthah, which he saw in a dream, warned him that his lofty rank required him not to cross the river. He therefore sent his army to the combat under the command

---

[1] "Manuel d'Histoire Ancienne," p. 289. Compare "Records of the Past," vol. iv., pp. 41—44.

of some of his father's generals, who were still living." Two features of Menephthah's character, as represented in Scripture, are here illustrated : his want of personal courage and his habit of departing from his promises with or without a pretext. The apparition of the god Phthah in a dream is clearly a convenient fiction, by means of which he might at once conceal his cowardice and excuse the forfeiture of his word.

The Egyptian monuments thus confirm three leading features in the character of Menephthah,— his superstitiousness, his want of courage, and his weak, shifty, false temper. They do, not, however, furnish much indication of his cruelty. This is, perhaps, sufficiently accounted for by their scantiness. Menephthah is a king of whom it has been said[1] that he " belongs to the number of those monarchs whose memory has been with difficulty preserved by a few monuments of inferior value, and a few inscriptions of but little importance." We have, in fact, but one inscription of any considerable length belonging to his reign.[2] It gives mainly an account of the Libyan war, in which he was not personally engaged. A tone of pride and arrogance common to the autobiographical memoirs of Egyptian kings

---

[1] Brugsch, " Histoire d'Egypte," p. 175.

[2] This inscription will be found translated in " Records of the Past," vol. iv., pp. 39—48, and in M. Chabas' " Recherches pour servir a l'Histoire de l'Egypte," pp. 84—94.

pervades it, but it contains few notices of any severities for which the monarch himself can be regarded as responsible. That he made slaves of the prisoners taken in the Libyan war[1] merely shows that he acted like other monarchs of the time. He speaks, however, of having in a Cushite war "slaughtered the people, and set fire to them, and netted, as men net birds, the entire country."[2] This last expression reminds one of a cruel Persian practice, whereby whole populations were exterminated, or reduced to slavery;[3] the preceding one, if it is to be taken literally, implies a still more extreme and unusual barbarity.

It was not be expected that the general series of events related in the first fourteen chapters of Exodus should obtain any direct mention in the historical records of Egypt. As M. Chabas remarks,[4] "Events of this kind were not entitled to be inscribed on the public monuments, where nothing was ever registered except successes and triumphs." The court historiographers would naturally refrain from all mention of the terrible plagues from which Egypt suffered during a whole year, as well as from any record of the disaster of the Red Sea; and the monarch would certainly not inscribe any account of

---

[1] "Records of the Past," vol. iv., p. 47, l. 63.
[2] Ibid., l. 67.
[3] Herod. iii. 149; vi. 31.
[4] "Recherches," etc., p. 152.

them upon his edifices. Still there are points of the narrative which admit of comparison with the records of the time, and in which an agreement or disagreement with those records would almost of necessity show itself; and these it is proposed to consider in the remainder of this chapter. Such are (1) the employment of forced labour in Egypt at this period of its history, and the method of its employment; (2) the inclusion, or non-inclusion, of the Hebrews among the forced labourers; (3) the construction at the period of "store-cities," and the names of the cities; (4) the military organization of the time; (5) the untimely loss of a son by the king under whom the Exodus took place; and (6) the existence or non-existence of any indication in the records of such exhaustion and weakness as might be expected to follow the events related in Exodus.

The use of forced labour by the Egyptian monarchs of the time, especially by Seti I. and Rameses II., is abundantly witnessed to by the monuments. The kings speak of it as a matter of course; the poets deplore it; the artists represent it. "It was the custom of the Egyptians to subject prisoners of war to this life of forced labour. A tomb of the time of Thothmes III. has furnished pictures which represent Asiatic captives making bricks, and working at buildings under the rod of task-masters—pictures which are a figured commentary on the verses of Exodus (ch. i. 11—14) which we have just cited. But under Rameses II. the unprecedented development of architectural works rendered the fatigues to which such wretches were exposed far more overwhelming."[1] Gangs of labourers were placed under the charge of an overseer armed with a stick, which he applied freely to their naked backs and shoulders on the slightest provocation. A certain definite amount of task-work was required every day of each labourer. Some worked at brick-making, some at stone-cutting, some at dragging blocks from the quarries, some at erecting edifices. Food was provided by the Government, and appears not to have been insufficient; but the hard work, and the exposure to the burning sun of Egypt, were exhausting in the extreme, and rendered their life a burden to those condemned to pass it in this sort of employ.

Whether the monuments indicate, or do not indicate, the inclusion of the Hebrews among the forced labourers of this period, depends on our acceptance or non-acceptance of a suggested identification.[2] Are we, or are we not, to regard the Hebrews as the same people with the Aperu or

---

[1] Lenormant, "Manuel d'Histoire Ancienne," vol. ii., p. 269, edition of 1883.

[2] On this identification, see Chabas, "Recherches pour servir à l'Histoire de l'Égypte," pp. 142—150; "Mélanges Égyptologiques," 2me Série, p. 108, *et seq.*

Apuriu? In favour of the identification, there is, in the first place, the close resemblance of the words. M. Chabas, indeed, overstates the case when he says[1] that the Egyptian Aperu is "the exact transcription of the Hebrew עברי." It is not so really, since the exact transcription would be "Aberu"; but it is a very near approach to an exact transcription. It falls short of exactness merely by the substitution of a *p* for a *b*, the two letters being closely cognate, and the ear of the Egyptians for foreign sounds not very accurate. In the next place, it is found that Rameses II. employs the Aperu in the building of his city of Rameses (Pa-Ramesu), which is exactly one of the works ascribed to the Hebrews in Exodus (ch. i. 11). Further, we must either accept the identity of the Hebrews with the Aperu, or we must suppose that the kings of this period had in their service at this time two sets of forced labourers quite unconnected, yet with names almost exactly alike. Against the identification, almost the sole point that can be urged, is the fact that Aperu are found still to be employed by the Egyptian kings after the Exodus is a thing of the past, as by Rameses III. and Rameses IV. But this objection seems to be sufficiently met by M. Chabas. "It is quite certain that, spread as the text of Scripture declares that they were over the whole of Egypt, the Hebrews

---

[1] Recherches," p. 142.

could not by any possibility respond universally to the appeal of Moses; perhaps some of them did not even wish to do so. Such was doubtless the case with those [Aperu] whom we find enrolled in regiments in the reigns of Rameses III. and Rameses IV."[1]

The construction of "store-cities" at the required period has received recent illustration of the most remarkable kind. The explorers employed by the "Egyptian Exploration Fund" have uncovered at Tel-el-Maskoutah, near Tel-el-Kebir, an ancient city, which the inscriptions found on the spot show to have been built, in part at any rate, by Rameses II., and which is of so peculiar a construction as to suggest at once to those engaged in the work the idea that it was built for a "store-city."[2] The town is altogether a square, enclosed by a brick wall twenty-two feet thick, and measuring six hundred and fifty feet along each side. The area contained within the wall is estimated at about ten acres. Nearly the whole of this space is occupied by solidly built square chambers, divided one from the other by brick walls from eight to ten feet thick, which are unpierced by window or door, or opening of any

---

[1] "Recherches," p. 163.
[2] See an article in the *British Quarterly Review* for July, 1883, pp. 110—115; and compare the letters on the same subject in the *Academy* for February 24th, March 3rd and 17th, and April 7th of the same year.

kind. About ten feet from the bottom, the walls show a row of recesses for beams, in some of which decayed wood still remains, indicating that the buildings were two-storeyed, having a lower room, which could only be entered by means of a trap door, used probably as a storehouse or magazine, and an upper one, in which the keeper of the store may have had his abode. Thus far the discovery is simply that of a "store-city," built partly by Rameses II.; but it further appears, from several short inscriptions, that the name of the city was Pa-Tum, or Pithom; and there is thus no reasonable doubt that one of the two cities built by the Israelites has been laid bare, and answers completely to the description given of it. Of the twin city, Rameses, the remains have not yet been identified. We know, however, from the inscriptions, that it was in the immediate vicinity of Tanis, and that it was built perhaps in part by Seti I., but mainly by his son Rameses II.

It lends additional interest to the discovery of Pithom that the city is found to be built almost entirely of brick. It was in brick-making that the Israelites are said in the Book of Exodus (ch. i. 14; v. 7—19) to have been principally employed. They are also said to have been occupied to some extent "in mortar" (ch. i. 14); and the bricks of the storechambers of Pithom are "laid with mortar in regular tiers."[1] They made their bricks "with straw" until

---

[1] *British Quarterly Review*, July 1883, p. 110.

no straw was given them, when they were reduced to straits (ch. v. 7—19). It is in accordance with this part of the narrative, and sheds some additional light upon it, to find that the bricks of the Pithom chambers, while generally containing a certain amount of straw, are in some instances destitute of it. The king's cruelty forced the Israelites to produce in some cases an inferior article.

The military organization of the Egyptians at the time of the Exodus is represented as very complete. The king is able almost at a moment's warning, to take the field with a force of six hundred *picked* chariots, and numerous others of a more ordinary description, together with a considerable body of footmen. It does not appear that he has any cavalry, for the word translated "horsemen" in our version probably designates the riders in the chariots. Each squadron of thirty chariots is apparently under the command of a "captain" (ch. xiv. 7). The entire force, large as it is, is ready to take the field in a few days, for otherwise the Israelites would have got beyond the Egyptian border before Pharaoh could have overtaken them. It acts promptly and bravely, and only suffers disaster through circumstances of an abnormal and indeed miraculous character. Now, it appears by the Egyptian monuments that the military system was brought to its highest perfection by Seti I. and Rameses II. It is certain that, in their time, the army was most carefully

NOTICES OF EGYPT IN EXODUS. 285

organized, divided into brigades,[1] and maintained in a state of constant preparation. The chariot force was regarded as of very much the highest importance, and amounted according to the lowest computation, to several thousands. It is doubtful whether any cavalry was employed, none appearing on the monuments, and the word so translated by many writers[2] being regarded by others as the proper designation of the troops who fought in chariots.[3] Infantry, however, in large well-disciplined bodies, always attended and supported the chariot force. Under Menephthah the system of his father and grandfather was still maintained, though no longer in full vigour. He required a fortnight to collect sufficient troops to meet the Libyan invasion.[4] He had then, however, to meet an army of trained soldiers, and had no need to hasten, since he occupied a strong position. Under the circumstances of the Exodus, it was necessary to be more prompt, and sufficient to collect a much

---

[1] "Records of the Past," vol. ii., p. 68.

[2] As generally in the "Records of the Past," and by M. Chabas in his "Recherches pour servir," etc., pp. 85, 88, 89, etc.

[3] M. Lenormant almost always replaces the "cavalry" of other translators by the expression *des chars* ("Manuel d'Histoire Ancienne," vol. ii., pp. 255, 256, etc.). He observes in one place, "The military education of the Egyptians did not include teaching men to ride, since they fought in chariots."

[4] "Records of the Past," vol. iv., p. 43.

smaller army. This he appears to have been able to do at the end of a few days.

It was scarcely to be expected that the Egyptian records would present any evidence on the subject of Menephthah's loss of a son by an untimely death. Curiously, however, it does happen that a monument at present in the Berlin Museum, contains a proof of his having suffered such a loss.[1] There is no description of the circumstances, but a mere indication of the bare fact. The confirmation thus lent to the Scriptural narrative is slight; but it has a value in a case where the entire force of the evidence consists in its being cumulative.

Three results would naturally follow on the occurrence of such circumstances as those recorded in Exodus. Egypt would be for a time weakened in a military point of view, and her glory, as a conquering power, would suffer temporary eclipse. The royal authority would be shaken, and encouragement afforded to the pretensions of any rival claimants of the throne. The loss of six hundred thousand labourers would bring to an end the period of the construction of great works, or, at the least, greatly check their rapid multiplication. Now this is exactly what all historians of Egypt agree to have been the general condition of things in Egypt in the later years of Menephthah and the period immediately following. Military expeditions cease until the time

---

[1] Brugsch, "Histoire d'Egypte," p. 175.

of Rameses III., a space of nearly forty years. The later years of Menephthah are disturbed by the rise of a pretender, Ammon-mes, who disputes the throne with his son, and according to Manetho,[1] occupies it for five years. Seti II., or Seti-Menephthah, has then a short reign; but another claimant is brought forward by a high official, and established in his place. Soon afterwards complete anarchy sets in, and continues for several years,[2] till a certain Setnekht is made king by the priests, and tranquillity once more restored. The construction of monuments during this period almost entirely ceases; and when Rameses III. shows the desire to emulate the architectural glories of former kings, he is compelled to work on a much smaller scale, and to content himself with the erection of comparatively few edifices.

---

[1] Ap. Syncell., "Chronographia," p. 72, C.

[2] See the "Great Harris Papyrus," translated by Dr. Eisenlohr in the "Transactions of the Society of Biblical Archæology," vol. i., p. 359, et seq.

CHAPTER V.

NOTICES IN EXODUS AND NUMBERS.

CHAPTER V.

NOTICES OF EGYPT IN EXODUS AND NUMBERS.

"THE children of Israel journeyed from Rameses to Succoth" (Exod. xii. 37). "It came to pass, when Pharaoh had let the people go, that God led them not [through] the way of the land of the Philistines, although that was near . . . But God led the people about, [through] the way of the wilderness of the Red Sea . . . And they took their journey from Succoth, and encamped in Etham, in the edge of the wilderness" (Exod. xiii. 17—20).

"Speak unto the children of Israel, that they turn and encamp before Pi-hahiroth, between Migdol and the sea, over against Baal-Zephon; before it shall ye encamp by the sea" (Exod. xiv. 2).

"These are the journeys of the children of Israel, which went forth out of the land of Egypt with their armies under the hand of Moses and Aaron. And Moses wrote their goings out according to their journeys by the commandment of the Lord: and these are their journeys according to their goings out.

And they departed from Rameses in the first month, on the fifteenth day of the first month . . . And the children of Israel removed from Rameses, and pitched in Succoth. And they departed from Succoth, and pitched in Etham, which is in the edge of the wilderness. And they removed from Etham, and turned again unto Pi-hahiroth, which is before Baal-Zephon: and they pitched before Migdol. And they departed from before Pi-hahiroth, and passed through the midst of the sea into the wilderness, and went three days' journey in the wilderness of Etham, and pitched in Marah. And they removed from Marah, and came unto Elim . . . And they removed from Elim, and encamped by the Red Sea" (Numb. xxxiii. 1—10).

Although the geographical problem connected with the Exodus of the Israelites from Egypt cannot be said to be as yet completely solved, yet the course of modern research has shed considerable light upon the route followed by the flying people, and the position of their various resting-places. The results arrived at may be regarded as tolerably assured, since they have not been reached without very searching criticism and the suggestion of many rival hypotheses. The boldest of these, started in the year 1874 by one of the first of modern Egyptologists, Dr. Brugsch,[1]

---

[1] The views of Dr. Brugsch were first propounded at the International Congress of Orientalists, held in 1874. They were afterwards published in the English translation of his "History of Egypt," London, 1879.

for a time shook to its foundation the fabric of earlier belief. The authority of its propounder was great, his acquaintance with the ancient geography of Egypt unrivalled, and his argument conducted with extreme skill and ingenuity; it was not to be wondered at, therefore, that his views obtained for a time very general credence. But researches conducted subsequently to the enunciation of his views, partly with the object of testing them, partly without any such object, have shown his theory to be untenable;[1] and opinion has recently reverted to the old channel, having gained by the discussion some additional precision and definiteness. We propose in the present chapter to consider the Exodus geographically, and to trace, as distinctly as possible, the "journeys" of the Israelites from their start on the day following the destruction of the first-born to their entrance on the "wilderness of Etham" after their passage of the Red Sea.

The point of departure is clearly stated both in Exodus (ch. xii. 37) and in Numbers (ch. xxxiii. 3, 5) to have been "Rameses." What does this mean? We hear in Scripture both of a "land of Rameses" (Gen. xlvii. 11), and of a city "Raamses," or Rameses. It is not disputed that these two words

---

[1] See Mr. Greville Chester's papers in the "Quarterly Statements" of the Palestine Exploration Fund, July, 1880, and April, 1881; and Mr. Stanley Poole's paper in the *British Quarterly Review* for July, 1883.

are the same; nor does it seem to be seriously doubted that the land received its name from the town. From which, then, are we to understand that the Israelites made their start? It has been argued strongly that "the land" is intended [1]; and with this contention we are so far agreed, that we should not suppose any general gathering of the people to the city of Rameses, but a movement from all parts of the land of Rameses or Goshen to the general muster at Succoth. Succoth seems to us to have been the first rendezvous. But a portion of the Israelites, and that the leading and guiding portion, started probably from the town. Menephthah resided at Pa-Ramesu, a suburb of Tanis. Moses and Aaron held communication with him during the night, after the first-born were slain. They must, therefore, have been in the town or in its immediate neighbourhood. They received permission to depart (Exod. xii. 31), and as soon as morning broke, they set off with the other Israelites of the neighbourhood. It is this start from the town of Rameses which the historian has in his eye; he needs a definite *terminus a quo*, from which to begin his account of the journeying (Numb. xxxiii. 5), and he finds it in this city, the seat of the court at the time. Rameses was in lat. 31°, long. 32°, nearly, towards the north-eastern corner of Egypt, about thirty miles almost due west of Pelu-

---

[1] See Dr. Trumbull's "Kadesh-Barnea" (New York, 1884), p. 382.

sium, from which, however, it was separated by a great marshy tract, the modern Lake Menzaleh, which in long. 32° 20' penetrates deep into the country, and renders a march to the south-east necessary in order to reach the eastern frontier of Egypt. The rendezvous must, consequently, have been appointed for some place in this direction; and it is in this direction that we must seek it.

This place is termed both in Exodus (ch. xii. 37, xiii. 20) and in Numbers (ch. xxxiii. 5, 6) "Succoth" —*i.e.*, "Tents" or "Booths"—an equivalent of the Greek Σκηναί, which is often used as a geographical designation. It has been proposed to identify Succoth with an Egyptian district called "Thuku" or "Thukut,"[1] and more recently with the newly-discovered town of Pithom[2] (Tel-el-Maskouteh). There is no evidence, however, that Pithom was ever called Succoth, nor would Tel-el-Maskouteh have been a convenient rendezvous for two millions of persons, with their flocks and herds. The Wady Toumilat offers but a thin thread of verdure along the line of the freshwater canal, and though a convenient route for those who came from the more southern part of the "land of Goshen," would have been very much out of the way for such as started from the more

---

[1] Brugsch, "History of Egypt," translated by Philip Smith, 2nd edit., pp. 370—4.
[2] Stanley Poole in the *British Quarterly Review*, July, 1883, p. 113.

northern portion, as from Tanis, or from the town of Goshen (Qosem) itself. But the district of Thukut, if it lay where Dr. Trumbull places it,[1] north and north-west of Lake Timseh, would be a very convenient place for a general muster, affording a wide space and abundant pasture in the spring-time, and easily reached both from south-west and north-west—in the one case by the Wady Toumilat, in the other by way of Tel-Dafneh and the western shore of Lake Ballah. This position for Thukut seems indeed to be definitively fixed by the discovery of the ruins of Pithom, the capital of Thukut, at Tel-el-Maskoutch, combined with the statement in an Egyptian text,[2] that Thukut was a region just within the Egyptian frontier, suited for grazing, and in the vicinity of some lakes. Dr. Brugsch's location of it on the southern shores of Lake Menzaleh became impossible from the moment that Tel-el-Maskoutch was proved to mark the site of Pithom.

It may, perhaps, be objected to the location of Succoth on the north and west of Lake Timseh, that the distance is thirty-five miles from Rameses (Tanis) and therefore could not have been traversed in a day. But nothing is said in Exodus, or elsewhere in Scripture, with respect to the length of time occupied by the journey between any two of the stations mentioned, except in one instance, when the time

---

[1] See "Kadesh-Barnea," pp. 392—5.
[2] Brugsch, "History of Egypt," vol. ii., p. 133.

occupied was "three days" (Exod. xv. 22; Numb. xxxiii. 8). It took a month for the multitude to reach the wilderness of Sin from their starting-point (Exod. xii. 18; xvi. 1); during this time we have only six stations mentioned; it took above a fortnight for them to move from the wilderness of Sin to the plain before Sinai (ch. xvi. 1; xix. 1); along this route are mentioned only three stations (Numb. xxxiii. 12—15). Thus there is every reason for supposing that the journey from station to station occupied, in most cases, several days.

The children of Israel "took their journey from Succoth and encamped in Etham," or "at Etham, in the edge of the wilderness" (Exod. xiii. 20). No name resembling Etham is to be found in the geographical nomenclature of Egypt, either native or classical. Hence it is suspected that the word is rather a common appellation than a proper name. "Khetam" in Egyptian meant "fortress"; and various *khetamu* are mentioned in the inscriptions— one near Pelusium, called the "khetam of Zor"; another near Tanis; a third, called the "khetam of King Menephthah," within the region of Thukut.[1] The eastern frontier was, in fact, guarded by a series of such fortresses, perhaps connected together by a wall or rampart; and especially the routes out of Egypt were thus guarded and watched. It was

---

[1] Trumbull, "Kadesh-Barnea," p. 329; Brugsch, "History of Egypt," vol. ii., p. 380.

probably to one of these "khetams"—that which guarded the way out of Egypt, known to the Hebrews as the "way of Shur" (Gen. xvi. 7)—that the march of the Israelites was directed from Succoth. The "khetam" lay "in the edge of the wilderness," and may perhaps be identified with that of King Menephthah. It was probably not far from the Bir Makdal of the maps, situated about ten miles east of the Suez Canal, east by north of Ismailia.

The multitude must have supposed that they were now about to enter the wilderness. They were "in its edge." Their leaders had doubtless brought with them the king's permission to pass the frontier fortress. The expectation must have been that on the morrow they would quit Egypt for ever. But here God interposed. Had the Israelites passed out of Egypt at this point, the march would naturally have been across the desert some way south of Lake Serbônis to the Wady El Arish, and thence along the coast of the Mediterranean to Gaza and the low tract of the Shefelch. But the nation was not yet in a fit condition to meet and contend with the warlike people of that rich and valuable region—the Philistines. God accordingly, who guided the march by the pillar of the cloud and of fire (ch. xiii. 21, 22), "led them not the way of the land of the Philistines, although that was near; for God said, Lest the people repent when they see war, and return to

Egypt: but God led the people about, the way of the wilderness of the Red Sea" (ib. 17, 18). Moreover, a direction was given through Moses to the people, "that they turn and encamp before Pi-hahiroth, between Migdol and the sea, over against Baal-Zephon" (ch. xiv. 2). It is clear that at this point the direction of the march was changed; and so far all are agreed. But was the "turn" towards the left or towards the right? Was the "sea" by which they were commanded to encamp the Mediterranean or the Red Sea?

It is the main point of Dr. Brugsch's theory that he holds "the sea" to have been the Mediterranean. He professes to find in this direction a Migdol, a Pi-hahiroth, and a Baal-Zephon. The Migdol is twenty miles from the Pi-hahiroth, and the Pi-hahiroth twenty-five from the Baal-Zephon, which is thus forty-five from the Migdol, for the three are nearly in a straight line. The Pi-hahiroth and the Baal-Zephon are not visible the one from the other.[1] Still, though these particulars of distance and position ill accord with the expressions used in Exod. xiv. 2 and Numb. xxxiii, 7, which imply proximity and the being within view, it would have been a most curious circumstance had there been on this side of the Isthmus of Suez, and also on the opposite one, three places similarly named within a

---

[1] Mr. Greville Chester in the "Quarterly Statement of the Palestine Exploration Fund," July, 1880, p. 154, note.

moderate distance of each other. But on examination it appears that only one of the three names is attached to any locality on the north side of the isthmus otherwise than by conjecture. Dr. Brugsch does not profess to have found in the remains of ancient Egypt any place called Pi-hahiroth or any called Baal-Zephon. He finds in Egyptian a word *khirot*, signifying "gulfs," and he finds in Diodorus a mention that there were βάραθρα, "pits," at the western end of Lake Serbonis. Out of these two facts he constructs an Egyptian Pi-khirot,[1] which he thinks may have been the original of the Pi-hahiroth of the Hebrews. Baal-Zephon he finds only mentioned in Egyptian documents as a God,— he conjectures his identity with Zeus Kasios,— and upon this pure conjecture locates his temple where one stood, erected to Zeus Kasios in post-Alexandrine times. If we put aside these two mere conjectures, there remains only a Migdol, which has a proved existence in these parts, though its exact emplacement is uncertain.

Migdol, however, is a generic term, meaning "a watch-tower." There are likely to have been many "Migdols" on the eastern frontier of Egypt, and it is maintained[2] that there are traces of at least three.

---

[1] "History of Egypt," vol. ii., p. 393. The real Egyptian original of Pi-hahiroth seems to have been "Pi-keheret," which is mentioned on a tablet of the time of Ptolemy Philadelphus, found at Tel-el-Maskouteh.

[2] Trumbull, "Kadesh-Barnea," pp. 374–8.

One of these, called by the Greeks Magdôlos, was certainly towards the north, not far from Pelusium; another, central, has left its name to Bir Makdal; a third, towards the south, is represented by the existing Muktala. This last may well be the Migdol of Exodus.

Dr. Brugsch's theory that Lake Serbônis is the true "Yam Suph," or "Sea of Weeds," wrongly understood by the Septuagint translators as "the Red Sea," has been completely disposed of by Mr. Greville Chester, who shows, first, that Lake Serbônis is almost wholly devoid of vegetation, either marine or lacustrine;[1] secondly, that the spit of land between it and the Mediterranean is not continuous but interrupted at the eastern extremity of the lake by a deep sea-channel;[2] thirdly, that there is no isthmus opposite El Gelse dividing the lake into two nearly equal portions,[3] as Dr. Brugsch supposed; and, fourthly, that the spit of land is above fifty miles long, and takes a lightly-equipped traveller *three days* to traverse,[4] instead of being passable in the course of a night. It may be added that, as the term "Yam Suph" is allowed by all, including Dr. Brugsch, to designate the Red Sea in Exod. xiii. 18 and Numb. xxxiii. 10, 11, it is

---

[1] "Quarterly Statement" of Palestine Exploration Fund for July, 1880, p. 155.
[2] Ibid., p. 157.   [3] Ibid., p. 154.   [4] Ibid., pp. 152—157.

inconceivable that the same writer should in the same narrative use it also of another far-distant sheet of water (Exod. xv. 4, 22).

The propriety of the name "Yam Suph," as applied to the Red Sea, has been well illustrated by Dr. Trumbull.[1] "Suph" in Hebrew means at once "sea-weed" (Jonah ii. 5), and "rushes" or "sedge" (Exod. ii. 3, etc.). The Red Sea is famous for the number and variety of its marine growths. "Weeds and corals are to be seen in such profusion and beauty at many places along the shores of the Red Sea, and again below its surface, as disclosed at low water, as almost to have the appearance of groves and gardens."[2] Again, "the *juncus acutus*, *arundo Ægyptiaca*, or *arundo Isaica*, grows commonly on the shore of the Red Sea, so that at this day a bay of the same is called *Ghubbet-el-bûs*, or "Reed Bay."[3] The observant naturalist, Klunzinger, says that, "Where the soil of the desert along that coast is kept moist by lagoons of sea water, the eye is gladdened by spreading meadows of green verdure. The coast flora of the desert, which requires the saline vapour of the sea, is peculiar. A celebrated plant is the *shora* (*Avicennia officinalis*), which forms large dense groves in the sea, these being laid bare

---

[1] "Kadesh-Barnea," pp. 353—356.
[2] Laborde, "Voyage de l'Arabie Pétrée," p. 5.
[3] Stickel, "Der Israeliten Auszug aus Ægypten" in "Studien und Kritiken" for 1850, p. 331.

only at very low ebb. Ships are laden with its wood, which is used as fuel, and many camels live altogether on its laurel-like leaves." He divides, indeed, the shore line of the Red Sea into the "outer shore zone," or the reef line, and the "inner shore *or sea-grass* zone." Even in the outer shore zone there "flourish also in many inlets of the sea thickets of the laurel-like shora shrub," as above described ; and there are "sea-grass pools." In the inner shore zone, " among the rocks, which are either bare or covered with a blackish and red mucilaginous sea-weed," there "grow green phanerogamous grasses of the family of the Naiadeæ."[1]

But if the sea intended in the directions given to Moses (Exod. xiv. 2) was the Red Sea, Migdol, Pi-hahiroth, and Baal-Zephon must be sought towards the south ; and the "turn" in the journey (ibid. and Numb. xxxiii. 7), of which we have spoken, must have been a turn to the right. It was to some extent a "turning *back*," as the Hebrew word used implies, a "return" into Egypt when the frontier had been reached, and might have been crossed. It looked like hesitation and doubt, like the commencement of an aimless, purposeless wandering. Hence the Pharaoh took heart, and made preparations for a pursuit at the head of an army (ch. xiv. 3, 5—9).

---

[1] Quoted from Dr. Trumbull's " Kadesh-Barnea," pp. 355—6.

If the " bitter lakes " were (as supposed by many [1]) connected at the time with the northern end of the Red Sea, as a marshy inlet, overflowed at high water, and Pi-hahiroth were near Muktala, the Israelites, to reach it, must have skirted the northern extremity of the lakes, and have proceeded southward along their western shores. A march of three days would bring them into the plain north-west of Suez, at the western edge of which the station Muktala (Migdol) is found. The Israelites "encamped between Migdol and the sea," for which there would be abundant room, as the distance is above ten miles. They were " beside Pi-hahiroth and before Baal-Zephon " (ch. xiv. 9). These conditions would be sufficiently answered if Pi-hahiroth were at Ajrud, which is thought to retain a trace of the name,[2] and Baal-Zephon were on the northeastern flank of Jebel Ataka. Baal-Zephon is not necessarily a Phœnician name, for the Egyptians had adopted " Baal " as a god long before the time of Menephthah, and Zephon (Zapouna or Typhon) was altogether Egyptian. There is no proof beyond the notices in Exodus that he had a temple, or a town named after him, in this quarter; but neither

---

[1] As Kurtz, Sharpe, Stanley Poole, Reginald Stuart Poole, Canon Cook, Lieutenant Conder, Burton, Villiers Stuart, Grätz, and others.

[2] So Ebers (" Gosen zum Sinai," p. 526); Kurtz (" Hist. of Old Covenant," vol. ii., p. 323), Keil and Delitzsch (" Bibl. Comment," on Exod. xiv. 2), etc.

is there any proof of his having had one in any other part of Egypt. It has been argued that the position on Jebel Ataka would be one exactly adapted to such a god as Baal-Zephon;[1] but we scarcely know enough of the Egyptian religion to be sure of this. We can only say that here, on the western coast of the Gulf of Suez, would be ample room for the encampment of the entire Israelitish host; that in this position it might well seem that "the wilderness had shut them in" (ch. xiv. 3); and that the host would be "before a Migdol" (Numb. xxxiii. 7), and perhaps "beside a Pi-ha-hiroth" (Exod. xiv. 9). The sea in front was but two or three miles across, and might easily have been passed in a night; the bottom was such as would naturally clog the Egyptian chariot wheels (ver. 25), and the further shore was destitute of springs, a true "wilderness" (ch. xv. 22), where the Israelites may well have gone "three days without water."

---

[1] Trumbull, "Kadesh-Barnea," p. 421.

CHAPTER. VI

NOTICES OF EGYPT IN EXODUS (continued).

CHAPTER VI.

THE NOTICES IN EXODUS (continued).

IN considering the Biblical notices of Egypt contained in the Book of Exodus, we have hitherto confined ourselves almost entirely to the main narrative, and indeed to such points of it as are capable of illustration from historical documents, monumental or literary. But the full force of the illustration which profane sources are capable of lending to the Scriptural account cannot be rightly estimated, unless we add to this some consideration of those various minor matters, incidentally touched upon, which constitute the *entourage* of the main narrative, and render it altogether so graphic and life-like. These touches must be either the natural utterances of one familiar with the country at the time, as Moses, the traditional author of Exodus, would have been, or the artful imitation of such utterances by a later writer, unfamiliar with the time, and probably with the scene, drawing upon his imagination or his stock of antiquarian knowledge. In the former case a general agreement between the Biblical portraiture and the facts as otherwise known to us might be confidently looked for; in the latter, there would be sure to appear on examination, repeated contradictions and discrepancies.

It will be the object of the present chapter to show that there is a close accord between the Scriptural notices and the facts as otherwise known to us in respect of almost all the minor matters of which we have spoken. These may be summed up under the following principal heads :—(*a*) the climate and productions of Egypt, (*b*) the dress and domestic habits of the people, (*c*) the ordinary food of the labouring classes, (*d*) customs connected with farming and cattle-keeping, and (*e*) miscellaneous customs.

The climate of Egypt is touched upon mainly in connection with the seventh plague, in ch. ix. We find there heavy rain (ver. 33), hail, thunder and lightning, mentioned as occurring in early spring, and doing great damage to the crops. The particular visitation is spoken of as miraculous in coming at the command of Moses (ver. 23), and as extraordinary in its intensity (ver. 24), but not as a thing previously unknown. On the contrary, it is implied that similar visitations of less severity were not unusual. Objection has been taken to the narrative on this account; and it has been represented as indicative of a great want of acquaintance with the climatic circumstances of the country, since rain and hail are, it has been said, unknown in Egypt. But the only ground for such a statement is the authority of the classical writers. Herodotus regarded rain in Upper Egypt as a prodigy,[1] and Mela goes so far as to call Egypt generally "a land devoid of showers."[2] But the observation of modern travellers runs counter to such views,[3] and supports the credit of the author of Exodus. In Upper Egypt, indeed, "very heavy rain is unusual, and happens only about once in ten years. Four or five showers fall there every year, after long intervals."[4] But in Lower Egypt, rain is as common in winter as it is in the south of Europe. Storms of great severity occur occasionally, more especially in February and March, when snow, hail, thunder and lightning are not uncommon. The Rev. T. H. Tooke "describes a storm of extreme severity, which lasted twenty-four hours, in the middle of February,"[5] as high up the valley as Beni-Hassan. Other travellers, as Seetzen and Willmann, speak of storms of thunder and hail in March. "The ravines in the valley of the kings' tombs near Thebes, and the precautions taken in the oldest temples at Thebes

---

[1] Herod, iii. 10.
[2] Pomp. Mel., "De Situ Orbis," i. 9; "Ægyptus terra expers imbrium."
[3] See the passages collected by Hengstenberg, "Egypt and the Books of Moses," pp. 117, 118.
[4] Wilkinson in Rawlinson's "Herodotus," vol. ii., p. 409, note 4.
[5] "Speaker's Commentary," vol. i., p. 285.

to guard the roofs against rain by lions' mouths, or gutters, for letting off the water from them,"[1] prove sufficiently that there was no great difference between ancient and modern times in respect of the rainfall of the Nile valley.

Among the cultivated products of Egypt mentioned in Exodus, the principal are, wheat, barley, flax, and rye, or spelt (ix. 32), to which may be added from the Book of Numbers (xi. 5) cucumbers, melons, onions, garlick, and leeks. Grains of wheat have been found abundantly in the coffins containing mummies, and " mummy wheat " is said to have been raised from such grains in various parts of Europe. The monuments, moreover, represent to us in numerous instances the growth of wheat, the mode in which it was cut, bound into sheaves, or gathered into baskets, and threshed by the tread of cattle on a threshing-floor.[2] Barley does not appear to be represented,[3] but its growth is manifest. It is mentioned as the ordinary food of the Egyptian horses,[4] and as one of the chief materials used in the making of bread.[5] It was also largely employed in the manufacture of

---

[1] Wilkinson, l.s.c. Compare "Ancient Egyptians," vol. ii. p. 426.

[2] See Wilkinson, "Ancient Egyptians," vol. ii., pp. 418—427.

[3] The Egyptian wheat being bearded, it is not easy to say in some cases whether barley or wheat is represented.

[4] " Records of the Past," vol. ii., p. 75.

[5] Ibid., vol. viii., p. 44.

beer.[1] Flax was likewise cultivated on an extensive scale to furnish the linen garments necessarily worn by the priests, and, preferentially by others, and needed also for mummy-cloths, corselets, and various other uses. Spelt, like wheat, is represented on the monuments,[2] and, according to Herodotus, was the grain ordinarily consumed by the Egyptians,[3] as is the *doora*—probably the same plant—at the present day. Herodotus also witnesses to the cultivation of onions and of garlick,[4] while that of cucumbers is attested by their being frequently figured in the tombs. The leeks of Egypt had the character of being superior to all others in the time of Pliny,[5] which would imply a long anterior cultivation. Melons are among the most abundant of the modern products, but their growth in ancient times seems not to be distinctly attested.

The abundant use of personal ornaments by the Egyptians, and especially of ornaments in silver and gold, implied in the direction given to the Israelites to "borrow" such things of their neighbours and lodgers before their departure from Egypt (ch. iii. 22), and in the "spoil" which they thus acquired (ch. xii. 36), is among the facts most copiously attested by

---

[1] Wilkinson, "Ancient Egyptians," vol. ii., p. 42.
[2] Ibid., p. 427.
[3] Herod., ii., 36.
[4] Ibid., ii. 125.
[5] Plin., "H N.," xix. 33

the extant remains. Ornaments in gold and silver have been found in the tombs, not only of the great and opulent, but even of comparatively poor persons; they were frequently worn by the men, and probably few women were without them. Among the articles obtained from the tombs are "rings, bracelets, armlets, necklaces, earrings, and numerous trinkets belonging to the toilet."[1] Most of these articles were common to the two sexes; but earrings were affected especially, if not exclusively, by the women.

Egyptian men of the upper class carried, as a matter of course, "walking sticks."[2] Hence the "rod" of Aaron was naturally brought into the presence of Pharaoh (ch. vii. 10); and the magicians had also "rods" in their hands (ib. ver. 12), which they "cast down" before Pharaoh, as Aaron had cast his. These "rods" or rather "sticks," are continually represented on the monuments: no Egyptian lord is without one;[3] at an entertainment there was an attendant whose especial duty it was to receive the sticks of the male guests on their arrival, and restore them at their departure.[4]

The Egyptians employed "furnaces" (ch. ix. 8) for various purposes, "ovens" (ch. viii. 3) for the

---

[1] Wilkinson, "Ancient Egyptians," vol. ii., p. 236.
[2] Ibid., vol. ii., p. 28; vol. iii., p. 447.
[3] Birch, "Egypt from the Earliest Times," p. 45; "The Egyptian lord . . . carried a wand or walking-stick as a sign of dignity or authority."
[4] Wilkinson, "Ancient Egyptians," vol. i., pl. xi., fig. 10.

baking of their bread, "kneading-troughs" (ibid.) for the formation of the dough, and "hand-mills" (ch. xi. 5) for the grinding of the corn into flour. "Their mills," says Sir Gardner Wilkinson, "were of simple and rude construction. They consisted of two circular stones, nearly flat, the lower one fixed, while the other turned on a pivot, or shaft rising from the centre of that beneath it; and the grain, descending through an aperture in the upper stone, immediately above the pivot, gradually underwent the process of grinding as it passed. It was turned by a woman, seated, and holding a handle fixed perpendicularly near the edge. . . . The stone of which the hand-mills were made was usually a hard grit."[1] Sir Gardner adds in a note that he draws these conclusions from the fragments of the old stones discovered among the ancient remains. The same writer witnesses to the use by the ancient Egyptians of furnaces, ovens, and kneading-troughs.[2]

One curious custom of an Egyptian household obtains incidental mention in the account of the first plague, viz., the storing of water in "vessels of wood and in vessels of stone" (ch. vii. 19). Water being exceedingly abundant in Egypt by reason of the Nile, with its numerous branches, natural and artificial, which conveyed the indispensable fluid

---

[1] Wilkinson, "Ancient Egyptians," vol. i., p. 359.
[2] Ibid., vol. ii., pp. 34, 192.

almost to every house, "storing" would have been quite unnecessary but for one circumstance. The Nile water during the period of the inundation is turbid, and requires to be kept for a considerable time before it becomes palatable and fit for use by the muddy particles sinking gradually to the bottom, and leaving pure water at the top. To produce this effect, it has always been, and still is, usual to keep the Nile water in jars, or in stone-troughs, until the sediment is deposited, and the fluid rendered fit for drinking.[1]

Another still more remarkable custom is brought under notice by the narrative in ch. i. "When ye do the office of a midwife to the Hebrew women," says the Pharaoh to Shiphrah and Puah, "*and see them upon the stools*, if it be a son, then ye shall kill him," etc. The incident is one which its delicate nature unfits for representation, and the monuments thus fail to confirm it; but a modern practice, peculiar, so far as we know, to Egypt, is probably the direct descendant of the ancient one, and at any rate lends it illustration. "Two or three days before the expected time of delivery," says Mr. Lane, in his account of the manners and customs of the modern Egyptians, "the *layah* (midwife) conveys to the house the *kursee elwiladeh*, a chair of a peculiar

---

[1] Wilkinson, "Modern Egyptians," vol. ii., p. 428. Compare Pococke, "Travels," vol. i., p. 312.

form, upon which the patient is to be seated during the birth."[1]

The ordinary food of the Israelites during the time of their sojourn in Egypt is stated in one place (Exod. xvi. 3) to have consisted of "bread" and "flesh." But from another we learn that it embraced also "fish" in abundance, and likewise the following vegetables: "cucumbers, melons, leeks, onions, and garlick" (Num. xi. 5). That bread was its staple may be gathered from the institution of the feast of unleavened bread (ch. xii. 15—20), as well as from the mention of "dough" (ibid. vers. 34, 39) as the only provision that they took with them, besides their beasts, when they quitted the country. Now "bread" was certainly "the staff of life" to the Egyptian nation, and the food on which they would naturally nourish their slaves. We find a king stating that he offered in a single temple loaves of three distinct kinds, viz., "best bread," "great loaves of bread for eating," and "loaves of barley bread," to the amount of 6,272,431.[2] He also offered to the same temple 5,279,552 bushels of corn.[3] "Bread" is the ordinary representative of food in Egyptian speech. The good man "gives *bread* to the hungry";[4] artisans labour for

---

[1] Lane. "Modern Egyptians," vol. iii., p. 142.
[2] "Records of the Past," vol. viii., p. 44, line 5.
[3] Ibid., p. 45, line 12.
[4] Birch, "Egypt from the Earliest Times," p. 46.

"bread";[1] "bread" is taken out to the rustics who work in the fields,[2] and is brought for the repast of young maidens.[3] Flesh, on the other hand, though largely consumed by the rich, was generally beyond the means of the poor; and the Israelites, longing after the "fleshpots" of Egypt can only be accounted for by supposing that the king nourished his labourers on a more generous diet than was obtainable by the working classes generally. It is not likely, however, that they received flesh often. We have probably in Num. xi. 5 the main constituents of their dietary in addition to bread. Fish, which they "did eat in Egypt freely," was undoubtedly one of the principal articles of food consumed by the lower orders. Herodotus says that a certain number of the poorer Egyptians "lived almost entirely on fish."[4] It was so abundant that it was necessarily cheap. The Nile produced several kinds, which were easily caught; and in Lake Mœris the abundance of the fish was such that the Pharaohs are said to have derived from the sale a revenue of above £94,000 a year.[5] Lake Menzaleh also, and the other lakes near the coast, must have yielded a considerable supply. The fishermen of Egypt

---

[1] "Records of the Past," vol. viii., p. 150.
[2] Ibid., vol. ii., p. 139.
[3] Ibid., vol. vi., p. 154.
[4] Herod., ii. 92.
[5] Ibid., ii. 149.

formed a numerous class,[1] and the salting and drying of fish furnished occupation to a large number of persons.[2] The quantity of vegetable food which the poorer Egyptians consumed is noted by Diodorus,[3] and Herodotus makes out that the labourers whom Khufu (Cheops) employed to build the great pyramid subsisted mainly, if not wholly, on radishes, onions, and garlick.[4] Cucurbitaceous vegetables are at present among the most abundant productions of the Egyptian soil, and the monuments frequently exhibit them.[5] On the whole, therefore, the dietary assigned to the Israelites in Egypt may be pronounced such as the country was well capable of furnishing, and such as agrees in most particulars with the ordinary food of the Egyptian labouring class.

The customs connected with farming and cattle-keeping noticed in Exodus and the later books of the Pentateuch include, besides the cultivation of certain cereals already mentioned, (*a*) the comparative lateness of the wheat and *doora* harvest (ch. ix. 31, 32); (*b*) the leaving of stubble in the fields after the gathering in of the crops (ch. v. 12); (*c*) the

---

[1] Herod., ii. 92, 95; "Records of the Past," vol. viii., p. 153.
[2] Wilkinson, "Ancient Egyptians," vol. ii., pp. 115—8.
[3] Diod. Sic., i. 80.
[4] Herod., ii. 125.
[5] Wilkinson, "Ancient Egyptians," vol. iii., pp. 419, 431.

general cultivation of the land *after the fashion of a garden* (Deut. xi. 10) ; (*d*) the employment of irrigation in such a way that the "foot" could direct the course of the life-giving fluid (ibid.) ; (*e*) the cultivation of fruit-trees (Exod. ix. 25 ; x. 15) ; and (*f*) the keeping of cattle, partly in the fields, partly in stalls, or sheds, where they were protected from the weather (ch. ix. 19—25). With respect to the first of these points, it may be observed that there is exactly the same difference now as that which the writer of Exodus notes,—"Barley ripens and flax blossoms about the middle of February or, at the latest, early in March,"[1] while the wheat harvest does not begin till April. There is thus a full month between the barley and the wheat harvest.[2] The doora is also a late crop.

The mode of reaping wheat which prevailed in ancient Egypt is amply represented upon the monuments, and appears to have been such as to leave abundant stubble in the fields, as implied in ch. v. 12. Not more than about a foot of the straw was cut with the ear, two feet or more being left.[3] The barley was probably reaped in the same way.

It is not, perhaps, quite clear what is meant in

---

[1] Canon Cook in the "Speaker's Commentary," vol. i., p. 286.

[2] Birch in Wilkinson's "Ancient Egyptians," vol. ii., p. 42, note.

Ibid, vol. ii., pp. 418—427.

Deut. xi. 10 by the land of Egypt being cultivated "as a garden of herbs"; but most probably the reference is, as Wilkinson suggests,[1] to the ordinary implement of cultivation, the plough, being largely dipensed with, and a slight dressing with the hoe, if even so much as that, used instead. Herodotus witnesses to the prevalence of this method of cultivation,[2] and the monuments occasionally represent it.

The absolute necessity of irrigation, and the nature of the irrigation, implied in the expression, "where thou sowedst thy seed, and wateredst it with thy foot" (Deut xi. 10), receive illustration from the pictures in the tombs, which show us the fields surrounded by broad canals, and intersected everywhere by cuttings from them, continually diminishing in size, until at last they are no more than rills banked up with a little mud, which the hand or "foot" might readily remove and replace, so turning the water in any direction that might be required by the cultivator.

Fruit-trees are represented on the monuments as largely cultivated and much valued. Among them the vine holds the foremost place. A sceptical critic was once bold enough to assert that the statements in the Pentateuch which implied the existence of the vine in Egypt were distinct evidence of "the late

---

[1] Wilkinson, "Ancient Egyptians," vol. ii., p. 389, note.
[2] Herod., ii. 14.

origin of the narrative."[1] But the tombs of Benihassan, which are anterior to the Exodus, contain "representations of the culture of the vine, the vintage, the stripping off and carrying away of the grapes, of two kinds of winepresses, the one moved by the strength of human arms, the other by mechanical power, the storing of the wine in bottles or jars, and its transportation into the cellar."[2] No one now doubts that the vine was cultivated in Egypt from a time long anterior to Moses. The fig and the date-bearing palm were likewise grown for the sake of the fruit, grapes, figs, and dates constituting the Egyptian lord's usual dessert,[3] while the last-named fruit was also made into a conserve,[4] which diversified the diet at rich men's tables.

The breeding and rearing of cattle was a regular part of the farmer's business in Egypt, and the wealth of individuals in flocks and herds was considerable. Three distinct kinds of cattle were affected—the long-horned, the short-horned, and the hornless.[5] "During the greater part of the year they were pastured in open fields, on the natural growth of the rich soil, or on artificial grasses, which

---

[1] Von Bohlen, "Die Genesis historisch-critisch erlautert," § 373.

[2] Champollion, quoted by Hengstenberg, "Egypt and the Books of Moses," p. 15.

[3] Birch, "Egypt from the Earliest Times," p. 45.

[4] Wilkinson, "Ancient Egyptians," vol. ii., p. 43.

[5] Ibid.

were cultivated for the purpose; but at the time of the inundation it was necessary to bring them in from the fields to the farm-yards or the villages, where they were kept in sheds or pens on ground artificially raised, so as to be beyond the reach of the river."[1] Thus the cattle generally had "houses" (Exod. ix. 20), *i.e.*, sheds or stalls, into which it was possible to bring them at short notice.

Among "miscellaneous customs" the following seem most worthy of notice: (*a*) the practice of making boats out of bulrushes (ch. ii. 3; compare Isa. xviii. 2), and (*b*) the position occupied by magic at the court of the Pharaohs. On the former point Sir Gardner Wilkinson remarks[2]: "There was a small kind of punt or canoe *made entirely of the papyrus*, bound together with bands of the same plant— the 'vessels of bulrushes' mentioned in Isa. xviii. 2." On the latter M. Maspero makes the following statement[3] "Magic was in Egypt a science, and the magician one of the most esteemed of learned men. The nobles themselves, the prince Khamuas and his brother, were adepts in supernatural arts, and decipherers of magic formularies, in which they had an entire belief. A prince who was a sorcerer would nowadays inspire a very moderate sentiment of

---

[1] Rawlinson, "History of Ancient Egypt," vol. i., pp. 171, 172.

[2] In Rawlinson's "Herodotus," vol. ii., p. 154, note.

[3] Quoted by M. Lenormant, "Manuel d' Histoire Ancienne," vol. ii., pp. 126—7.

esteem. In Egypt the profession of magic was not incompatible with royalty, and the sorcerers of a Pharaoh had not uncommonly the Pharaoh himself for their pupil." The magical texts form a considerable proportion of the MSS. which have come down to us from ancient times, particularly from the nineteenth dynasty; and the composition of some of them was ascribed to a Divine source.

CHAPTER VII.

NOTICES OF EGYPT IN THE FIRST BOOK OF KINGS.

CHAPTER VII.

NOTICES OF EGYPT IN THE FIRST BOOK OF KINGS.

IT is, at first sight, surprising that there is no mention of Egypt in connection with the history of the Israelites between the Exodus and the reign of Solomon. The interval is one of, at least, three hundred—perhaps of four hundred—years. During its earlier portion, and again about a century before its close, the Egyptian monarchs conducted expeditions into Northern Syria, if not even into Mesopotamia, which might have been expected to have brought them into contact with the Hebrew people; but the Hebrew records of the time are entirely silent on the subject, and indeed only mention Egypt retrospectively, as the place where Israel had once suffered affliction.[1] Perhaps the earlier expeditions—those of Rameses III.[2]—may have taken place while Israel was still detained in

---

[1] Josh. i. 10, xxiv. 4—7, 14, 17; 1 Sam. ii. 27, vi. 6, x. 18, xii. 6—8.

[2] Brugsch, "History of Egypt," vol. ii., p. 152.

the "Wilderness of the Wanderings," in which case there would naturally have been no collision between the two peoples; while those of Rameses XII.[1] and of Her-hor[2] (about B.C. 1130—1100), having Syria rather than Palestine for their object, may have been conducted along the coast route, by way of Philistia and Phœnicia, into Cœle-Syria, and so have left the Israelite territory untouched, or nearly untouched. The main explanation, however, of the disappearance of Egypt from the narrative, is to be found in her general depression and weakness during the period in question, which prevented any real conquests from being made, or any large armies sent into Western Asia, as in the earlier times of Thothmes III., Amenhotep II., Seti, and Rameses II., or in the later ones of Sheshonk and Neku. This depression is very marked in the Egyptian remains, which show no really great or conquering monarch between Rameses III. and Sheshonk I. During this space, which is that of the Judges and first two kings in Israel, Egypt really ceased to be an aggressive power.

The Scriptural notices of Egypt belonging to the reign of Solomon are the following:—

1. "Solomon made affinity with Pharaoh, king of Egypt, and took Pharaoh's daughter, and brought her into the city of David" (1 Kings iii. 1).

---

[1] Brugsch, "History of Egypt," vol. ii., pp. 184-7; Birch, "Egypt from the Earliest Times," pp. 149-153.
[2] Birch, p. 154.

2. "Pharaoh, king of Egypt, had gone up and taken Gezer, and burnt it with fire, and slain the Canaanites that dwelt in the city, and given it for a present unto his daughter, Solomon's wife" (1 Kings ix. 16).

3. "Solomon had horses brought out of Egypt, and linen yarn; the king's merchants received the linen yarn at a price. And a chariot came up and went out of Egypt for six hundred shekels of silver, and an horse for a hundred and fifty: and so for all, the kings of the Hittites, and for the kings of Syria, did they bring them out by their means" (1 Kings x. 28, 29).

4. "The Lord stirred up an adversary unto Solomon, Hadad the Edomite: he was of the king's seed in Edom. For it came to pass, when David was in Edom, and Joab, the captain of the host, was gone up to bury the slain, after he had smitten every male in Edom, . . . that Hadad fled, he and certain Edomites of his father's servants with him, to go into Egypt, Hadad being yet a little child; and they arose out of Midian, and came to Paran; and they took men with them out of Paran, and they came to Egypt, unto Pharaoh, king of Egypt, which gave him an house, and appointed him victuals, and gave him land. And Hadad found great favour in the sight of Pharaoh, so that he gave him to wife the sister of his own wife, the sister of Tahpenes the queen; and the sister of Tahpenes bare him

Genubath, his son, whom Tahpenes weaned in Pharaoh's house: and Genubath was in Pharaoh's household, among the sons of Pharaoh" (1 Kings xi. 14—20).

5. "Solomon sought to kill Jeroboam. And Jeroboam arose and fled into Egypt, unto Shishak, . . . and was in Egypt unto the death of Solomon" (1 Kings xi. 40).

There is nothing surprising in the willingness of a Pharaoh of the twenty-first dynasty to give a daughter in marriage to the foreign monarch of a neighbouring country. Even in the most flourishing times the kings of Egypt had been willing to form matrimonial alliances with the Ethiopian royal house, and had both taken Ethiopian princesses for their own wives[1] and given their daughters in marriage to Ethiopian monarchs. The last king of the twentieth dynasty married a "princess of Baktan"[2] —a Syrian or Mesopotamian; and even the great Rameses married a Hittite.[3] According to 1 Chron. iv. 18, there was one Pharaoh who allowed a daughter of his to marry a mere ordinary Israelite. To "make affinity" with a prince of Solomon's rank and position would have been beneath the dignity of few Egyptian monarchs; it was probably felt as a

---

[1] Birch, "Egypt from the Earliest Times," pp. 81, 107, etc.
[2] "Records of the Past," vol. iv., p. 57.
[3] Lenormant, "Manuel d'Histoire Ancienne," vol. ii., p. 264.

highly satisfactory connection by the weak Tanite Pharaoh whose daughter made so good a match.

With which of the Tanite monarchs it was that Solomon thus allied himself is uncertain. M. Lenormant fixes definitely on Hor-Pasebensha,[1] or Pasebensha II., the last king of the dynasty; but an earlier monarch is more probable. Solomon's marriage was early in his reign (1 Kings iii. 1), and he reigned forty years (ch. xi. 42), during the last five or ten of which he would seem to have been contemporary with Shishak (ch. xi. 40). When he ascended the throne, the king who reigned in Egypt was probably either Pasebensha I. or Pinetem II. Unfortunately these monarchs have left such scanty remains, that we know next to nothing concerning them.

The conquest of Gezer by this Pharaoh, whoever he was, and its transference to Solomon *as his wife's dowry* (ch. ix. 16), though it cannot be confirmed from Egyptian history, may be illustrated from Assyrian. Sargon tells us in one of his inscriptions that, having conquered the country of Cilicia with some difficulty, on account of its great natural strength, he made it over to Ambris, king of Tubal, who had married one of his daughters, as the princess's dowry.[2]

---

[1] Lenormant, "Manuel d'Histoire Ancienne," vol. ii., p. 329.
[2] "Ancient Monarchies," vol. ii., p. 150, note 6.

The establishment of commercial relations between Palestine and Syria on the one hand and Egypt on the other (ch. x. 28, 29) is exactly what might have been expected to follow on the matrimonial alliance concluded between Solomon and his Egyptian contemporary. When Rameses II. allied himself with the Hittite royal house, interchange of commodities between Egypt and Syria is the immediate consequence. Corn is sent by sea from the valley of the Nile to the Syrian mountain tract for the support of the "children of Heth,"[1] who doubtless made a return in timber, or some other products of their own soil. In Solomon's time the Egyptian commodities imported by the Western Asiatics were different. Long practice had perfected in Egypt the manufacture of chariots, and these had become indispensable to the Hittite and Syrian kings for the maintenance of their independence against the encroachments of Assyria. Each king of these peoples—and there were several kings of each[2]—maintained a war force of several hundred chariots,[3] for each of which were needed two well-trained horses. These Egypt supplied, together (if our translators are right) with "linen yarn," also a commodity known to have been produced largely in that country.[4]

[1] "Records of the Past," vol. iv., p. 43, l. 24.
[2] See 2 Sam. viii. 3—12, x. 6—16, 1 Kings, x. 29, 2 Kings, vii. 6, and the Assyrian inscriptions *passim*.
[3] "Ancient Monarchies," vol. ii., p. 103, note 7.
[4] Herod., ii. 37, 182, iii. 47 ; Plin., "H. N." xix. 1.

The story of Hadad's flight to Egypt and hospitable reception by an Egyptian Pharaoh, whose queen's name was Tahpenes, admits of no illustration from profane sources. We do not know the names borne by the queens of the later monarchs of the twenty-first dynasty, and we have thus no means of identifying the Pharaoh intended. No doubt Egypt was at all times open as a refuge to political exiles; but there must have been special reasons for the high favour shown to Hadad. Perhaps he was already connected by blood with the Tanite monarchs; perhaps Edom had been in alliance with Egypt before David conquered it.

Jeroboam's flight to Shishak brings before us an Egyptian monarch who is fortunately unmistakable. Hitherto the sacred writers have been content, when mentioning Egyptian kings, to speak of them by their recognised official title of "Pharaoh."[1] Now for the first time is this habit broken through, and the actual proper name of an Egyptian monarch presented to us. The Hebrew Shishak (שִׁישַׁק) represent almost exactly the Egyptian name ordinarily written "Sheshenk," but sometimes "Sheshek,"[2] and expressed in the fragments of Manetho by Sesonchis (Σέσωγχις).[3] This is a name well known to Egypto-

---

[1] See above, Ch. I. p. 221.
[2] Lepsius, "Ueber die XXII. Ægyptische Konigs-dynastie pp. 267, 289.
[3] Syncellus, "Chronographia," pp. 73D, 74D.

logists. Wholly absent from all the earlier Egyptian monuments, it appears suddenly in those of the twenty-second (Bubastite) dynasty, where it is borne by no less than four monarchs, besides occurring also among the names of private individuals. This abundance would be somewhat puzzling were it not for the fact that one only of the four monarchs is a warrior, or leads any expedition beyond the borders.[1] The records of the time leave no doubt that the prince who received Jeroboam was Sheshonk I., the founder of the Bubastite line, the son of Namrot and Tentespeh, the first king of the twenty-second dynasty.

"It came to pass in the fifth year of King Rehoboam that Shishak, king of Egypt, came up against Jerusalem; and he took away the treasures of the house of the Lord, and the treasures of the king's house; he even took away all; and he took away all the shields of gold which Solomon had made" (1 Kings xiv. 25, 26).

With this may be compared 2 Chron. xii. 1—9:

"And it came to pass, when Rehoboam had established the kingdom, and had strengthened himself, he forsook the law of the Lord, and all Israel with him; and it came to pass, that in the fifth year of King Rehoboam Shishak, king of Egypt, came

---

[1] Lenormant, "Manuel d'Histoire Ancienne," vol. ii., p. 340.

up against Jerusalem, because they had transgressed against the Lord, with twelve hundred chariots and threescore thousand horsemen; and the people were without number that came with him out of Egypt— the Lubims, and the Sukkiims, and the Ethiopians. And he took the fenced cities which pertained to Judah, and came to Jerusalem. Then came Shemaiah the prophet to Rehoboam, and to the princes of Judah that were gathered together to Jerusalem because of Shishak, and said unto them, Thus saith the Lord, Ye have forsaken Me, and therefore have I also left you in the hand of Shishak. Whereupon the princes of Israel and the king humbled themselves, and they said, The Lord is righteous. And when the Lord saw that they humbled themselves, the word of the Lord came to Shemaiah saying, They have humbled themselves; therefore I will not destroy them, but I will grant them some deliverance; and My wrath shall not be poured out upon Jerusalem by the hand of Shishak. *Nevertheless they shall be his servants*, that they may may know My service, and the service of the kingdoms of the countries. So Shishak, king of Egypt, came up against Jerusalem, and took away the treasures of the house of the Lord, and the treasures of the king's house; he took all; he carried away also the shields of gold which Solomon had made."

The Palestinian expedition of Sheshonk I. forms

the subject of a remarkable bas-relief,[1] which, on his return from it, he caused to be executed in commemoration of its complete success. Selecting the Great Temple of Karnak, at Thebes, which Seti I. and Rameses II. had already adorned profusely with representations of their victories, he built against its southern external wall a fresh portico or colonnade, known to Egyptologists as "the portico of the Bubastites," and carved upon the wall itself, to the east of his portico, a memorial of his grand campaign. First, he represented himself in his war costume, holding by the hair of their heads with his left hand thirty-eight captive Asiatic chiefs, and with an iron mace uplifted in his right threatening them with destruction. Further, he caused himself to be figured a second time, and represented in the act of leading captive a hundred and thirty-three cities or tribes, each specified by name and personified in an individual form, accompanied by a cartouche containing their respective names. In the physiognomies of these ideal figures the critical acumen or lively imagination of a French historian sees rendered "with marvellous ethnographic exactness" the Jewish type of countenance[2]; but less gifted travellers do not find anything very peculiar in the profiles, which,

---

[1] For a representation of this monument, see the "Denkmäler" of Lepsius, part iii., Pls. 252 and 253*a*.

[2] Lenormant, "Manual d'Histoire Ancienne," vol. ii., p. 340.

whether representing Jews or Arabs, are almost exactly alike.

The list of names contained in the record is very much more interesting than the array of countenances accompanying them. They have been carefully transcribed, and compared with those which occur in the Hebrew Scriptures, both by Mr. Reginald Stuart Poole[1] and by Dr. Brugsch.[2] It results from the comparison, first, that of the ninety names which are legible about forty or forty-five may be pretty certainly identified either with Palestinian towns or districts or with Arab tribes of the neighbourhood ; secondly, that the Arab tribe names are in several instances repeated ; and thirdly, that the Palestinian town names are divisible into three classes : (*a*) cities of Judah proper, (*b*) Levitical cities within the limits of the kingdom of Israel, and (*c*) Canaanite cities within the same limits. To the first class belong Adoraim (called Adurma), Aijalon (called Ayulon), and Shoco (called Shauke), which were among the "fenced cities" that Rehoboam fortified in anticipa- of Sheshonk's attack (2 Chron. xi. 5—10); also Gibeon (Kebeana), Alemeth (Beith'almoth), Beth-Tappuah (Beith-Tapuh), Telem (Zalema), Azem (Aauzamaa), and Lebaoth (Libith). To the second

---

[1] See the article on SHISHAK in Smith's "Dictionary of the Bible," vol. iii.

[2] "Geschichte Ægyptens unter den Pharaonen," pp. 660—662.

class may be assigned Taanach (Ta'ankau), mentioned as a Levitical city in Josh. xxi. 25; Rehob (Rehabau), mentioned in Josh. xxi. 31 and 1 Chron. vi. 75; Mahanaim (Mahunema), mentioned Josh. xxi. 38, 1 Chron. vi. 80; Beth-horon (Beith-Huaron), mentioned Josh. xxi. 22, 1 Chron. vi. 68; Kedemoth (Kademoth), mentioned Josh. xxi. 37, 1 Chron. vi. 79; Bileam (Bilema), mentioned 1 Chron. vi. 70; Golan (Galenaa) mentioned Josh. xxi 27, 1 Chron. vi. 71; and Anem (Anama), mentioned in 1 Chron. vi. 73. As belonging to the third class we can only fix positively on Beth-shan (Beith-shan-ra) and Megiddo (Maketu); but Rabbith, Shunem, Hapharaim, and Edrei, which are also contained in Sheshonk's list of his conquests, may be suspected of having retained a Canaanite element in their population.

This list is remarkable both for what it contains and for what it omits. The omission of most of those strongholds towards the south, which Rehoboam fortified against Egypt, as Hebron, Lachish, Azekah, Mareshah, Gath, Adullam, Bethzur, and Tekoa (2 Chron. xi. 6—10), is perhaps to be explained by the illegibility of twelve names at the beginning of the list, where these cities, as the first attacked, would most probably have been mentioned. The omission of Jerusalem might also be accounted for in the same way. Or the fact may have been that Jerusalem itself was not taken. Like Hezekiah, on the first invasion of Sennacherib (2 Kings

xviii. 13—16). Rehoboam may have surrendered his treasures (1 Kings xiv. 26), to save his city from the horrors of capture. This was, perhaps, the fulfilment of God's promise by the mouth of Shemaiah —" I will grant them some deliverance, and My wrath shall not be poured upon Jerusalem by the hand of Shishak" (2 Chron. xii. 7). The Egyptian monarch, on receiving the treasures and the submission of Rehoboam (ibid. ver. 8), may have consented to respect the city.

But, as he could not mention Jerusalem among his actual conquests, he supplied the place where the name would naturally have occurred with an inscription of a peculiar kind. The cartouche borne by one of the earlier of the ideal figures contains the epigraph "YUTeH MALeK," in which Egyptologists generally recognise a boast either that the "king" or the "kingdom of Judah" made submission to the conqueror. "Yuteh Malek" is, we think, most properly read as "Judah, a kingdom." By introducing the words, Sheshonk wished to mark that besides subduing cities and districts and tribes, he had in one case conquered a country which was under the government of a king.

The fact that a large proportion of the towns mentioned as taken are in the territories not of Rehoboam, against whom Sheshonk "went up" (1 Kings xiv. 25), but of Jeroboam, his *protégé* and friend, whom his expedition was doubtless intended to assist, and the further fact that these towns were chiefly Levitical or Canaanite, would seem to show that Jeroboam, in the earlier part of his reign, had considerable opposition to encounter within the limits of his own kingdom. The disaffection of those Levites whose possessions lay within his territories is sufficiently indicated in Chronicles by the account which is there given (2 Chron. xi. 13, 14) of a number of them leaving their possessions and "resorting to Rehoboam throughout all their coasts." It is probable that such as remained were equally hostile, and that Jeroboam used the arms of his ally to punish them. At the same time, he was enabled by Egyptian aid to reduce the few Canaanite cities which still maintained their independence, as Gezer had done until conquered by the Pharaoh who gave his daughter to Solomon (2 Kings ix. 16)

The army with which Sheshonk invaded Palestine is more numerous than we should have anticipated, and some corruption in the numbers may be suspected. It is composed, however, exactly as the monuments would have led us to expect, almost wholly of foreign mercenaries (2 Chron. xii. 3), Libyans, Ethiopians, and others. The Egyptian armies of the time consisted, for the most part, of Maxyes and other Berber tribes from the north-west, and of Ethiopians and negroes from the south.[1] Sheshonk

---

[1] Lenormant, "Manuel d'Histoire Ancienne," vol. ii., pp. 340, 341.

who was himself of foreign descent, placed far more dependence on these foreign troops than on the native Egyptian levies.

"Asa had an army of men that bare targets and spears... And there came out against them Zerah the Ethiopian with an host of a thousand thousand and three hundred chariots, and came unto Mareshah. Then Asa went out against him, and they set the battle in array in the valley of Zephathah at Mareshah. And Asa cried unto the Lord,... so the Lord smote the Ethiopians before Asa and before Judah, and the Ethiopians fled. And Asa and the people that were with him pursued them unto Gerar; and the Ethiopians were overthrown, that they could not recover themselves" (2 Chron. xiv. 8—13).

The Egyptians do not record unsuccessful expeditions, and thus the monuments contain no mention of this attack on Asa. It appears to have been provoked by Asa's rebellion, which is glanced at in 2 Chron. xiv. 6. The Egyptian monarch who sent or led the expedition was probably Osorchon (Uasarkan) II., whose name the Hebrews contracted into Zerach (זֶרַח). He was, perhaps, an Ethiopian on his mother's side. Asa's defeat of his vast army is the most glorious victory ever obtained by an Israelite monarch, and secured his country from any Egyptian attack for above three centuries.

CHAPTER VIII.

THE NOTICES OF EGYPT IN THE SECOND BOOK OF KINGS.

CHAPTER VIII.

THE NOTICES OF EGYPT IN THE SECOND BOOK OF KINGS.

"IN the twelfth year of Ahaz, king of Judah, began Hoshea, the son of Elah, to reign in Samaria. . . . Against him came up Shalmaneser, king of Assyria; and Hoshea became his servant, and gave him presents. And the king of Assyria found conspiracy in Hoshea, for he had sent messengers to So, king of Egypt, and brought no present to the king of Assyria, as he had done year by year; therefore the king of Assyria shut him up, and bound him in prison." (2 Kings xvii. 1—4).

It is not very easy to identify the "king of Egypt" here mentioned, as one with whom Hoshea, the son of Elah, sought to ally himself, with any of the known Pharaohs. "So" is a name that seems at first sight very unlike those borne by Egyptian monarchs, which are never monosyllabic, and in no case end in the letter *o*. A reference to the Hebrew text removes, however, much of the difficulty, since the word rendered by "So" in our version is found to be one of three letters, סוא, all of which may be consonants. As the Masoretic pointing, which our translators followed, is of small authority, and in proper names of scarcely any authority at all, we are entitled to give to each of the three letters its consonant force, and, supplying short vowels, to render the Hebrew סוא by "Seveh." Now "Seveh" is, very near indeed to the Manethonian "Sevech-us," whom the Sebennytic priest makes the second monarch of his twenty-fifth dynasty; and "Sevech-us" is a natural Greek equivalent of the Egyptian "Shebek" or "Shabak," a name borne by a well-known Pharaoh (the first king of the same dynasty), which both Herodotus and Manetho render by "Sabacôs." It has been generally allowed that So (or Seveh) must represent one or other of these, but critics are not yet agreed which is to be preferred of the two.[1] To us it seems that both the name itself and the necessities of the chronology point to the first king rather than to the second; and we consequently regard Hoshea as having turned in his distress to seek the aid of the monarch whom the Egyptians knew as Shabak, and the Greeks as Sabacôs or Sabaco.[2]

The application implies an entire change in the

---
[1] The general opinion is in favour of Shabak; but some, like Hekekyan Bey ("Chronology of Siriadic Monuments," p. 106), prefer Shabatok.

[2] Herod. ii. 139; Manetho ap. Syncell., "Chronograph.," p. 74, B.

condition of political affairs in the East, and in the relations of state to state, from those which prevailed when Egyptian monarchs last figured in the sacred narrative, two hundred or two hundred and fifty years earlier. Then Egypt was an aggressive power, bent on establishing her influence over Palestine, and from time to time invading Asia with large armies in the hope of making extensive conquests.[1] She was the chief enemy feared by the petty kingdoms and loosely aggregated tribes of South-western Asia, the only power in their neighbourhood that possessed large bodies of disciplined troops and an instinct of self-aggrandisement. But all this was now altered. Egypt from the time of Osarkon II., had steadily declined in strength; her monarchs had been inactive and unwarlike, her policy one of abstention from all enterprise. The inveterate evil of disintegration with which her ill-shaped territory was naturally threatened, and which had from time to time shown itself in her history, once more made its appearance. There arose a practice of giving appanages to the princes of the royal house, which tended to become hereditary, and trenched on the sovereignty of the nominal monarch. "Egypt found herself divided into a certain number of principalities, some of which contained only a few towns, while others extended over several adjacent cantons. Ere long the chiefs of these principalities were bold

---

[1] 2 Chron. xii. 3; xiv. 9.

enough to reject the suzerainty of the Pharaoh; relying upon their bands of Libyan mercenaries, they not only usurped the functions of royalty, but even the title of king, while the legitimate reigning house, relegated to a corner of the Delta, with difficulty preserved a remnant of its old authority."[1] By the close of the twenty-second dynasty, "Egypt had arrived at such a point of disintegration as to find herself portioned out among nearly twenty princes, of whom four at least assumed the cartouche and the other emblems of royalty."[2]

Meanwhile, as if to counterbalance the paralysis and decrepitude of the Egyptian state, there had arisen on the other side of Syria and Palestine a great power, continually increasing in strength, with the same instinct of aggrandisement which had formerly possessed Egypt, and with even greater aptitudes for war and conquest. Assyria, from about B.C. 880, or a little earlier, began to press westward upon the nations dwelling between the Euphrates and the Mediterranean, and to threaten them with subjugation. Asshur-nazir-pal took Carchemish, conquered Northern Syria, and forced the Phœnician cities to make their submission to him.[3] His son, Shalmaneser II., engaged in wars with Hamath, Damascus, and Samaria; defeated Benhadad, Hazael,

---

[1] Lenormant, "Manuel d'Histoire Ancienne," vol. ii., p. 341.
[2] Ibid., p. 342.
[3] "Ancient Monarchies," vol. ii., pp. 88, 89.

and Ahab; and made Jehu take up the position of a tributary.[1] The successors of these two warlike princes "fairly maintained the empire which they had received,"[2] and even pushed their expeditions into Philistia and Edom. After a lull in the war-storm, which lasted from about B.C. 780 to 750, it recommenced with increased fury. Tiglath-Pileser II. crushed the kingdom of Damascus, and greatly crippled that of Samaria, besides which he reduced the Philistines and several tribes of Arabs. He was succeeded by Shalmaneser IV., the monarch mentioned in 2 Kings xvii. 3.

The situation was thus the following. The petty states of Palestine and Syria had been suffering from the attacks of the Assyrians for a century and a half. One after another, the greater part of them had succumbed. First they were made tributaries; then they were absorbed into the conquering state and became mere provinces. Hoshea found his kingdom threatened with the fate which had befallen so many others. He had the courage to make an effort to save it. Casting an anxious glance over the entire political position, he thought that he saw in the Egyptian monarch of the time a possible deliverer. For there had been quite recently a revolution in Egypt. The weak and indolent native monarchs had been thrust aside, and superseded by a stronger

---

[1] "Ancient Monarchies," vol. ii., pp. 102—106.
[2] Sayce, "Ancient Empires of the East," p. 375.

and fiercer foreign race from the neighbouring
Ethiopia. "So," or Shabak, was one of these
foreigners, and wielded the resources of two countries,
his adopted and his native one. It was reasonable
to expect that he would see the danger which
menaced Egypt from the new masters of Western
Asia, and the desirability of maintaining the barrier
between his own dominions and the Assyrian, which
the still unconquered tribes and kingdoms of Syria
and Palestine were capable of constituting. There
were others besides Samaria ripe for revolt.[1] It
would have been a wise policy on the part of the
Egyptian monarch to have fomented the disaffection,
and supported with his full force the movement in
favour of independence which was in progress.

Hoshea's "messengers," under these circumstances,
sought the court of Shabak, which appears to have
been fixed at Memphis, in Lower Egypt.[2] It would
seem that they were received with favour, and that
material aid was promised, since Hoshea almost
immediately broke into open revolt by withholding
the tribute due to his Assyrian suzerain. With the
utmost promptness Shalmaneser marched against
him, seized his person, and carried him off to
Nineveh. Shabak made no effort in his defence.

---

[1] As Tyre, which actually revolted a year or two later; and
Hamath, Arpad, Simyra, and Damascus, which revolted from
Sargon in B.C. 721.

[2] Rawlinson, "History of Ancient Egypt," vol. ii., p. 446.

The first attempt of the people of God to "call to Egypt" (Hos. vii. 11) thus proved a most disastrous failure: the king, who had "trusted upon the staff of the bruised reed" (2 Kings xviii. 21), was ruined by his misplaced confidence, and within a few years his capital was taken (ibid. ver. 6), and his people carried into captivity (ibid,).

"And Rabshakeh said, ... Speak ye now to Hezekiah, Thus saith the great king, the king of Assyria, What confidence is this wherein thou trustest? Thou sayest—but they are but vain words—I have counsel and strength for the war. Now on whom dost thou trust, that thou rebellest against me? Now, behold, thou trustest upon the staff of this bruised reed, even upon Egypt, on which if a man lean, it will go into his hand and pierce it; so is Pharaoh, king of Egypt, unto all that trust on him" (ch. xviii. 19—21).

"When he" (*i.e.*, Sennacherib) "heard say of Tirhakah, king of Ethiopia, Behold, he is come out to fight against thee, he sent messengers again unto Hezekiah, saying, Let not thy God in whom thou trustest deceive thee, saying, Jerusalem shall not be delivered into the hand of the king of Assyria" (ch. xix. vers. 9, 10).

Another act in the drama has been opened. The kingdom of Samaria having been conquered and absorbed by the terrible Assyrians, it is Judæa's turn to be threatened with a similar fate. Not that she

is now threatened for the first time. Before Samaria
had fallen, Ahaz, the father of Hezekiah, placed
himself voluntarily under the Assyrian suzerainty,
consenting to become the vassal of Tiglath-Pileser
(2 Kings xvi. 7—10). Hezekiah threw off the
Assyrian yoke (ch. xviii. 7); but it was reimposed
upon him, first, as it would seem, by Sargon,[1] and
again (about B.C. 701) by Sennacherib (ibid. vers.
13—16). The Jewish monarch was, however, at no
time a submissive or willing vassal; and he had no
sooner bowed his neck to Sennacherib's yoke than
he began to make preparations for recovering his
independence. Like his brother monarch in Samaria,
he thought that he saw in Egypt his best ally and
protector. We may gather from Sennacherib's
reproaches in this chapter, as well as from passages
in the prophecies of Isaiah, that a formal embassy
was sent, either to Tirhakah at Napata, or to
his representative in Lower Egypt, with an offer
of alliance and a request for armed assistance,
especially chariots and horsemen (ibid. vers. 23, 24).
As in the former instance, the answer received was
favourable. Tirhakah was an enterprising monarch,
who left a name behind which marks him as one of
the greatest of Egypt's later kings.[2] He saw the

---

[1] Sargon claims in his inscriptions to have conquered Jerusalem (see Mr. Cheyne's "Isaiah," vol. i., p. 69). Various passages of Isaiah are thought to have reference to this conquest.

[2] Megasthenes, Fr. 80.

wisdom of upholding the independence of Judæa, and, accepting the alliance proffered by Hezekiah, probably gave an assurance of help, should Sennacherib attempt to punish his revolted vassal.

The occasion for fulfilling his promise soon arrived. Sennacherib, in B.C. 700 or 699, once more proceeded into Palestine,[1] and, sending a general to frighten Hezekiah into submission (ibid. ver. 17), himself marched on towards the south. He had received information of the alliance that had been concluded between Judæa and Egypt (vers. 21, 24), and regarding Tirhakah as his chief enemy, pressed forward to encounter his troops. Tirhakah, on his part, remained faithful to his ally, and put his army in motion to meet Sennacherib (ch. xix. 9).

This boldness is quite in accordance with Tirhakah's character. He was an enterprising prince, engaged in many wars, and a determined opponent of the Assyrians. His name is read on the Egyptian monuments as Tahark or Tahrak: and his face, which appears on them, is expressive of strong determination. The Assyrian inscriptions tell us that, in the later part of his life, he carried on a war for many years with Esarhaddon and his son, Asshur-

---

[1] M. Lenormant considers that the embassy of Rabshakeh and destruction of Sennacherib's host fell in the same year as his first invasion ("Manuel d'Histoire Ancienne," vol. ii., p. 361); but it seems to me more probable that they were separated by a short interval.

bani-pal.[1] If his star ultimately paled before that of the latter, it was not from any lack of courage, or resolution, or good faith on his part. He struggled gallantly against the Assyrian power for above thirty years, was never wanting to his confederates, and, if he did not quite deserve the high eulogies of the Greeks, was, at any rate, among the most distinguished monarchs of his race and period.

"In his" (Josiah's) "days Pharaoh-Nechoh, king of Egypt, went up against the king of Assyria to the river Euphrates; and King Josiah went against him; and he slew him at Megiddo, when he had seen him. . . . And the people of the land took Jehoahaz, the son of Josiah, and anointed him, and made him king in his father's stead. . . . And Pharaoh-Nechoh put him in bands at Riblah, in the land of Hamath, that he might not reign in Jerusalem, and put the land to a tribute of an hundred talents of silver and a talent of gold. And Pharaoh-Nechoh made Eliakim, the son of Josiah, king in the room of Josiah his father, and turned his name to Jehoiakim, and took Jehoahaz away; and he came to Egypt, and died there" (ch. xxiii. 29—34)

An interval of ninety years separates this notice from the one last considered. The position of affairs is once more completely changed. Although the present passage, taken by itself, does not give any indication of what had occurred, it is quite certain

---

[1] G. Smith, "History of Asshur-bani-pal," pp. 15—47.

that, in the interval between Tirhakah's war with Sennacherib and "Pharaoh-Necho's" invasion of Palestine, the empire of Assyria had come to an end. Necho was on his way "to fight against Carchemish by Euphrates" (2 Chron. xxxv. 20) with "the house wherewith he had war" (ibid.); and that house was not the old one of the Sargonidæ, wherewith Tirhakah had contended, but a new "house" which had recently come into power, and which held its court, not at Nineveh, but at Babylon (Jer. xlvi. 2). The exact year of the fall of Assyria is indeed uncertain;[1] but all authorities agree that it had taken place before the date of Necho's expedition, which was in B.C. 608. By "king of Assyria," in ver. 29, we must therefore understand king of Babylon, just as in Ezra vi. 22 we must understand by "king of Assyria" king of Persia. The Babylonian monarch, Nabopolassar, had taken a share in the great war by which the empire of the Assyrians was brought to an end,[2] and had succeeded to Assyria's rights in Western Mesopotamia, Syria, and Palestine. He was probably regarded by Josiah as his suzerain, and therefore entitled to such help as he could render him.

While these changes had taken place in Asia, in Africa also the condition of affairs was very much altered. The Ethiopian dynasty, after its long

---

[1] The opinion of scholars varies between B.C. 625 and B.C. 610.
[2] "Ancient Monarchies," vol. ii., p. 232.

struggle against Assyria, had been forced to yield, had given up the contest, and retired from Egypt altogether.[1] Assyria had for a time held Egypt under her sway, and, acting in the spirit of the maxim, "Divide et impera," had split up the country among no fewer than twenty princes. Of these some had been Assyrians, but the greater part natives. A Necho (Neku), the grandfather of the antagonist of Josiah, had held the first place among the twenty, being assigned the governments of Memphis and Sais, together with almost the whole of the Western Delta. He had been succeeded after a time by his son Psamatik, the Psammetichus of the Greeks, who had taken advantage of the growing weakness of Assyria during the later half of the seventh century to raise the standard of revolt, and had succeeded, by the assistance of Gyges, king of Lydia, and of numerous Greek and Carian mercenaries, in establishing his own independence and uniting all Egypt under his sway. A period of great prosperity had then set in. Psamatik I., a prudent, and at the same time a brave and warlike prince, raised Egypt from a state of extreme depression to a height which she had only previously reached under the Osirtasens, the Thothmeses, and the Ramessides. During the rapid decline and decay of Assyrian power which followed upon the death of Asshur-bani-

---

[1] Lenormant, "Manuel d'Histoire Ancienne," vol. ii., pp. 377, 378.

pal (B.C. 626), he extended his sway over Philistia and Phœnicia, thus resuming the policy of aggression upon Asia which had been laid aside, at any rate from the time of the first Sheshonk. The opportunity seemed good for re-establishing Egyptian influence in this quarter, now that Assyria was approaching her end, and Babylon had not yet stepped into the position of her successor.

The "Pharaoh-Nechoh" of the present chapter is undoubtedly Neku II., the son and successor of Psamatik I. and the grandson of the first Neku. He succeeded his father in B.C. 611 or 610, and held the throne till B.C. 595 or 594. He left behind him a high character for courage and enterprise. "We must see in him," says Dr. Wiedemann,[1] according to the narratives of the Greek historians, one of the most enterprising and excellent sovereigns of all Egyptian antiquity." After two or three years of preparation for war, he led his forces into Palestine by the coast road commonly followed by his predecessors, through Philistia and Sharon to Megiddo, on the high ground separating the plain of Sharon from that of Esdraelon. Here, on a battlefield celebrated alike in ancient and in modern times, he was confronted by Josiah, the Jewish monarch, who had recently united under his sway the greater

---

[1] "Geschichte Ægyptens von Psammetich I. bis auf Alexander den Grossen," p. 147.

portion of the two kingdoms of Israel and Judah.[1] Necho, according to the author of Chronicles, endeavoured to avoid engaging his troops, first by assuring him that his quarrel was not with him, but with the royal house of Babylon (2 Chron. xxxiii. 21), and then by urging that he had received a Divine commission to attack his enemy. Assertions of this kind were probably not unusual in the mouths of Egyptian princes, who regarded themselves as the favourites of Heaven, sons of the sun, and under constant Divine protection. We have an example in Piankhi, one of the Ethiopian monarchs of Egypt, who, when marching against the native princes that had revolted from him, declares,[2] "I am born of the loins, created from the egg, of the Deity. . . . I have not acted without His knowing: He ordained that I should [so] act." Neither argument had any effect on the resolution of the Jewish king; he probably deemed himself bound, as a faithful vassal, to bar the way of his suzerain's enemy; and Necho, finding him thus resolved, was compelled to engage his forces. The battle, commonly known as that of Megiddo, seems to be mentioned by Herodotus[3] as the battle of Magdolum, wherein he says that Neko (Necho) defeated the "Palestinian Syrians," which appears to be his name for the Jews. There is

---

[1] 2 Kings xxiii. 15—19; 2 Chron. xxxiv. 6 9.
[2] "Records of the Past," vol. ii., p. 91, l. 69.
[3] Herod., ii. 159.

reason to believe that the chief adversaries of the Jews on this occasion were the Greek and Carian mercenaries in the Egyptian service, since Necho was so pleased at their behaviour that he sent the arms which he had worn in the battle as an offering to a Greek temple in Asia Minor.

The success of Necho in detaching Syria from the Babylonian empire, and attaching it to his own, implied in the narrative of Kings, and in Jer. xlvi. 2, is alluded to in a fragment of Berosus.[1] Berosus, as a Babylonian, ignores Necho's independent position, and speaks of him as the "satrap" of the western provinces, who had caused them to "revolt." He regards the "revolt" as extending to Egypt, Syria, and Phœnicia, and as lasting until, in B.C. 605, Nebuchadnezzar was sent by his father to re-establish the dominion of Babylon in the far west.

---

[1] Beros. in the "Fragm. Hist. Gr." of C. Müller, vol. ii., Fr. 14

CHAPTER IX.

THE NOTICES OF EGYPT IN THE BOOK OF THE PROPHET ISAIAH.

CHAPTER IX.

THE NOTICES OF EGYPT IN THE BOOK OF THE PROPHET ISAIAH.

"THE burden of Egypt. Behold, the Lord rideth upon a swift cloud, and shall come into Egypt; and the idols of Egypt shall be moved at His presence, and the heart of Egypt shall melt in the midst of it. And I will set the Egyptians against the Egyptians; and they shall fight every one against his brother, and every one against his neighbour; city against city, and kingdom against kingdom. And the spirit of Egypt shall fail in the midst thereof. . . and they shall seek to the idols, and to the charmers, and to them that have familiar spirits, and to the wizards. And the Egyptians will I give over into the hands of a cruel lord; and a fierce king shall rule over them, saith the Lord, the Lord of hosts. . . Surely the princes of Zoan are fools; the counsel of the wise counsellors of Pharaoh is become brutish; how say ye unto Pharaoh, I am the son of the wise, the son of ancient kings? Where are they? where are thy wise men? and let them tell thee now, and let them know what the Lord hath purposed upon Egypt. The princes of Zoan are become fools, the princes of Noph are deceived; they have also seduced Egypt, even they that are the stay of the tribes thereof" (Isa. xix. 1—13).

It was a principal part of the mission of Isaiah during the reign of Hezekiah to dissuade the Jews from placing their dependence on Egypt in the struggle wherein they were engaged, with the prophet's entire consent and approval, against the Assyrians. Egypt, it was revealed to him, was no sure stay, no trustworthy ally, no powerful protector; she would fail in time of need, either unwilling or unable to give effectual help. (See ch. xx. 6; xxx. 3, 7; xxxi. 1—3.) Nor was this the worst. So long as king and people put their trust in an "arm of flesh," and did not rely upon God, God's arm was straitened, and He could not work the miraculous deliverance, which He was prepared to work, "because of their unbelief." Isaiah's prophecies with respect to Egypt are thus, almost entirely, depreciatory, and denunciatory. He is bent on showing that she is a power on whom no dependence can be wisely placed, in the hope that he may thereby prevent Hezekiah and his princes from contracting any alliance with the Egyptian monarch.

In this first prophecy he announces two calamities as about to befall Egypt, either of which is sufficient to render her an utterly worthless ally The first of these calamities is civil war. The Egyptians are about to "fight every one against his brother, and every one against his neighbour; city against city, and kingdom against kingdom. It is a remarkable illustration of this prophecy to find, as we do, from an inscription of Piankhi-Merammon,[1] that about B.C. 735 Egypt was divided up among no fewer than twenty-two princes, of whom four bore the title of "king," and that a civil war raged among them for some considerable time. Tafnekht, prince of Sais, began the disturbance by a series of skilfully arranged encroachments upon his neighbours. "During several years he laid siege successively to the fortresses which were held by the independent military chiefs and the petty princes of the western portion of Lower Egypt. Once master of all the territory to the west of the middle branch of the Nile, Tafnekht, respecting the dominion of the dynasty of Tanis over the Eastern Delta, proceeded to mount the stream, in order to make himself master of Central Egypt, and even with the intention of essaying the conquest of Upper Egypt, which was in the possession of the Ethiopian kings of Napata at this period. The stronghold of Meri-tum, now Meydoum, the district of Lake Mœris, the city of Heracleopolis, with its king Pefaabast, and that of Hermopolis, with its king Osorkon, recognised his authority as sovereign.

---

[1] See "Records of the Past," vol. ii., pp. 81—104; and compare Brugsch, "Geschichte Ægyptens," pp. 682—707.

He also made himself master of Aphroditopolis, and, pursuing his career of success, was in course of conquering the canton of Ouab, with its capital, Pa-matsets, when the chiefs of the upper and lower country who had not yet bowed their heads to his yoke invoked the aid of the Ethiopian monarch."[1] Piankhi gladly responded to the call, and in the course of one or two campaigns succeeded in despoiling Tafnekht of all his conquests, and in restoring Egypt to tranquillity. He then reigned for some years in peace; but at his death disturbances broke out afresh. Bocchoris, or Bok-en-ranf, who succeeded Tafnekht at Sais, had a reign as troubled as his predecessor's. "It was," says M. Lenormant,[2] "an incessant struggle against the petty princes, a continuous series of wars, first for the subjection of the Delta and Central Egypt, nay, even temporarily of the Thebaid, and then for the preservation of his conquests, and the maintenance with much difficulty of a precarious dominion." In the end Bocchoris succumbed to Shabak, the successor of Piankhi, who punished his rebellion, as he considered it, by burning him alive.[3] A third occasion of civil war, belonging to a somewhat later date, is mentioned by Herodotus. Psammetichus, the founder of the twenty-sixth

---

[1] Lenormant, "Manuel d'Histoire Ancienne," vol. ii., p. 344.

[2] Ibid., p. 349.

[3] Manetho ap. Syncell., "Chronograph.," p. 74, B.

dynasty, had to contend, according to this author,[1] with eleven of his brother princes before he succeeded in uniting all Egypt under his sceptre. Briefly, it may be said that Egypt, from about B.C. 735 to B.C. 650, suffered from a continued series of civil wars, which rendered her exceptionally weak, and caused her to fall an easy prey alternately to the Ethiopians and the Assyrians.

The other calamity prophesied is that of conquest by a foreign king of a fierce and cruel temper. "The Egyptians will I give over into the hands of a cruel lord; and a fierce king shall rule over them, saith the Lord" (ver. 4). The Egyptian and Assyrian records show that, between the years B.C. 750 and B.C. 650, Egypt was conquered at least five times, and was ruled by at least eight foreign monarchs. The first conquest—that of Piankhi Merammon—was certainly not a subjection to a "fierce and cruel lord," for Piankhi was a remarkably mild and clement prince, who did not even punish rebellion with any severity.[2] Shabak, the next conqueror after Piankhi, was cruel; but he can scarcely be the monarch intended, since he was accepted as a legitimate Pharaoh; the "princes of Zoan and Noph" were his counsellors; and, if the prophecy touches him at all, it is as the deceived and misled Pharaoh of ver. 11, not as the "fierce king"

---

[1] Herod., ii. 152.
[2] Rawlinson, "History of Ancient Egypt," vol. ii., p. 443.

of ver. 4. The same may be said of his successors, Shabatak and Tirhakah, who were closely connected with Noph (here Napata), and were recognised as legitimate Pharaohs. It is to an Assyrian, not to an Ethiopian, conqueror that the prophecy must refer, and hence doubtless the introduction of Assyria by name into the later part of the prophecy, which in a certain sense balances the earlier (vers. 23—25). Two successive Assyrian monarchs conquered Egypt, Esarhaddon, and Asshur-bani-pal. Either of the two would correspond well to the description of the "fierce king and cruel lord." Esarhaddon, who had Manasseh brought before him with a hook passed through his jaws (2 Chron. xxxiii. 11), who broke up Egypt into twenty governments and changed the names of the towns,[1] who usually executed rebels, and is said by his son to have appointed governors over the various provinces of Egypt for the express purpose of slaying and plundering its people,[2] was certainly a severe and harsh monarch, who might well answer to the description of Isaiah; and Asshur-bani-pal, his successor, who rivetted the Assyrian yoke on the reluctant country, was a yet more cruel and relentless tyrant. Asshur-bani-pal burnt alive his own brother, Saul-Mugina, caused several of his prisoners to be chained and flayed, tore out the tongues of others by the roots, punished

---

[1] G. Smith, "History of Asshur-bani-pal," pp. 34, 35.
[2] Ibid., p. 16.

many by mutilation, and was altogether the most cruel and bloodthirsty of all the Assyrian monarchs of whom any record has come down to us.[1] It is probably his conquest of Egypt in B.C. 668—666 which Isaiah's prophecy announces, though it is quite possible that Isaiah may have himself expected an earlier accomplishment of the prediction.[2]

"In the year that Tartan came unto Ashdod, when Sargon, the king of Assyria, sent him, and fought against Ashdod, and took it, at the same time spake the Lord by Isaiah, the son of Amoz, saying, Go and loose the sackcloth from off thy loins, and put off thy shoe from thy foot. And he did so, walking naked and barefoot. And the Lord said, Like as my servant Isaiah hath walked naked and barefoot three years for a sign and wonder upon Egypt and upon Ethiopia, so shall the king of Assyria lead away the Egyptians prisoners, and the Ethiopians captives, young and old, naked and barefoot, even with their buttocks uncovered, to the shame of Egypt. And they shall be afraid and ashamed of Ethiopia their expectation, and of Egypt their glory. And the inhabitant of this isle shall say in that day, Behold, such is our expectation, whither we flee for help to be delivered from the king of Assyria: and how shall we escape?" (Isa. xx. 1—6).

---

[1] See "Ancient Monarchies," vol. ii., p. 206.
[2] As Mr. Cheyne supposes: "Comment on Isaiah," vol. i., pp. 112, 113.

The general warning contained in Isaiah's "burden of Egypt" failed altogether of its intended effect. In Israel Hoshea, about B.C. 724, entered into alliance with Shabak (So), and thereby provoked the ruin which fell both on himself and his country. The lesson was lost on Hezekiah and his counsellors, who, as the attitude of the Assyrians became more and more threatening, inclined more and more to follow Hoshea's example and place themselves under the protection of Egypt. Egypt was at this time, as already explained, closely connected with Ethiopia, which under Piankhi, Shabak, Shabatok, and Tirhakah, exercised the rights of a suzerain power, permitting, however, to certain native Egyptian princes a delegated sovereignty. Hence the close connection in which we find Ethiopia and Egypt placed in the present prophecy. In the year that the Assyrian Tartan, or commander-in-chief, took Ashdod, having been assigned the task by Sargon, king of Assyria, the successor of Shalmaneser IV., and father of Sennacherib—probably the year B.C. 714—Isaiah was directed to renew his warning against trust in these African powers. They had become the "glory" and the "expectation" of his countrymen, whither they were ready to "flee for help" (vers. 5, 6). In order to impress the Jews with the folly of their vain hopes, Isaiah was instructed to announce a coming victory of Assyria over combined Egypt and Ethiopia, the result of which would be a great removal of captives, belonging to both nations, from the banks of the Nile to those of the Tigris, to the great "shame" of the conquered and the great glory of the conquerors. To arrest the attention of his nation, he was to take the garb of a prisoner himself, and to go barefoot and "naked," *i.e.*, clad in a single scant tunic, for three years, at the end of which time his prophecy would be accomplished. The prophecy seems to have had its first accomplishment when, in B.C. 711, Ashdod revolted from Assyria, under promise of support from the Ethiopian Pharaoh of the period, and was captured, with its garrison, which is likely to have consisted in part of Egyptians and Ethiopians. We are expressly told that the prisoners were on this occasion transported into Assyria, their place being supplied by captives taken in some of Sargon's eastern wars.[1]

Ten years later, in the reign of Sennacherib, there was another occasion of collision between Assyria and Egypt in a war provoked by the revolt of Ekron. In the battle of Eltekeh (B.C. 701) both Ethiopians and Egyptians are expressly declared to have been engaged, and many prisoners of both nations to have been taken.[2] These were, no doubt, carried off by the conqueror.

Later, in the wars of Esarhaddon and Asshurbani-pal with Tirhakah, there must have been nu-

---
[1] "Ancient Monarchies," vol. ii., p. 147.
[2] "Records of the Past," vol. i., pp. 36, 37.

merous occasions of a similar kind.[1] The entire course of the struggle between Assyria on the one hand and Ethiopia and Egypt on the other was adverse to the latter people until the strength of Assyria collapsed at home, and she (about B C. 650) withdrew her forces from Egypt to the defence of her own territory.

"Woe to the rebellious children, saith the Lord, that take counsel, but not of Me; and that cover with a covering, but not of My Spirit, that they may add sin to sin; that walk to go down into Egypt, and have not asked at My mouth, to strengthen themselves in the strength of Pharaoh, and to trust in the shadow of Egypt! Therefore shall the strength of Pharaoh be your shame, and the trust in the shadow of Egypt your confusion. For his princes were at Zoan, and his ambassadors came to Hanes. They were all ashamed of a people that could not profit them, nor be an help nor profit, but a shame and also a reproach. The burden of the beasts of the south: into the land of trouble and anguish, from whence come the young and old lion, the viper and fiery flying serpent, they will carry their riches upon the shoulders of young asses, and their treasures upon the bunches of camels, to a people that shall not profit them. For the Egyptians shall help in vain, and to no purpose; therefore have I cried con-

---

[1] See Mr. George Smith's "History of Asshur-bani-pal," pp. 16, 19, 23, 54, etc.

cerning this,—Their strength is to sit still" (Isa. xxx. 1—7).

"Woe to them that go down to Egypt for help; and stay on horses, and trust in chariots, because they are many; and in horsemen, because they are very strong; but they look not unto the Holy One of Israel, neither seek the Lord! . . . Now the Egyptians are men, and not God, and their horses flesh, and not spirit. When the Lord shall stretch out His hand, both he that helpeth shall fall, and he that is holpen shall fall down, and they all shall fall together. For thus hath the Lord spoken unto me, Like as the lion and the young lion roaring on his prey, when a multitude of shepherds is called forth against him, he will not be afraid of their voice nor abase himself for the noise of them; so shall the Lord of hosts come down to fight for Mount Zion and for the hill thereof. As birds flying, so will the Lord of hosts defend Jerusalem; . . . He will preserve it" (Isa. xxxi. 1—5).

Matters have now progressed a stage. Isaiah's warnings are not only unheeded, but set at nought. Alarmed at the advances that Sennacherib has made and is making, convinced, not perhaps without reason, that the policy of Assyria is to leave him the mere shadow of independence, Hezekiah has taken the final plunge. Declining to ask counsel of God's prophet (ver. 1), he has sent ambassadors of high rank (ver. 4), accompanied by a train of camels and asses, laden with rich presents, (ver. 6), to the court of the vassal Pharaoh to whom is committed the government of Lower Egypt. "His" (*i.e.*, Hezekiah's) "princes are at Zoan" (Tanis); "his ambassadors have come to Hanes." He has made application for a force of chariots and cavalry (ch. xxxvi. 9). He has probably sent a prayer to the Ethiopian suzerain of the country, requesting him to move to his relief. The thing is done, and cannot be undone; and it remains only for the prophet to make a declaration, first that it has been done against God's will (vers. 1, 9, 12), and secondly, that it will be of no avail—nothing will come of it—the Egyptians will give no effectual help (vers. 5, 7). The historical chapters of Isaiah, especially chapters xxxvi. and xxxvii., are the sequel to this intimation. They show that Hezekiah received no help at all from the subordinate Pharaoh, who was probably Shabatok, and that though Tirhakah did move on his behalf (ch. xxxvii. 9), yet that he neither engaged the forces of Sennacherib, nor seriously troubled him. The relief of Hezekiah, and the relief of Egypt itself—whose subjection to Assyria was thereby deferred for a generation—came from another quarter. When Hezekiah gave up his trust in any arm of flesh, and made his appeal to God, spreading before Him the blasphemous letter of Sennacherib (ibid. vers. 14— 20), then Isaiah was commissioned to assure him of a miraculous deliverance. "Then" ("that night,"

2 Kings xix. 35), " the angel of the Lord went forth, and smote in the camp of the Assyrians an hundred and fourscore and five thousand ; and when they arose early in the morning, behold, they were all dead corpses " (Isa. xxxvii. 36). The deliverance itself, and its miraculous, or at any rate its marvellous character, was acknowledged by the Egyptians, no less than by the Israelites. When, two hundred and fifty years afterwards, Herodotus visited Egypt, he was informed that "Sennacherib, king of the Arabians and Assyrians, having marched a great army into Egypt, was met at Pelusium by the Egyptian monarch. As the two hosts lay there opposite one another, there came in the night a number of field-mice, which devoured all the quivers and bow strings of the enemy, and ate the thongs by which they managed their shields. Next morning they commenced their flight, and great multitudes fell, as they had no arms with which to defend themselves."[1]

" In that day shall five cities in the land of Egypt speak the language of Canaan, and swear to the Lord of hosts ; one shall be called, The city of destruction. In that day shall there be an altar to the Lord in the midst of the land of Egypt, and a pillar at the border thereof to the Lord. And it shall be for a sign and for a witness unto the Lord of hosts in the land of Egypt : for they shall cry unto the Lord because of the oppressors, and He shall send them a

---

[1] Herod., ii. 141.

saviour, and a great one, and he shall deliver them. And the Lord shall be known to Egypt, and the Egyptians shall know the Lord in that day, and shall do sacrifice and oblation ; yea, they shall vow a vow unto the Lord, and perform it. And the Lord shall smite Egypt : He shall smite and heal it ; and they shall return even to the Lord, and He shall be entreated of them, and shall heal them" (Isa. xix. 18—22).

This prophecy has been called a mere expression of Isaiah's earnest *wish* for the conversion of Egypt to the worship of the true God ;[1] but it is at any rate a wish which had a remarkable fulfilment. About the year B.C. 170, Onias, the son of Onias III., the high-priest, quitted Palestine, and sought refuge with Ptolemy Philometor, who readily protected him on account of the hostility between the two royal houses of Egypt and of Syria. While a refugee at his court, Onias, regarding the position of his brethren in Palestine, oppressed by Antiochus Epiphanes, as well-nigh hopeless, conceived the idea of founding and maintaining a temple in Egypt itself, which should be free from the corruptions then creeping in at Jerusalem, and should be a rallying-point to the Jewish nation, should the temple on Mount Zion be destroyed or made a heathen fane. Under these circumstances he addressed an appeal to Ptolemy and his wife Cleopatra for the grant of a

---
[1] Stanley, " Lectures on the Jewish Church," vol. iii., p. 251.

site. "In the district of Heliopolis, a part of Egypt already consecrated by the memory of Moses (Gen. xli. 45), he had observed a spot where a sanctuary of Bubastis (Pasht), a goddess of the country, was languishing among the thousand other Egyptian sanctuaries. This place he requested for himself, and it was reported that Ptolemy granted it with the jesting remark that he wondered how Onias could think of making a sanctuary out of a spot which, though inhabited by sacred animals, was yet in the Judæan sense polluted, for the animals were among those reckoned unclean by the Judæans. *In the sanctuary itself was placed an altar resembling that at Jerusalem.* Instead of the seven-lighted candlestick, which seems to have been regarded as too holy to be imitated, a single golden lamp was suspended in it by a golden chain. The sacred house was built somewhat in the form of a tower"—the general style of the building being apparently not Jewish, but Egyptian[1]—"the fore-court was enclosed with a wall of brick and gates of stone, and the whole of the fortified little town, with the district which gathered round the temple, was probably called Oneiôn."[2]

This temple continued to exist from B.C. 170 to B.C. 73, when it was destroyed by the Romans. It was greatly venerated by the bulk of the Egyptian Jews,

---
[1] Stanley, "Lectures on the Jewish Church," vol. iii, p. 252.
[2] Ewald, "History of Israel," vol. v., p. 356, E.T. Compare Joseph., "Ant. Jud.," xiii. 3, § 2.

who brought thither their sacrifices and their offerings. Jews flocked to the towns in its neighbourhood; and it may well be, though the actual fact cannot be proved, that then at least " five cities in the land of Egypt spoke" (Hebrew) "the language of Canaan," one of them being Ir-ha-kheres, "the city of the sun," the ancient Heliopolis.[1] At the same time the great synagogue of Alexandria, at the extreme "border" of the land, where it was most commonly approached by strangers, stood "as a pillar" (ch. xix. 19) "for a sign and for a witness unto the Lord of hosts," showing that Jehovah was worshipped in the land openly, and with the goodwill of the Government, and indicating that Egypt—so long Jehovah's enemy—had been, at least partially, converted to His service.

---

[1] See Mr. R. S. Poole's article on IR-HA-HERES in Smith's "Dict. of the Bible," vol. i., p. 870.

CHAPTER X.

THE NOTICES OF EGYPT IN THE BOOKS OF JEREMIAH AND EZEKIEL.

CHAPTER X.

*THE NOTICES OF EGYPT IN THE BOOKS OF
JEREMIAH AND EZEKIEL.*

THE prophecies of Jeremiah have suffered greatly by disarrangement; and the historical notices which they contain, more especially those that concern Egypt, are wholly out of their proper chronological order. We propose, therefore, in the present paper to follow the actual order of time rather than that of Jeremiah's chapters according to our translators' arrangement,[1] and we consequently commence with one of the latest of his notices, namely, that contained in the earlier portion of his forty-sixth chapter:—

" The word of the Lord which came to Jeremiah the prophet against the Gentiles, against Egypt, against the army of Pharaoh-Necho, king of Egypt, which was by the river Euphrates in Carchemish, which Nebuchadnezzar, king of Babylon, smote in the fourth year of Jehoiakim, the son of Josiah, king

---

[1] Our translators follow the Hebrew. The Septuagint arrangement is quite different.

of Judah. Order ye the buckler and shield, and draw near to battle. Harness the horses; and get up, ye horsemen, and stand forth with your helmets; furbish the spears, and put on the brigandines. Wherefore have I seen them dismayed and turned away back? and their mighty ones are beaten down, and are fled apace, and look not back: for fear was round about, saith the Lord. Let not the swift flee away, nor the mighty man escape; they shall stumble and fall towards the north, by the river Euphrates. Who is this that cometh up as a flood, whose waters are moved as the rivers? Egypt riseth up like a flood, and his waters are moved like the rivers; and he saith, I will go up and cover the earth; I will destroy the city and the inhabitants thereof. Come up, ye horses, and rage, ye chariots; and let the mighty men come forth; the Ethiopians and the Libyans, that handle the shield; and the Lydians, that handle and bend the bow. For this is the day of the Lord God of hosts, a day of vengeance, that he may avenge him of his adversaries; and the sword shall devour, and it shall be satiate and made drunk with their blood; for the Lord God of hosts hath a sacrifice in the north country by the river Euphrates. Go up into Gilead, and take balm, O virgin, the daughter of Egypt; in vain shalt thou use many medicines; for thou shalt not be cured. The nations have heard of thy shame, and thy cry hath filled the land; for the mighty man hath stumbled against the mighty, and they are fallen both together" (Jer. xlvi. 1—12).

In this passage we have the fullest account that has come down to us of one of the most important among the "decisive battles of the world." The contending powers are Egypt and Babylon, the contending princes Neko (Pharaoh-Necho), the son of Psamatik I., and Nebuchadnezzar, the son of Nabopolassar—the founder of the second empire of the Chaldæans. We have already seen[1] how Neko, having (in B.C. 608) defeated Josiah, king of Judah, at Megiddo, on the border of the great plain of Esdraelon, pressed forward to meet the "house with which he had war at Carchemish by Euphrates" (2 Chron. xxxv. 20). Complete success for the time attended his expedition. He made himself master of the whole tract of territory intervening between the "river of Egypt" (Wady-el-Arish) on the one hand and the river Euphrates on the other (2 Kings xxiv. 7). Syria in its widest extent, Phœnicia, Philistia, and Judæa submitted to him. It seemed as if the days of the Thothmeses and Amenhoteps were about to return, and Egypt to be once more the predominant power in the Eastern world, the "lady of nations," the sovereign at one and the same time of Africa and of Asia. Had Babylon acquiesced in the loss of territory, her prestige would have been gone, and her empire would probably have soon

---
[1] Supra, p. 358.

crumbled into dust. Egypt and Media would have stood face to face as the two rivals for supremacy; and possibly the entire course of the world's later history might have been changed.

But Nabopolassar appreciated aright the importance of the crisis, and before Egypt had had time to consolidate her power in the newly-conquered provinces, resolved on making a great effort to recover them. In the year B.C. 605—three years after Neko's great success—having collected his troops and made his preparations, he sent his son and heir, Nebuchadnezzar, at the head of a large army, to reconquer the lost territory. Nebuchadnezzar marched upon Carchemish, the strong frontier fortress near the Euphrates, which had originally been the capital of the early Hittite kingdom, and the site of which is now marked by the ruins called "Jerablus" or "Jerabus."[1] Here he found Neko encamped at the head of a considerable force, in part, no doubt, Egyptians, but mainly Ethiopians, Libyans, and Greco-Carians from Asia Minor, perhaps the "Lydians" of Jeremiah (ver. 9).[2] The battle poetically described by Jeremiah was fought. The Egyptian force of foot, horse, and chariots was

---

[1] Sayce, "Ancient Empires of the East," p. 425.
[2] "Lud" in the Hebrew Scriptures ordinarily designates an African people (see Gen. x. 13; 1 Chron. i. 11; Isa. lxvi. 19; Ezek. xxx. 5). But here the "Lydians" may be meant. Gyges had furnished the original Greco-Carian force.

completely defeated; a great carnage took place (ver. 10); and the few survivors fled away in dismay (ver. 5), evacuating province after province, and retiring within their own frontier. Nebuchadnezzar followed on their traces, at least as far south as Jerusalem, where he received the submission of Jehoiakim (2 Kings xxiv. 1), and from which he carried off a portion of the temple treasures (Dan. i. 1). He would probably have gone further and invaded Egypt had not news reached him (late in B.C. 605) of his father's decease, which necessitated his own immediate return to his capital. Accompanied by a small force lightly equipped, he crossed the desert by way of Damascus and Tadmor, while the heavy-armed troops, the baggage, and the prisoners made their way to Babylon by the usual but circuitous route, down the valley of the Orontes, across Northern Syria to Carchemish, and then along the banks of the Euphrates.

We have one profane account of this expedition, entering far less into details than Jeremiah, but in complete accord with his statements, and supplying various points of interest, which have been worked into the above narrative. The Babylonian historian, Berosus,[1] as quoted by Josephus, says, speaking of Nebuchadnezzar: "When his father, Nabopolassar, heard that the satrap appointed to govern Egypt,

---

[1] Fr. 14 in the "Fr. Hist. Gr." of C. Müller, vol. ii., p. 506.

and the districts of Cœlesyria and Phœnicia, had revolted from him, as he was not himself able any longer to endure hardships, he assigned a certain portion of his army to his son, Nebuchadnezzar, who was in the flower of his youth, and sent him against the rebel. And when Nebuchadnezzar had fallen in with him, and engaged him in battle, he defeated him, and from this beginning proceeded to bring the country under his own rule. Now it chanced that his father, Nabopolassar, just at this time fell sick, and departed this life, having reigned one-and-twenty years. Nebuchadnezzar shortly after heard of his father's decease, and, having arranged the affairs of Egypt and the other countries, and appointed certain of his friends to conduct to Babylon the captives which he had taken from the Jews, the Phœnicians, the Syrians, and the parts about Egypt, together with the heavy-armed troops and the baggage, started himself with a very small escort, and, travelling by the way of the wilderness, reached Babylon."

"The word of the Lord that came to Jeremiah the prophet against the Philistines, before that Pharaoh smote Gaza. Thus saith the Lord, Behold, waters rise up out of the north, and shall be an overflowing flood, and shall overflow the land, and all that is therein; the city and them that dwell therein; then the men shall cry, and all the inhabitants of the land shall howl. At the noise of the stamping of the hoofs of his strong horses, at the rushing of his chariots, and at the rumbling of his wheels, the fathers shall not look back to their children for feebleness of hands; because of the day that cometh to spoil all the Philistines, and to cut off from Tyrus and Zidon every helper that remaineth; for the Lord will spoil the Philistines, the remnant of the country of Caphtor. Baldness is come upon Gaza; Ashkelon is cut off with the remnant of their valley: how long wilt thou cut thyself? O thou sword of the Lord, how long will it be ere thou be quiet? Put up thyself into thy scabbard; rest and be still. How can it be quiet, seeing the Lord hath given it a charge against Ashkelon, and against the sea-shore? There hath He appointed it" (Jer. xlvii. 1—7).

We are, first of all, informed here that a certain prophecy was delivered, "before that Pharaoh smote Gaza." In this statement it is implied that, at some date in the ministry of Jeremiah, the strong Philistine town of Gaza (Jud. xvi. 1—3) was taken by a king of Egypt. Now the kings of Egypt contemporary with Jeremiah's ministry would seem to have been Psamatik I., Neko, Psamatik II., and Uaphra or "Pharaoh-Hophra." Does it appear from profane sources that Gaza was besieged and taken by any one of these monarchs?

This question may be answered in the affirmative. Herodotus tells us that after the battle of Magdolum (Megiddo), Neko took "Kadytis," a large city in

Syria.[1] This Kadytis he afterwards describes as lying upon the coast between Phœnicia and Lake Serbonis.[2] It was at one time identified with Jerusalem, because the Arabs call that city "Al Kods"—"the Holy"; and more recently it has been conjectured to represent the Hittite city of "Kadesh" on the Orontes;[3] but its position on or near the sea militates against both these hypotheses. Gaza is called "Gazetu" in the hieroglyphical inscriptions of Egypt,[4] and "Khazitu" in the cuneiform inscriptions of Assyria, of which forms "Kadytis" is a fair rendering. Hence recent editors of Herodotus regard it as "plain" that the Kadytis, which he says that Neko took, was Gaza.[5]

It is doubtful whether the remainder of the prophecy refers in any way to Egypt. The "waters that rise up out of the north" are usually taken by the commentators for the army of Nebuchadnezzar, either when he invaded Syria after the battle of Carchemish (B.C. 605), or subsequently when he advanced to the sieges of Jerusalem and Tyre (B.C. 598). The description in ver. 3 would suit a Babylonian army as well as an Egyptian, and the characteristic of "noise" seems to belong to Babylon *especially* (chs. iv. 29; viii. 16; Ezek. xxvi. 10).

---

[1] Herod., ii. 159.   [2] Ibid., iii. 5.
[3] Lenormant, "Manuel d'Histoire Ancienne," vol. ii., p. 391.
[4] "Records of the Past," vol. ii., p. 115; Brugsch, "Geschichte Ægyptens," p. 295.
[5] Sayce, "Ancient Empires," p. 216, note 4.

There is not, however, any distinct evidence that Nebuchadnezzar at any time led a hostile expedition into Philistia, while we know of Neko that he did so; and as his expedition seems to have been made on his return from Carchemish, his army would on this occasion have "risen up out of the north" (ver. 2). The note of time in ver. 1 is also more apposite if Neko's expedition is intended, since the prophet would then have inserted the date, in order to draw attention to the fact that the word of the Lord announcing a great invasion of Philistia came to him before the event.

"And King Zedekiah, the son of Josiah, reigned instead of Coniah, the son of Jehoiakim. . . . Then Pharaoh's army was come forth out of Egypt; and when the Chaldæans that besieged Jerusalem heard tidings of them, they departed from Jerusalem. Then came the word of the Lord unto the prophet Jeremiah, saying, Thus saith the Lord, the God of Israel, Thus shall ye say unto the king of Judah that sent you to inquire of me, Behold, Pharaoh's army, which is come forth to help you, shall return to Egypt into their own land. And the Chaldæans shall come again, and fight against this city, and take it, and burn it with fire" (Jer. xxxvii. 1—10).

"He (Zedekiah) rebelled against him (Nebuchadnezzar) in sending his ambassadors into Egypt, that they might give him horses and much people. Shall he prosper? Shall he escape that doeth such things?

Or shall he break the covenant, and be delivered? As I live, saith the Lord, surely in the place where the king dwelleth that made him king, whose oath he despised, even with him in the midst of Babylon he shall die. Neither shall Pharaoh with his mighty army and great company make for him in the war, by casting mounts and building forts, to cut off many persons" (Ezek. xvii. 15—17).

The Pharaoh contemporary with the later years of Zedekiah, the last king of Judah, who reigned from B.C. 597 to B.C. 586, was undoubtedly Ua-ap-ra,[1] whom the Greeks called "Apries,"[2] and whom Jeremiah in one place speaks of as "Pharaoh-Hophra" (ch. xliv. 30). Apries ascended the throne in B.C. 591, and reigned alone nineteen years (to B.C. 572), after which he was for six years more joint-king with Amasis.[3] It would seem that very soon after his accession Zedekiah made overtures to him for an alliance (Ezek. xvii. 15), transferring to him the allegiance which he owed to Babylon, and making a request for a large body of troops, horse and foot (ibid.). It is in accordance with the bold and aggressive character assigned to Apries by the Greeks[4] to

---

[1] Brugsch ("Geschichte Ægyptens," p. 734) gives the name as "Uah-ab-ra," Birch ("Egypt from the Earliest Times," p. 180) as "Uah-hap-ra."

[2] Herod., ii. 161; Diod. Sic., i. 68. Manetho, however, calls him "Uaphris."

[3] Wiedemann, "Geschichte Ægyptens," p. 121.

[4] Herod., l.s.c.; Diod. Sic., l.s.c.

find that he at once accepted Zedekiah's offer, and prepared to bear his part in the war. "Pharaoh's army went forth out of Egypt" (Jer. xxxvii. 5) with the object of "helping" Zedekiah (ibid. ver. 7); and the movement was so far successful that the army of the Chaldæans, which had commenced the siege of Jerusalem, "broke up from before it for fear of Pharaoh's army" (ibid. ver. 11). Nebuchadnezzar, who was directing the siege, marched away to encounter the Egyptians, and either terrified them into a retreat, or actually engaged and defeated them.[1] The foundation was thus laid of that enmity between the two kings which, later in Egyptian history, is found to have had very important consequences. Apries, for the time, submitted, and led his army back within his own frontier, leaving the unfortunate Jewish monarch to his fate.

"Then came the word of the Lord unto Jeremiah in Tahpanhes, saying, Take great stones in thine hand, and hide them in the clay in the brick-kiln, which is at the entry of Pharaoh's house in Tahpanhes, in the sight of the men of Judah; and say unto them, Thus saith the Lord of hosts, the God of Israel, Behold, I will send and take Nebuchadnezzar, the king of Babylon, my servant, and will set his throne upon these stones that I have hid; and he shall spread his royal pavilion over them. And when he cometh, he shall smite the land of

---

[1] So Josephus, "Ant. Jud.," x. 7, § 3.

Egypt, and deliver such as are for death to death; and such as are for captivity to captivity; and such as are for the sword to the sword. And I will kindle a fire in the houses of the gods of Egypt; and he shall burn them, and carry them away captives; and he shall array himself with the land of Egypt, as a shepherd putteth on his garment; and he shall go forth from thence in peace. He shall break also the images of Beth-shemesh, that is in the land of Egypt; and the houses of the gods of the Egyptians shall he burn with fire" (Jer. xliii. 8—13).

"The word that the Lord spake to Jeremiah the prophet, how Nebuchadnezzar, king of Babylon, should come and smite the land of Egypt. Declare ye in Egypt, and publish in Migdol, and publish in Noph and in Tahpanhes; say ye, Stand fast, and prepare thee; for the sword shall devour round about thee. Why are thy valiant men swept away? They stood not because the Lord did drive them. He made many to fall; yea, one fell upon another; and they said, Arise, and let us go again to our own people and to the land of our nativity from the oppressing sword. They did cry there, Pharaoh, king of Egypt, is but a noise; he hath passed the time appointed. . . . O thou daughter dwelling in Egypt, furnish thyself to go into captivity; for Noph shall be waste and desolate without an inhabitant. Egypt is like a very fair heifer; but destruction cometh; it cometh out of the north. Also her hired

men are in the midst of her like fatted bullocks;
for they also are turned back and are fled away
together; they did not stand, because the day of
their calamity was come upon them, and the time
of their visitation. . . . The Lord of hosts, the God
of Israel saith, Behold, I will punish the multitude
of No, and Pharaoh, and Egypt, with their gods,
and their kings; even Pharaoh, and all them that
trust in him; and I will deliver them into the hand
of those that seek their lives, and into the hand of
Nebuchadnezzar, king of Babylon, and into the hand
of his servants: and afterward it shall be inhabited,
as in the days of old, saith the Lord" (Jer. xlvi.
13—26).

On the fact of there having been at least one
invasion of Egypt by Nebuchadnezzar subsequently
to his capture of Jerusalem in B.C. 586, it is only
necessary to refer the reader to ch. vii. of the
First Part of this work.[1] It was there shown that
two wholly independent documents, one Egyptian,
the other Babylonian, prove the invasion to have
taken place, while the Egyptian one, though seeking
to minimize the success of the invaders, necessarily
implies an occupation of the whole of Egypt. The
general Hor, who is "governor of the regions of the
south," admits that the Asiatics penetrated to the
extreme southern border of Egypt (comp. Ezek. xxix.
10; xxx. 6), and claims credit for not having "let

---

[1] See pp. 117—120.

them advance quite into Nubia."[1] His account of his careful restoration of the temple of Kneph at Elephantine[2] indicates that it had suffered damage at the hands of the invaders, and is a comment on the expression "the houses of the gods of the Egyptians shall he burn with fire" (Jer. xliii. 13). The representation of the army by which Egypt was defended as one of "hired" men (ibid. xlvi. 21), who said one to another, when they were defeated, "Arise, and let us go again to our own people and to the land of our nativity from the oppressing sword" (ibid. ver. 16), accords well with all that we know of the Egyptian military force of the time, which consisted, not of native soldiers, but of foreign mercenaries, Ethiopians, Libyans, Carians, and Greeks.[3] The date of the expedition, Nebuchadnezzar's thirty-seventh year,[4] or B.C. 568, falls exactly into the time when Apries and Amasis were joint-kings of Egypt, and explains the apparent discrepancy between the two documents, one of which speaks of Apries as king, while the other certainly did not name Apries, and probably named Amasis.[5] The conjoint reign would

---

[1] "Records of the Past," vol. vi., p. 83.

[2] Ibid., p. 82, lines 25, 36, 40.

[3] Herod. ii. 163; Jer. xlvi. 9, etc.

[4] "Transactions of Society of Biblical Archæology," vol. vii., p. 222.

[5] The name is partially obliterated, but evidently ended in "-su." The Egyptian name of Amasis, Aahmes, terminated in s. That of Apries, Ua-ap-ra, contained no s.

even seem to be indicated by the mention of "kings" in ch. xlvi. 25.

"I will give Pharaoh-Hophra, king of Egypt, into the hand of his enemies, and into the hand of them that seek his life, as I gave Zedekiah, king of Judah, into the hand of Nebuchadnezzar, king of Babylon, his enemy, and that sought his life" (Jer. xl. 30).

There would seem to be no doubt that this prophecy was fulfilled to the letter, and that Pharaoh-Hophra (Ua-apra) fell into the power of his enemies and suffered a violent death. But it is not altogether clear who these enemies were, or how his death was brought about. Herodotus relates[1] that the reverses which befell him arose out of an unsuccessful expedition against Cyrênê, in which Apries was thought to have intentionally sacrificed the lives of some thousands of his soldiers. A mutiny followed, and Amasis, having been sent to put it down, was induced to place himself at its head. The result was a civil war, in which the rebel chief was successful. Apries fell into his hands, and was at first treated with kindness, allowed to inhabit the royal palace[2] and (we must suppose) to retain the title of king. But after six years, during which both monarchs reigned, but Amasis alone governed, dissatisfaction with this condition of things showed itself among the Egyptians, who persuaded Amasis to allow them to put Apries to death. The story is not, intrinsically, very pro-

---
[1] Herod., ii. 161—163.   [2] Ibid., 169.

bable; and it is contradicted by Josephus, who
ascribes the execution of Apries to Nebuchadnezzar.[1]
That monarch may not improbably have borne Apries
a grudge on account of the aid which he gave to
Zedekiah, and also of his aggressions upon the
Phoenician cities,[2] and, though the adversary with
whom he contended in the field may have been
Amasis, he may yet have let his main vengeance
fall upon Apries, whom he no doubt looked on as
a rebel, as he had looked upon Neko.[3] Amasis
may have obtained easier terms of peace by the
surrender of his fellow-king, or may even have been
allowed to retain the throne in consequence of his
complaisance. Most probably he accepted the position
of a vassal monarch, a position which he may have
retained until Nabonidus was threatened by Cyrus
(B.C. 547), or even until the fall of Babylon in
B.C. 538. During this period Egypt was a "base
kingdom" (Ezek. xxix. 14), "the basest of the kingdoms" (ibid. ver. 15), if its former exaltation was
kept in view.

---

[1] "Ant. Jud.," x. 9, § 7.
[2] Herod., ii. 161; Diod. Sic., i. 68.
[3] Berosus, Fr. 14.

CHAPTER XI.

NOTICES OF EGYPT IN DANIEL.

CHAPTER XI.

NOTICES OF EGYPT IN DANIEL.

THE notices of Egypt in the Book of Daniel have the peculiarity that they are absolutely and entirely prophetical. Daniel is not individually brought into any contact with Egypt, nor does Egypt play any part in the stirring events of the time wherein he lives. Egypt had, in fact, fallen to the rank of a very second-rate power after the battle of Carchemish (B.C. 605), and counted for little in the political struggles of the time, which had for their locality the great Iranian plateau, together with the broad valley of the Tigris and the Euphrates. Daniel, who was contemporary, as he tells us (chs. i.—vi.), with Nebuchadnezzar, Belshazzar, Darius the Mede, and Cyrus the Great, must have died about B.C. 534, or at any rate before B.C. 529—the year of Cyrus' decease. His notices of Egypt belong to a date more than two centuries later. It is given him to see in vision a sort of sketch of the history of the world from his own time to the coming of the kingdom of the Messiah ; and in this "apocalyptic vision" or rather series of visions, the future of Egypt is placed before him, in some detail, during a space of some century and a half, from about B.C. 323 to B.C. 168.

It is scarcely necessary to say that the genuineness and authenticity of the entire Book of Daniel have been fiercely assailed, both in remote times and in our own day. But the arguments of the assailants have never been regarded as of any weight by the Church; and the Book has maintained its place in the Canon through all ecclesiastical ages and throughout Christendom. It is impossible in a paper like the present to enter into this great controversy, which has employed the pens of more than twenty critics of repute during the present century, and which cannot be said to have been set at rest even by the admirable labours of Auberlen, Hengstenberg, and Pusey. We shall here, of necessity, assume the genuineness and authenticity of the Book, and especially of the chapter (ch. xi.) which bears upon the history of Egypt; we shall regard it, not as a *vaticinium post eventum*— the composition of a nameless author in the time of Antiochus Epiphanes—but as the genuine utterance of Daniel himself in the year to which he assigns it —"the first year of Darius the Mede" (ch. xi. 1), or B.C. 538-7. As the prophecy is too long to be conveniently treated as a whole, we shall break it up into portions, and endeavour to show how far its various parts are confirmed or illustrated by profane authors.

"Now I will show thee the truth. Behold, there shall stand up yet three kings in Persia ; and the fourth shall be far richer than they all ; and by his strength through his riches he shall stir up all against the realm of Grecia. And a mighty king shall stand up, that shall rule with great dominion, and do according to his will. And when he shall stand up, his kingdom shall be broken, and shall be divided toward the four winds of heaven, and not to his posterity, nor according to the dominion which he ruled ; for his kingdom shall be plucked up, even for others beside those" (Dan. xi. 2—4).

This first section of the prophecy has no direct bearing upon Egypt. Its object is to bridge the interval between the date of the vision and the point at which the history of Egypt is to be taken up. The date of the vision is B.C. 538-7, the first year of Darius the Mede in Babylon, and the first of Cyrus (by whom Darius had been set up) in Persia. Egyptian history is to be taken up from B.C. 323, at which point, after a long period of subjection to Persia, Egypt became once more an independent and important kingdom. What are to be the main events, the great landmarks, of the interval ? The angel who speaks to Daniel thus enumerates them : (1) There will be three kings in Persia, followed by a fourth richer and stronger than any of them, who will lead a great expedition into Greece. (2) A mighty king will stand up, greater apparently than even the

Persian kings, who will "rule with great dominion, and do according to his will." (3) After this king has "stood up" for a while, his kingdom will be broken, "divided toward the four winds of heaven," not descending to his posterity, either as a whole, or in any of its fragments, but falling into the hands of "others beside those"—*i.e.*, of persons not his descendants. Now, profane history relates[1] that three kings ruled in Persia after Cyrus the Great, viz., Cambyses (from B.C. 529 to B.C. 522), Bardes or Smerdis (during seven months of B.C. 522), and Darius, the son of Hystaspes (from B.C. 521 to B.C. 486), and that these were then followed by Xerxes, the son of Darius,[2] under whom Persia was at the height of its power and prosperity, until in his fifth year he "stirred up all against the realm of Grecia," and made that great expedition which still remains one of the most marvellous events in the world's entire history. This expedition fell into B.C. 480, and was followed by a gradual diminution of Persian power, and by wars of no great moment, until, in B.C. 335, a "mighty king" stood up, viz., Alexander the Great, who ruled a greater dominion than had been held by any previous monarch, since it reached from the Adriatic to the Sutlej, and from the Danube to Syene. The wide sovereignty and autocratic pride

---

[1] See especially Herod., ii. 1, iii. 67, 68, confirmed by the Behistun inscription.

[2] Herod., vii. 4, *et. seq.*

of Alexander are well expressed by the words "that shall rule with great dominion, and do according to his will" (ver. 3); for Alexander brooked no restraint, and was practically a more absolute despot than any Persian king had ever been. At his death, as is well known, his kingdom was "broken up." Though he left behind him an illegitimate son, Hercules, and had also a posthumous child by Roxana, called Alexander, yet neither of them ever succeeded to any portion of his dominions. These fell at first to the ten generals, Ptolemy, Pithon, Antigonus, Eumenes, Leonnatus, Lysimachus, Menander, Asander, Philotas, Laomedon, and ultimately to Ptolemy, Seleucus, Antipater, Antigonus, Eumenes, Clitus, and Cassander.

"And the king of the south shall be strong, and one of his princes [and he] shall be strong above him and have dominion; his dominion shall be a great dominion. And in the end of years they shall join themselves together; for the king's daughter of the south shall come to the king of the north to make an agreement; but she shall not retain the power of the arm; neither shall he stand, nor his arm; but she shall be given up, and they that brought her, and he that begat her, and he that strengthened her in these times" (Dan. xi. 5, 6).

That the king of Egypt is meant by "the king of the south" might be presumed from the fact that Egypt formed the most southern portion of the dominions of Alexander;[1] but it is placed beyond dispute or cavil by the mention of Egypt as the country to which the king of the south carried his captives, in ver. 8. Profane history shows us that, after the death of Alexander (B.C. 323), Ptolemy Lagi, who had governed Egypt as Alexander's lieutenant from its conquest (B.C. 332), assumed the regal authority, and after a little time the regal name, in that country, and ruled it from B.C. 323 to B.C. 283—a space of forty years.[2] He is justly characterised as "strong," since he was able to enlarge his original territories by the addition of Phœnicia, Palestine, Cyprus, and the Cyrenaica; and, though he was sometimes defeated, he was upon the whole one of the most warlike and successful of the princes among whom Alexander's kingdom was partitioned. Another, however, of the princes is truly said to have been "strong above him." The Syrian was undoubtedly the greatest of the kingdoms into which the Macedonian monarchy became broken up; and Seleucus Nicator, its first ruler, was a more powerful sovereign than Ptolemy Lagi. Seleucus ruled from the Mediterranean to the Indus, and from the Jaxartes to the Indian Ocean, having thus a territory

---

[1] The mouths of the Indus are about parallel with the most southern portion of Egypt, but though visited by Alexander, they can hardly be regarded as within his permanent dominions.

[2] Grote, "History of Greece," vol. viii., p. 533; Heeren, "Manual of Ancient History," p. 249.

five or six times as large as that of Ptolemy. His dominion was emphatically "a great dominion." It was the representative in Western Asia of the great monarchy which had existed in that region from the time of Nimrod, and exceeded in dimensions every such monarchy except the Persian. Seleucus and Ptolemy Lagi maintained, on the whole, friendly relations; and the struggle between the kings of the north and of the south was deferred to the reigns of their successors.

Daniel's statement that "in the end of years" the kings of the north and of the south "shall join themselves together" implies a previous rupture and struggle, which is found to have taken place in the reigns of Ptolemy II. (Philadelphus) and Antiochus Soter. A permanent jealousy, and many occasional causes of quarrel, set the two powers in hostility the one to the other; and in B.C. 264 Antiochus made an expedition against Egypt, which resulted in complete failure,[1] leaving a stain on the Syrian arms which it was regarded as necessary to efface. Antiochus II. (Theus) consequently renewed the war in B.C. 260, and a long contest followed without any very decided advantage to either side, until, in B.C. 250, negotiations for peace were set on foot—the two kings "associated themselves" (marginal rendering), and in the following year (B.C. 249) it was

---

[1] Heeren, p. 236; Smith, "Dict. of Greek and Roman Biography," vol. iii., p. 586.

arranged that Ptolemy II. should give his daughter Berenicé, in marriage to Antiochus Theus, who repudiated his previous wife, Laodicé, in order to make way for her.[1] The wedding took place; and thus "the king's daughter of the south came to the king of the north to make (*i.e.*, cement) an agreement" (ver. 6). But the well-meant attempt at peace failed. In B.C. 247, on the death of Ptolemy II., Antiochus Theus repudiated his Egyptian wife, and recalled Laodicé, who shortly poisoned her husband, and caused Berenicé also to be put to death.[2] Thus this princess "did not retain the power of the arm" (*i.e.*, the secular authority); neither did her husband retain his power, or "stand." The attempted arrangement entirely fell through. Berenicé herself and her son ("he whom she brought forth," marginal rendering) suffered death; and the entire party concerned in the transaction was discredited and placed under a cloud.

"But out of a branch of her roots shall one stand up in his estate, which shall come with an army, and shall enter into the fortress of the king of the north, and shall deal against them, and shall prevail, and shall also carry captives into Egypt their gods, with their princes, and with their precious vessels of silver and of gold; and he shall continue more years than the king of the north" (Dan. xi. 7, 8).

---

[1] "Hieronym. ad Dan.," xi. 6; Polyb., v. 18, § 10; Athen. "Deipn.," ii., p. 45.
[2] Heeren, l.s.c.

There are some errors of translation in this passage which require to be removed before its statements can be properly compared with those of profane historians. Modern criticism thus renders the passage [1]—"But a branch of her roots shall rise up in his place, which shall come against the host, and enter into the strong places, of the king of the north, and shall deal against them, and shall prevail, and shall also carry captive into Egypt their gods, with their images, and with their precious vessels of silver and of gold ; and [then] for some years he shall stand aloof from the king of the north." History tells that a branch from the same roots as Berenicé, her brother Ptolemy Euergetes, in the year after her murder (B.C. 245), made war upon Seleucus II. (Callinicus), the son of Antiochus Theus and Laodicé, who was implicated in the bloody deed, and, having invaded Syria made himself master of various "strong places" in the country, as especially of Seleucia, near Antioch, a most important city.[2] He "prevailed" in the war most completely, capturing Antioch, and reducing to temporary subjection the whole of the eastern provinces—Mesopotamia, Babylonia, Susiania, Media, and Persia.[3] He stated in an inscription which he set up at Adulé that among the treasures which he

---

[1] See the "Speaker's Commentary," vol. vi., pp. 374, 375.

[2] Polyb., v. 58, § 11.

[3] See the "Inscription of Adulé," quoted by Clinton ("Fasti Hellenici," vol. iii., p. 383, note o).

carried off from Asia were holy relics (ἱερά) removed from Egypt by the Persians,[1] and no doubt, together with these, he would, like other conquerors, include in his booty the "gods and images" of the defeated nations. After the war had lasted four years, Euergetes "stood aloof" from the king of the north, consenting on account of some internal troubles in his own dominions to conclude a truce with Callinicus for ten years.

"But his sons shall be stirred up and shall assemble a multitude of great forces; and one shall certainly come, and overflow, and pass through; then shall he return, and be stirred up, even to his fortress. And the king of the south shall be moved with choler, and shall come forth and fight with him, even with the king of the north: and he shall set forth a great multitude; but the multitude shall be given into his hand. And when he hath taken away the multitude, his heart shall be lifted up; and he shall cast down many ten thousands; but he shall not be strengthened by it" (Dan. xi. 10—12).

The construction of the Hebrew is such as to render it uncertain *whose* sons are intended in the opening clause of this passage, whether those of the king of the north or of the south. The *nexus*, however, of the clause with those that follow makes it tolerably clear that the attack this time is on the

---

[1] See the "Inscription of Adulé," quoted by Clinton ("Fasti Hellinici," vol. iii., p. 383, note o).

part of the northern monarch, against whom the king of the south "comes forth, moved with choler" (ver. 11), anxious to repel what he regards as an unprovoked assault. Now Callinicus had two sons, who reigned one after the other—Seleucus III. (Ceraunus) from B.C. 226 to 223, and Antiochus III. (the Great) from B.C. 223 to 187. Of these, the elder, Seleucus, is said by Jerome[1] to have invaded Egypt in combination with his brother, Antiochus, and to have waged a war with Euergetes; but the silence of profane historians throws some doubt on this statement. "One" of the sons, however, Antiochus the Great, most "certainly," "came, and overflowed, and passed through" the territories of Egypt, attacking Ptolemy Philopator, the son of Euergetes, with great vigour in B.C. 219, and in B.C. 218 repeatedly defeating his forces, and conquering the greater part of Palestine, including Samaria and Gilead.[2] From these conquests he "returned" for the winter to "his fortress" of Ptolemaïs,[3] whence he made great efforts to have everything in readiness for a further attack upon his adversary in the ensuing year. In the spring he set forth on his march southward, passed through Gaza, and encamped at Raphia (now *Refah*), a small town near the coast, on the road to Egypt.[4]

---

[1] Comment. in Dan., xi. 10.
[2] Polyb., v. 59–70.
[3] Ibid., v. 71, § 11.
[4] Ibid., v. 80, § 4.

Meanwhile Philopator, "moved with choler," had quitted Alexandria, at the head of an army of seventy-five thousand men, supported by seventy-three elephants, and had marched to Pelusium, whence, after resting a few days, he proceeded along the coast to Rhinocolura, and thence towards Raphia, where he encamped over against the army of Antiochus. The Syrian forces were somewhat less numerous than his own, amounting to only sixty-eight thousand, but they were stronger in cavalry and in elephants. After some unimportant skirmishing, the two hosts engaged each other, and though the Syrian right defeated the Egyptian left, and the Asiatic elephants of Antiochus proved greatly superior to the African ones of his adversary, yet the battle resulted in a decisive victory for the Egyptians, who slew ten thousand of the enemy, and took above four thousand prisoners.[1] The Syrian "multitude" was thus "given into Ptolemy's hand," and a portion of it "taken away" into Egypt. His victory naturally "lifted up" Ptolemy's "heart"; he was greatly elated, and is said after the battle to have "abandoned himself to a life of licentiousness."[2] No real advantage resulted to him from his having "cast down many ten thousands"; the Syrian kingdom remained more powerful than his own, and was certain to

---

[1] Polyb., v. 81—86.
[2] "Speaker's Commentary," vol. vi., p. 376.

revenge the defeat of Raphia when a favourable opportunity offered.

"The king of the north shall return, and shall set forth a multitude greater than the former, and shall certainly come after certain years with a great army and with much riches. And in those times shall there many stand up against the king of the south; also the robbers of thy people shall exalt themselves to establish the vision; but they shall fall. So the king of the north shall come and cast up a mount and take the most famed cities, and the arms of the south shall not withstand, neither his chosen people, neither shall there be any strength to withstand. But he that cometh against him shall do according to his will, and none shall stand before him; and he shall stand in the glorious land, which by his hand shall be consumed. He shall also set his face to enter with the strength of his whole kingdom, and upright ones with him; thus shall he do; and he shall give him the daughter of women, corrupting her; but she shall not stand on his side, neither be for him" (Dan. xi. 13—17).

In B.C. 204, thirteen years after the battle of Raphia, Antiochus the Great "returned" to the attack upon Egypt. Having made alliance with Philip III. of Macedon,[1] he invaded Cœle-Syria and Palestine with a great army,[2] and with the goodwill

---

[1] Polyb., xv. 20; Liv., xxxi. 14.
[2] Smith, "Dict. of the Bible," vol. i., p. 74.

of the inhabitants, whom the cruelties and exactions of Philopator had disgusted, occupied the entire region to the borders of Egypt, "the robbers" (rather "captains") of the Jewish people joining with him "to establish the vision." A turn in the war subjected these rebels to the vengeance of Ptolemy, who recovered Jerusalem in B.C. 200, and took severe measures against the inhabitants.[1] Two years later Antiochus once more gathered his forces, and marched southward. One after another the strongholds of Syria and Palestine fell into his hands. "The arms of the south" were not able to "withstand" him.[2] At Panias, near the sources of the Jordan, he entirely defeated Scopas, the chief general of the Egyptian monarch,[3] after which he besieged him in Sidon, which he took, and a little later retook Jerusalem. He then "completely established himself in Palestine," occupying "the glorious land," which was no doubt "consumed" by having to furnish supplies for his army. But he did not press forward into Egypt. He "set his face" to establish "equal conditions" (ver. 17, marginal rendering). He arranged a marriage between his daughter, Cleopatra, and Ptolemy Epiphanes, who had succeeded his father, Philopator, pledging himself to give over Cœle-Syria and Palestine

---

[1] Joseph., "Ant. Jud.," xii. 3, § 3.
[2] Appian, "Syriaca," § 1; Liv. xxxviii. 19.
[3] Polyb., xvi. 18, § 2; 39, § 3; Joseph., l.s.c.

to Egypt as her dowry.[1] He had no intention, however, of fulfilling this part of the contract. The provinces were not made over, and Egypt was rather exasperated than conciliated by the transaction. Cleopatra herself, instead of supporting her father's interests, opposed them. Declining to "stand on his side," or " be for him," she maintained her husband's rights, and joined with him in looking to Rome for their vindication and establishment.

---

[1] Polyb., xxviii. 17, § 9; Appian, "Syriaca," § 4.

CHAPTER XII.

THE NOTICES OF EGYPT IN DANIEL.

CHAPTER XII.

NOTICES OF EGYPT IN DANIEL.

"AFTER this shall he turn his face unto the isles, and shall take many: but a prince for his own behalf shall cause the reproach offered by him to cease; without his own reproach he shall cause it to turn upon him. Then he shall turn his face toward the fort of his own land: but he shall stumble and fall, and not be found. There shall stand up in his estate a raiser of taxes in the glory of the kingdom: but within few days shall he be destroyed, neither in anger, nor in battle" (Dan. xi. 18—20).

In the prophetical books of the Old Testament and even in some of the historical ones (Gen. x. 5; Esth. x. 1), the expression translated "the isles," or "the islands," designates primarily the shores and isles of European Greece—the "maritime tracts" which invited the colonist and the conqueror to brave the terrors of the deep, and journey westward from Asia, in search of "fresh fields and pastures new." Antiochus the Great, shortly after concluding his peace with Philopator, undertook an aggressive movement in this direction.¹ Crossing the Hellespont in B.C. 197, he took possession of the Chersonese, with its city of Lysimachia. Five years later, having made alliance with the Ætolians, he moved into Central Greece, landing at Demetrias, and soon afterwards making himself master of Chalcis, thereby throwing out a challenge to the Romans, which they were not slow to accept. Rome could not allow the establishment of an Asiatic power in Europe; and her "prince" for the time being, the consul Ma. Acilius Glabrio, soon "caused the reproach," which Antiochus had "offered" the Romans, "to cease," turning it back upon Antiochus himself² by the decisive victory of Thermopylæ.³ Antiochus was forced to quit Greece in haste,⁴ and "turned his face towards the fort" (*i.e.*, the various strongholds) "of his own land," whither he retreated in the autumn of B.C. 191. But Rome followed up her advantage. The Roman admiral, Æmilius, swept the fleet of Antiochus from the sea.⁵ Her generals, the two Scipios, Asiaticus and Africanus, invaded Asia in force; and in B.C. 190 was fought the great battle of Magnesia,⁶ which at

---

¹ See Liv., xxxv. 23, 43; Polyb., xviii. 32.
² This seems to be the true meaning of the last clause of ver. 18. (See "Speaker's Commentary," vol. vi., p. 379.)
³ Liv., xxxvi. 18, 19.   ⁴ Ibid., xxxvi. 21.
⁵ Liv. xxxvii. 30.
⁶ Polyb., xxi. 13, xxii. 8; Liv., xxxvii. 42; Appian, "Syriaca," §§ 33—37.

once and for ever established the predominance of the Roman arms over those of the Syrian kingdom, and made Rome arbiter of the destinies of the East. At Magnesia Antiochus "stumbled and fell" with a fall from which there was no recovery, either for himself or for his kingdom. It did not suit Rome at once to enter into possession; but from the date of the Magnesian defeat Syria lay at her mercy and was practically her vassal. Shortly afterwards (B.C. 187) Antiochus "was not found." He made an expedition into the eastern provinces,[1] to collect money for the payment of the Roman war contribution, and never returned from it. Rumour said that his exactions provoked a tumult in the distant Elymais, and that he fell a victim to the fury of the plundered people.[2] He was succeeded by his son, Seleucus IV. (Philopator), who seems to be called "a raiser of taxes" on account of the burdens which the weight of the Roman indemnity compelled him to lay on his subjects, and "the glory of the kingdom" in derision.[3] He was a weak and undistinguished monarch, whose short reign of eleven years was wholly uneventful. His treasurer, Heliodorus, murdered him treacherously in cold blood,[4] not having any grievance

---

[1] Porphyr. ap. Euseb., "Chron. Can.," i. 40, § 12.
[2] Justin, xxxii. 2; Strab., xvi., p. 744.
[3] Our version gives "*in* the glory of the kingdom"; but the word "in" is wanting in the original.
[4] Appian, "Syriaca," § 45.

against him, but simply in the hope of succeeding to his dominions. Thus he was "destroyed, neither in anger, nor in battle," by an ambitious subject.

"And in his estate shall stand up a vile person, to whom they shall not give the honour of the kingdom: but he shall come in peaceably, and obtain the kingdom by flatteries. And with the arms of a flood shall they be overflown before him; yea, also the prince of the covenant. And after the league made with him he shall work deceitfully; for he shall come up, and shall become strong with a small people. He shall enter peaceably even upon the fattest places of the province; and he shall do that which his fathers have not done, nor his fathers' fathers: he shall scatter among them the prey, and spoil, and riches; yea, and he shall forecast his devices against the strongholds, even for a time" (Dan. xi. 21—24).

Antiochus Epiphanes, who succeeded his brother, Seleucus IV., is almost certainly intended by the 'vile person" of this passage. He was a man of an extraordinary character. Dean Stanley calls him "one of those strange characters in whom an eccentricity touching insanity on the left and genius on the right combined with absolute power and lawless passion to produce a portentous result, thus bearing out the two names by which he was known—*Epiphanes*, "the Brilliant," and *Epimanes*, "the Madman."[1]

---

[1] Stanley, "Lectures on the Jewish Church," vol. iii., p. 288.

He was a "fantastic creature, without dignity or self-control, who caricatured the manners and dress of the august Roman magistrates, startled young revellers by bursting in on them with pipe and horn, tumbled with the bathers on the slippery marble pavement, and, in the procession which he organized at Daphné, appeared riding in and out on a hack pony, playing the part of chief waiter, mountebank, and jester."[1] He was not the legitimate heir to the throne, and "the honour of the kingdom" was in no way formally conferred on him. Nor did he establish himself by force of arms. On the contrary, he "came in peaceably," under the auspices of Eumenes of Pergamus,[2] and "obtained the kingdom" by bribes, cajolery, and "flatteries." He courted the favour of the Syrian lower classes, of Rome, and of the Hellenising party among the Jews. At a later date, "with the arms of a flood," he "overflowed," and carried all before him, sweeping through Cœle-Syria and Palestine into Egypt,[3] and receiving the submission of Jason,[4] the high-priest of the Jews, or "prince of the covenant," who "made a league" with him, engaging to support his interests in Judæa, and to pay him an annual tribute of four hundred and forty silver talents. Antiochus, however, after this

---

[1] Stanley, "Lectures on the Jewish Church," vol. iii., p 289.
[2] Appian, l.s.c.
[3] 1 Mac. i. 17; Appian, "Syriaca," § 66.
[4] 2 Mac. iv. 7—10.

league, "worked deceitfully," transferring the high-priesthood from Jason to his brother Menelaus on receipt of a bribe, and forcing Jason to become a fugitive from his country.[1] After this he was able, through the support of Menelaus, to "become strong" in Palestine, without maintaining there more than a "small" army. He "entered peaceably upon the fattest places of the province," his authority being generally recognised throughout the fertile tract between Syria Proper and Egypt, though it belonged of right to Ptolemy. That he maintained his influence in the tract by means of a lavish expenditure of money, though not distinctly stated by profane historians, is probable enough, since it was certainly the method by which he soon afterwards maintained it in Egypt.[2]

"And he shall stir up his power and his courage against the king of the south with a great army, and the king of the south shall be stirred up to battle with a very great and mighty army; but he shall not stand; for they shall forecast devices against him. Yea, they that feed of the portion of his meat shall destroy him, and his army shall overflow; and many shall fall down slain. And both these kings' hearts shall be to do mischief, and they shall speak lies at one table; but it shall not prosper; for yet the end shall be at the time appointed" (Dan. xi. 25—27).

---

[1] 2 Mac. iv. 23, 26.   [2] Polyb., xxviii. 17.

Epiphanes invaded Egypt several times during the earlier portion of his reign. The prophetic vision vouchsafed to Daniel did not very clearly distinguish between the several attacks. If the present passage is to be assigned to any particular year, it must be to B.C. 171, when Epiphanes "entered Egypt with a great multitude, with chariots, and elephants, and horsemen, and with a great navy" (1 Mac. i. 17). Egypt was then under the sovereignty of Ptolemy VI. (Philometor), who, however, was still a minor, under the tutelage of Eulæus and Lennæus, who exercised the royal authority as regents.[1] These chiefs collected as large a force as they could to resist the Syrian monarch; but the result of the battle, which took place near Pelusium,[2] was the complete defeat of the Egyptians and the temporary subjection of the larger part of Egypt to the authority of Antiochus. Ptolemy Philometor fell into his enemy's hands, but was honourably treated, the policy of Antiochus being to cajole Philometor into believing that he was his friend, bent on supporting his authority against that of his brother, Physcon, who had a strong party in the country, especially at Alexandria. We have no full account, in any profane writer, of the history of the period; but it is quite possible that the loss of the battle of Pelusium was owing to treachery on the part of some of Philometor's ministers (ver. 26;

---

[1] Polyb., xxviii. 17; Hieronym ad Dan., xi.
[2] Liv., xliv. 19; Polyb., xxviii. 17.

and it is certain that in the intercourse between him and Epiphanes each king was trying to deceive and overreach the other (ver. 27). Nothing decisive was accomplished, however, as yet; "the end" was reserved for "the time appointed" (ibid.).

"Then shall he return into his land with great riches; and his heart shall be against the holy covenant; and he shall do exploits, and return to his own land. At the time appointed he shall return, and come toward the south; but it shall not be as the former, or as the latter" (rather "it shall not be at the latter time as at the former"). "For the ships of Chittim shall come against him; therefore he shall be grieved and return, and have indignation against the holy covenant" (Dan. xi. 28—30).

That Epiphanes on his first invasion of Egypt obtained a considerable booty, which he carried off into Syria, is confirmed by the First Book of Maccabees (i. 19). That on his return, or soon after, his "heart was against the holy covenant," appears both from 1 Mac. i. 20—24 and from 2 Mac. v. 11—21. That after one or two years he "returned," and once more "came toward the south," is also certain, as, likewise, that he did not fare this time so well as previously, since though success attended his arms, he was "compelled by the ambassadors of various northern kingdoms," supported by the "ships of Chittim"—*i.e.*, the fleets of Rome and Rhodes —"to surrender against his will almost all the advantages that he had gained."[1] This time he returned from Egypt in extreme ill-temper, and vented his spleen on the Jews by renewed attacks and oppressions.

"And at the time of the end shall the king of the south push at him; and the king of the north shall come against him" (*i.e.*, against the king of the south), "like a whirlwind, with chariots, and with horsemen, and with many ships, and he shall enter into the countries, and shall overflow and pass over. And he shall enter also into the glorious land, and many countries shall be overthrown; but these shall escape out of his hand, even Edom, and Moab, and the chief of the children of Ammon. He shall stretch forth also his hand upon the countries; and the land of Egypt shall not escape. But he shall have power over the treasures of gold and of silver, and over all the precious things of Egypt; and the Libyans and the Ethiopians shall be at his steps. But tidings out of the east and out of the north shall trouble him; therefore shall he go forth with great fury to destroy, and utterly to make away many. And he shall plant the tabernacle of his palace between the seas in the glorious holy mountain; yet he shall come to his end, and none shall help him" (Dan. xi. 40—45).

The closing scene of the war between the kings of the north and of the south—Epiphanes and the

---
[1] Ewald, "History of the Jews," vol. v., p. 297.

brothers Philometor and Physcon—came in B.C. 168. Epiphanes having withdrawn into Syria for the winter, leaving his supposed ally, Philometor, at Memphis, and his open enemy, Physcon, in Alexandria, was staggered by the information that, during his absence, the hostile brothers had made up their differences, and that Physcon had agreed to receive Philometor into Alexandria,[1] at which place the reconciled enemies were now holding their court conjointly. An embassy, which met Epiphanes at Rhinocolura, politely suggested to him that the end for which he had been waging war—the establishment of Philometor's authority—was accomplished, and that nothing remained for him but to sheath his sword and return home. This was felt by Antiochus as a deadly blow struck at his schemes—a "push" on the part of the "king of the south," which required to be met by the promptest and most energetic measures. He at once broke up his camp, and marched into Egypt as an open enemy. With the speed of a "whirlwind," he advanced upon Pelusium, "with chariots, and with horsemen, and with many ships" (ver. 40); thence, in a more leisurely fashion, he proceeded to march upon Alexandria. Egypt generally submitted to him. The "treasures of gold and silver" and "all the precious things of Egypt" were placed at his disposal by the inhabitants; contingents of Egyptian troops were pressed into his service,[2] and "the Libyans

---

[1] Liv., xlv. 11. [2] Ibid., xlv. 12.

and the Ethiopians," long employed as auxiliaries by the monarchs of Egypt, whether native or foreign, were (as a matter of course) " at his steps " (ver. 43). He was drawing near Alexandria with the intention of renewing the siege, and with an almost certain prospect of reducing the place within a few months, when an unexpected obstacle was interposed. The prophetic vision speaks of "tidings out of the east and out of the north." The "tidings" told of the near approach of a small body of Romans. These proved to be ambassadors. At their head was a man who has left an imperishable name in history, C. Popillius Lænas. This bold and haughty envoy, approaching with his small retinue the master of countless legions, held out to him a small tablet, containing a short senatorial decree. "Read this," he said, "at once." The cautious Greek cast his eye over the document, and perceived that it was a positive command to him to desist from hostilities against those who were "the friends of the Roman people." Unwilling to see the prize of victory snatched from his grasp at the moment of success, and hoping to temporize, Antiochus replied that he would consult his friends on the senatorial proposals and let the envoys have an answer. Popillius had a wand in his hand, the emblem of the ambassadorial office. Hastily tracing with it a circle on the sand round Antiochus, "Consult," he said, "and give your answer before you overstep this line." The Syrian monarch was so astonished and so dismayed, that he replied, with the utmost meekness—"I will do as the senate decrees."[1] Thus were baffled and confounded the ambitious designs of the "great king," who regarded himself as the successor of Cyrus, Darius, and Xerxes, and the living representative of Alexander the Great. A brief sentence uttered by a Roman civilian brought a great war to an end, and prohibited its renewal.

Epiphanes retired from Egypt in greater dudgeon than ever, "deeply grieved, and groaning in spirit," as Polybius says,[2] and sought a species of consolation in increased severity towards the Jews. It was now that he accomplished his last acts of impiety and cruelty upon that unfortunate people, sending against them "Apollonius, that detestable ringleader, with an army of two-and-twenty thousand, commanding him to slay all those who were in their best age, and to sell the women and the younger sort" (2 Mac. v. 24), and soon afterwards polluting the temple in Jerusalem, and wholly forbidding the exercise of the Jewish religion. It was this issue to the wars between the "kings of the north and of the south" that gave to them their great importance in the theocratic history, and rendered them a fitting subject for so long a prophecy as that which we have been considering. Their entire result was to bring out,

---

[1] Polyb., xxix. 11, §§ 1—6; Liv., xlv. 12.
[2] Βαρυνόμενος μὲν καὶ στένων (xxix. 11, § 8).

more strongly than it had ever been brought out before, the Roman influence over the affairs of the East, to intensify the antagonism between Rome and Syria, to place Egypt under a permanent Roman protectorate, and to make Rome the natural ally and defender of every petty nationality which had any inclination to assert itself against Syria and could do so with the least hope of success. The close connection between the Roman and Jewish peoples, which, beginning with the embassy of Judas Maccabæus in B.C. 161 (1 Mac. viii. 17—32), and terminated in the destruction of Jerusalem by Titus in A.D. 70, was the consequence of the Syro-Egyptian struggle, and especially of the war between Epiphanes and Philometor, which therefore worthily occupies a very considerable space in the prophetical synopsis of Daniel.

The ultimate fates of Egypt and Babylon, as represented to us in Scripture, offer a remarkable contrast. Babylon is to "become heaps" (Jer. li. 37), to be "wholly desolate" (ibid. l. 13), "not to be inhabited" (Isa. xiii. 20). Egypt is to be a "base kingdom" (Ezek. xxix. 14)—"the basest of the kingdoms" (ibid. ver. 15), but still to remain a kingdom. It is not "to exalt itself any more above the nations"; it is to be "diminished"; it is no more to have any "rule over the nations" (ibid.), or to be "the confidence of the house of Israel." But it is to maintain a certain position among the powers of the earth, a certain separateness, a certain *low* consideration. Now this is exactly what has been the general position of Egypt from her conquest by Cambyses to the present day. Under the Persians she was a sort of outlying kingdom, rather than an ordinary satrapy. She frequently revolted and established a temporary independence, but was soon coerced into subjection. During the earlier portion of the Ptolemaic period she rose to considerable influence and prosperity; but still she was never more than a second-rate power. Syria always, and Macedonia sometimes, was superior to her in extent of dominion and importance (Dan. xi. 5). Rome made her a province, but a province with a certain separateness, under regulations which were peculiar.[1] Under the Mohammedans, whether Arabs, Saracens, or Turks, she has still for the most part been secondary, either an actual dependency on some greater state, or at any rate overshadowed by rivals of superior dignity. A veil hangs over the future; but, so far as human sagacity can forecast, there seems to be little likelihood of any vital change in her position. With peculiar characteristics and an isolated position, she must almost of necessity maintain her separate and distinct individuality, even though she become a dependency on a European power. On the other hand, she has exhibited under

---

[1] Tacit., "Ann.," ii. 59.

recent circumstances no elements of greatness, and remains emphatically "a base kingdom," if not even "the basest of the kingdoms." There seem to be no elements out of which her revival and reconstitution as a great monarchy could be possible.

THE END.

14

www.ingramcontent.com/pod-product-compliance
Lightning Source LLC
Chambersburg PA
CBHW020534300426
44111CB00008B/657